The Laurel Great Lives and Thought series is designed to present to the general reader and to students the best that has been expressed in the history of ideas, together with full-length portraits of the thinkers and doers whose contributions have left an indelible imprint upon the world's course.

The scope of the series is universal: every aspect of human experience—politics, history, sociology, religion, philosophy, psychology, science, literature, etc.—will receive its merited attention. The author-editors of THE GREAT LIVES AND THOUGHT are chosen both for their knowledge of the subject and for their ability to write lucidly.

Charles Warren Everett was a member of the English Department at Columbia University and College from 1927 until his recent retirement. From 1940 to 1942 he was an expert consultant to the Secretary of War. Professor Everett is the editor of THE LIMITS OF JURISPRUDENCE DEFINED by Bentham (1945). A contributor to JEREMY BENTHAM AND THE LAW (1948), he delivered the Bentham Bicentenary Lecture in London in 1948. He is a member of the executive body of the Bentham Committee, which is preparing a thirty-two volume edition of Bentham's works.

Edgar Johnson, the General Editor, was formerly Chairman of the Department of English at City College of the City University of New York. He is the author of a definitive biography of Dickens and of ONE MIGHTY TORRENT: THE DRAMA OF BIOGRAPHY.

JEREMY BENTHAM

CHARLES W. EVERETT

General Editor, Edgar Johnson

THE LAUREL GREAT LIVES AND THOUGHT

Published by Dell Publishing Co., Inc.
750 Third Avenue, New York, N. Y. 10017
Copyright © 1966 by Dell Publishing Co., Inc.
Laurel ® TM 674623, Dell Publishing Co., Inc.
First printing: January, 1966
Printed in the U. S. A.

Typography by R. Scudellari

Contents

A Selective Bibliography

A full Bentham bibliography, by the present writer, was annexed to the translation of Élie Halévy's *Formation of Philosophical Radicalism* published in New York in 1926 by Harcourt, Brace. Some of the important books written since then, as well as the most important on that list, are here mentioned for those who wish to read further.

PUBLISHED WORKS

The Works of Jeremy Bentham, published under the superintendence of his executor, John Bowring. 11 vols. Edinburgh, 1838–43. The life of Bentham contained in Vols. X and XI of this edition is the source of all later biographies, but is somewhat misleading. Bowring probably took down the reminiscences of Bentham's old age correctly, but Bentham's memory was not very accurate after he passed the age of seventy.

A Comment on the Commentaries of Sir William Blackstone. Edited by C. W. Everett. Oxford: The Clarendon Press, 1928.

The Limits of Jurisprudence Defined. Edited by C. W. Everett. New York: Columbia University Press, 1945.

Jeremy Bentham's Economic Writings. 3 vols. Edited by Werner Stark. New York: Burt Franklin, 1952.

BOOKS ABOUT BENTHAM

The most important analysis of Bentham's work from a technical point of view is to be found in *History of English Law*, Vol. 13, by Sir William Molesworth. London, 1952.

The most important philosophical analysis is to be found in Halévy's work, referred to above.

Jeremy Bentham and the Law, edited by G. W. Keeton and George Schwarzenberger, London, 1948, is a collection of essays by various specialists.

Bentham and the Ethics of Today, by David Baumgardt. Princeton: Princeton University Press, 1952. Baumgardt had been professor of philosophy at Berlin before Hitler came to power. It was, in fact, Hitlerism that turned his attention to Bentham. As he concludes in the book, pp. 524–25, "Bentham was far more aware of the ethical weight of the problem of Machiavellianism than all the critics he has hitherto had to face." "In comparison with Bentham's critical method, all the conservative theories of morals, which presently dominate the field, are as dogmatic and uncritical as is Nietzsche's or Machiavelli's or modern fascist ethics."

Jeremy Bentham: An Odyssey of Ideas, by Mary Peter Mack. London: Heinemann, 1963.

A History of English Criminal Law and its Administration from 1750 (Vol. III of *Crosscurrents in the Movement for the Reform of the Police*), by Leon Radzinowicz. New York, 1957.

Certain older works retain some importance for special reasons:

The English Utilitarians. Leslie Stephen. 3 vols. London, 1900. Vol. I is a biography of Bentham.

Jeremy Bentham, by Charles Milner Atkinson. London, 1905.

Three Criminal Law Reformers, by Coleman Phillipson. London, 1923.

Two excellent articles by Graham Wallas should also be mentioned: "Jeremy Bentham," *Political Science Quarterly,* March, 1923; and "Bentham as Political Inventor," *Contemporary Review,* March, 1926.

Foreword

Jeremy Bentham lived for 84 years, from 1748 to 1832, and for 60 years he worked steadily toward his aim of becoming the "Newton of legislation." His published works amount to some ten millions of words, and his unpublished manuscripts make up almost an equal bulk.

The range of his experience of the world is almost as impressive. He had seen France in 1764 under the old regime, and he corresponded at length with Mirabeau during the French Revolution. He had visited Turkey when criticism of the Sultan's unlimited rule was met by the response, "The Sultan is too just and merciful to abuse his power." He had seen Bulgarian and Cossack headmen administering the customs of barbaric tribes; in Russia he had watched for two years Potemkin's attempt to make Russia a Western nation by edict from St. Petersburg, backed by the power of Catherine the Great. In England, he was the friend of Joseph Priestley and of Sir Samuel Romilly; at Bowood, Lord Shelburne's country seat, he had played chess with William Pitt, and he had played violin sonatas with Lady Shelburne at the harpsichord.

Probably he was the only human being ever to be on terms of intimacy with *both* Aaron Burr and John Quincy Adams. Burr, as an exile in 1808, lived as Bentham's guest for some months and borrowed £200 of him, every penny of which he repaid. John Quincy Adams brought a letter to Bentham from President Madison when he came to London as American minister in 1815, and the two men soon fell into taking long walks around the London parks, often before breakfast. Burr and Adams had read Bentham, as had Madison. Bentham may have had few readers in English, but they were choice ones.

Étienne Dumont of Geneva had translated some of Bentham's manuscript material into French as early as 1802 in the three volumes of the *Traités de législation civile et pénale*. The *Traités* were widely read, by Mohammedans, by Greeks, and by Russians, by Bolívar in Venezuela and by Livingston in Louisiana. They were retranslated into Spanish, Polish, Italian, Hungarian, Portuguese, Russian, and German. The only place they were not very well known to political thinkers was England.

That foreigners should hold Bentham in respect seemed strange enough to some of his contemporaries. "His name is little known in England," wrote Hazlitt in 1825, "better in Europe, best of all in the plains of Chile and the mines of Mexico. He has offered constitutions for the New World, and legislated for future times. . . . Mr. Hobhouse is a greater man at the hustings, Lord Rolle at Plymouth Dock; but Mr. Bentham would carry it hollow, on the score of popularity, at Paris or Pegu." Borrow, carrying the light of Protestantism to darkest Spain, recounts the story of an *alcalde* whose admiration of Jeremy Bentham was almost too much for Borrow's gravity. Under arrest as a Carlist spy, Borrow was taken before the *alcalde* of Corcuvion, who promptly released him with apologies:

ALCALDE: Surely it was very ridiculous that they should have arrested you as a Carlist.

MYSELF: Not only as a Carlist, but as Don Carlos himself.

ALCALDE: Oh! most ridiculous; mistake a countryman of the grand Baintham for such a Goth!

MYSELF: Excuse me, sir, you speak of the grand somebody.

ALCALDE: The grand Baintham. He who has invented laws for all the world. I hope shortly to see them adopted in this unhappy country of ours.

MYSELF: Oh! you mean Jeremy Bentham. Yes! very remarkable man in his way.

ALCALDE: In his way! in all ways. The most universal
   genius which the world ever produced—a Solon, a
   Plato, and a Lope de Vega.

MYSELF: I have never read his writings. I have no
   doubt that he was a Solon; and, as you say, a
   Plato. I should scarcely have thought, however,
   that he could be ranked as a poet with Lope de
   Vega.

ALCALDE: How surprising! I see, indeed, that you
   know nothing of his writings, though an Englishman.
   Now, here am I, a simple *alcalde* of Galicia,
   yet I possess all the writings of Baintham on that
   shelf, and I study them day and night.

MYSELF: You doubtless, Sir, possess the English
   language.

ALCALDE: I do. I mean, that part of it which is contained
   in the writings of Baintham. . . . But it is
   late; I must find you a lodging for the night. I
   know one close by which will just suit you. Let
   us repair thither this moment. Stay, I think I see
   a book in your hand.

MYSELF: The New Testament.

ALCALDE: What book is that?

MYSELF: A portion of the sacred writings, the Bible.

ALCALDE: Why do you carry such a book with you?

MYSELF: One of my principal motives in visiting
   Finisterra was to carry this book to that wild place.

ALCALDE: Ha, Ha! how very singular. Yes, I remember,
   I have heard that the English highly prize
   this eccentric book. How very singular that the
   countrymen of the grand Baintham should set any
   value upon that old monkish book!*

Among the countrymen of "the grand Baintham"
there was, it is true, a Benthamite group, and this group
was influential out of all proportion to its numbers. In
1808 Bentham had made the acquaintance of a brilliant
young Scottish journalist, James Mill, who had assisted

---

*George Borrow, *The Bible in Spain* (2 vols., London: John Murray, 1896), Vol. II, p. 40.

in forming the school of which the reformer had dreamed in his youth. Through Mill, Bentham met Francis Place, a practical politician who, from the position of tailor and trade-union secretary, had become a most effective propagandist and election manager. In 1824 Bentham founded the *Westminster Review,* which numbered among its contributors James Mill, John Stuart Mill, John Austin, George Grote, Bowring, Roebuck, Fonblanque, Bingham, Graham, and Eyton Tooke. In Parliament, Bentham's reforms were advocated by Romilly and Burdett, and even Brougham said that he had sat at the feet of Gamaliel.

Since most of the Radical group were young men, the Benthamic influence could be expected to continue long after Bentham's death. The volumes that poured steadily from his pen were to be used by his disciples as source books for legislation. Edwin Chadwick, the father of modern sanitation, took from the incomplete *Constitutional Code* the details of the New Poor Law of 1834, and of the Act establishing a proper census of vital statistics in 1836. From the same work, Parkes and Place drafted the Municipal Reform Act of 1835. The division and organization of the work of governmental departments, the extension of the franchise, the reform of the land laws, the parcel post, a national system of education, the modern police force, the establishment of a permanent civil service based on competitive examinations—all these were, for the most part, the carrying out of plans carefully worked out by Bentham. Of course, since modern reformers have often been men of great experience and intelligence, concrete alterations have frequently differed markedly from Bentham's somewhat overfussy planning. The great changes in legislative drafting in Britain, for example, begun by Symonds and carried on so brilliantly in our own time by Sir Cecil Carr, follow Bentham's concepts, but have developed techniques and skills in historical and legal analysis unthought of by Bentham.

Though much has been used of Bentham's suggestiveness and inventiveness, much remains to take. In fact, it is only at this late date that he appears to be coming into his own. A Bentham Committee has been formed in London, under the chairmanship of Lord Cohen, Lord Justice of Appeal, and its membership includes some of the most distinguished jurists, historians, philosophers, and economists of the United Kingdom. Much work has already been done, with the support of the Rockefeller Foundation, and the Committee have announced the prospective publication of 32 volumes of Bentham's works, a considerable part of which is to be taken from his as yet unpublished manuscripts.

The main collection of Bentham's publications at the present time is to be found in John Bowring's *Works of Bentham,* published in 11 volumes in 1843. The 11 volumes are double column in very small type, with about 600,000 words to each volume. References in this book to Bentham's published work are to this edition.

The chief collection of Bentham mss. is in the library of University College, London, and amounts to 173 boxes or portfolios, containing three or four hundred pages each. References in this book to Bentham's unpublished mss. are to this collection. There are also something like 1,600 letters of Bentham's in the British Museum, of which Bowring published about 250.

Most of the letters published in this book were not known to Bowring and are taken from the mss.

In the text several of Bentham's most important works have been presented in abbreviated form, but always using Bentham's own words and presenting the material as fully as possible in the space available. In the first section a brief account is given of Bentham's education and life, but stress is laid on the nature of his ideas rather than on his relations with people.

—CHARLES EVERETT

LIFE

part 1 AND WORK

Jeremy Bentham was born on February 15, 1748, in Church Lane, Houndsditch, London, then a most respectable neighborhood. His father, Jeremiah Bentham, was a prosperous and ambitious attorney, though his ambitions centered on his son and heir rather than on his own career. He had increased his own inheritance by judicious dealings in real estate, he thought he knew the ways of the world, and he was prepared to furnish his son with the kind of education needed to reach high position. Jeremy was duly baptized in the newly completed church of St. Botolph Aldgate, and the father began making his plans.

Education was a simple thing to Jeremiah Bentham. He was in no doubt either as to the ends to be attained by education, nor the means to be employed to attain the ends. The end desired was either money or some equivalent form of power: the training must be both technical and social. The technical training that offered the most possibilities was law, for law was involved in almost all human relationships, and was so arranged that its practitioner could profit if the machinery of society ran well, and could profit still more if it ran ill. Jeremy should be a lawyer. But Jeremiah Bentham, who knew his way about in the world, knew that the study of law was not enough. Even more important was social training. The social training of young Jeremy must be one that would render him agreeable to his betters, and that would tend to bring him into their society. Jeremiah was quite sure that for one man who attains distinction through mastery of his craft or profession, there are three who cling to the skirts of the great and by them are lifted into power. Jeremy should therefore have masters in dancing, French, drawing, and music, and should enter one of the great public schools and a fashionable college at the University.

Jeremiah Bentham had brushed up his own Latin and Greek in order to act as teacher, and Jeremy learned Latin grammar and the Greek alphabet on his father's knee. To the end of his life, Jeremiah Bentham kept scraps of Latin written by Jeremy at the age of five. Good work was rewarded by praise and fine clothes. A typical entry in the father's diary is: "10 December, 1753. Paid Mr. Robert Hartley for double allepine for Jerry's coat and breeches, to his pink waistcoat 0 12 3." Jeremy excelled in music as in letters. With his miniature violin the undersized boy had learned to scrape Foote's Minuet at the age of five, and had gone on to Corelli and Handel in a way to delight his teachers. When he was seven, his mother could write casually but proudly to his father: "After dinner and Jerry had given our friends a specimen of his Proficiency in Musick by playing a Sonata or two out of a collection which Mr. Evans had by him of Handel's— we proceeded to Mrs. Morell's."

He was sent to Westminster School at the age of seven, and he was to spend there every winter from his seventh to his twelfth year.

In 1760 Jeremy was considered to have reaped the full benefit of Westminster, and no time was lost in arranging for his entrance to the university, so that on June 28 his father was able to record in his journal:

Aujourd'hui à midi, set out with my friend, Mr. William Brown, and my son Jeremy, from London for Oxford. Lay at Orkney's Arms, by Maidenhead bridge. Got to Oxford at dinner, *après midi.* Entered my son at Queen's College; and he subscribed the statutes of the University in the apartment of Dr. Browne, the Provost of Queen's, he being the present vice-chancellor; and by his recommendation, I placed my son under the care of Mr. Jacob Jefferson, as his tutor—paying Mr. Jefferson for caution-money, £ 8; entrance to Butler, &c. 10 s.; matriculation, 17 s. 6

d.; table fees, 10 s. The age of my dear son, upon his being admitted of the University this day, is twelve years, three months, and thirteen days.

The library that Jeremy took with him when he went again to settle at the University in October was in itself a commentary on his education past and to come. Of the 60 volumes, only 12 were in English, and the 12 included Buchanan's *Psalms*, the *Rational Catechism, The English Common Prayer Book,* Milton's *Paradise Lost* and *Paradise Regained,* Potter's *Elements of Arithmetic.* But there were six volumes of Cicero, and at least one volume each of Ovid, Horace, Terence, Virgil, Juvenal, Sallust, Pliny, Anacreon, Lucian, Demosthenes, and Homer. His training had been the conventional one for a gentleman, and might even lead to classical scholarship.

At regular intervals he wrote dutiful letters to his father describing his progress. "Dear papa," he wrote,

We have lectures twice a day from Mr. Jefferson, at 11 o'clock in the morning and 9 at night, except on Tuesday and Fridays (when we have publick lectures by the Greek lecturer, Mr. Hodgkin) and holydays. Mr. Jefferson does not intend beginning with me in Logick yet a while: On Saturday we all received the Sacrament: upon which account we were lectured in Greek Testament 3 days before, and as many after that day. To prepare myself for that awful duty, I read *Nelson on the Sacrament* which Mr. Jefferson lent me, and intended to fast that morning; but it would not do, for I began to grow sick for want of victuals; and so was forced to eat a bit of breakfast with Mr. Cooper, with whom I have lived this ten days. [November 6, 1760.]

At home there were developments that interested him greatly. Brother Samuel was showing a precocity that promised great things. Jeremy wrote (November 6, 1760): "Pray give my duty to Grandmamma and love to brother Sammy with a kiss, who I hope still goes on to improve in polite literature, as he used to do." Brother Sammy, aged four, having replied to this proffer of affection with his own hand, the young collegian found it necessary to call attention to his own maturity by requesting, "Pray tell Sam not to direct to me Master when he writes to your dutiful and affectionate son."

Samuel himself soon attained a certain maturity of his own, for Jeremy wrote (June 12, 1761), "It was with great pleasure that I received your letter, as it gave me such a surprising account of dear Sammy's improvement, which is so great that it quite astonished me when I read your account of him, as he could not spell above 10 to 15 words at most when I went away from home, and those monosyllables. I long to see him in his breeches, which I daresay become him extremely well."

On March 10, 1762, Jeremy first broached the possibility of studying physics with Dr. Bliss. He wrote,

I have finished Homer's *Iliad,* and also the Ethic Compendium; I think of looking over the *Odyssey* as I intend to be examined in it, good part of which I read at School. Mr. Jefferson began Natural Philosophy with us yesterday, but whether we shall improve much or not I can't tell, as he has no apparatus—but today Dr. Bliss's lectures will begin, and I hope I may attend his next course, which will be next Year.

Apparently his father made no objection to the proposal, for the next year Jeremy took the course, and was disappointed by the unsatisfactory results of the experiments:

We have gone through the science of Mechanics with Mr. Bliss, having finished on Saturday; and yesterday we begun upon Opticks: there are two more remaining, Hydrostatics, and Pneumatics. Mr. Bliss seems to be a very good sort of a man, but I doubt is not very well qualified for his Office, in the practical Way I mean, for he is oblig'd to make excuses for almost any Experiment, they not succeeding according to expectation: in the Speculative part, I believe he is by no means deficient.

In 1763, being then sixteen years of age, Bentham took his Bachelor's degree, and in November of the same year began to eat dinners in Lincoln's Inn and to attend the Court of King's Bench, where his father had secured for him a student's seat. His career seemed to have begun under fair auspices. In December he returned to Oxford to hear Blackstone's lectures.

But Jeremy Bentham was spending part of his time in ways that were much less profitable. He was reading widely, particularly in the works of Montesquieu, Hume, Priestley, Hartley, Beccaria, and Helvetius, and he was experimenting in chemistry and physics. These experiments were hampered by lack of money, for Bentham had only £103 a year—"and for these allowances," he said, "I was to appear as a gentleman, with lace and embroidery on occasion. I had four guineas to pay my laundress, four guineas to my barber, and two to my shoeblack." But in spite of money embarrassments, he had fitted up a laboratory in a closet, cutting a hole to admit enough light; he had put half a guinea into phials and had bargained with a chemist for the sweepings of his shop. The place often smelled to heaven and brought remonstrances from Bentham's neighbors. Unexpected visitors must have been surprised at the new method of studying law. "I was, I remember," he told Bowring, "reading Montesquieu, when the Archbishop of York called on me, to solicit my vote for Jenkinson and Hay. Prodigiously courteous was his grace; though I was only half dressed, and I was busy, too, on chemistry, evaporating urine in order to obtain phosphorus."

Bentham's reading was leading him into other paths quite as foreign to an attorney's career as was chemistry. In Hume's *Essays* he had come upon the first mention of the principle of utility, though he felt that the idea attached to it was a vague one, as it was used sim-

ply as synonymous with conduciveness to an end, and
with no intimation of happiness as connected with the
idea. Hartley's *On Man* gave him certain hints for the
construction of a rational psychology; and Barrington's
Observations on the Statutes, which he read in 1766,
showed him how considerable were the defects in the
existing body of law. He picked up a reading knowledge
of Italian, and read Beccaria's *Dei Delitti* shortly after
its anonymous appearance in 1764, and in Beccaria he
may have noticed the phrase *"la massima felicità de-
visa nel maggior numero."* In the year 1768 he came
upon the expression "the greatest good of the greatest
number" at the end of Priestley's *Essay on Government,* and says that he cried out, like Archimedes, in an
inward ecstasy, "Eureka!" The next year he read *De
l'esprit* of Helvetius, the special significance of which
was that it pointed out for him his own proper genius.
If genius was identical with invention or production, as
Helvetius led him to think, then the discovery had an
immediate and personal application. "Have I a genius
for anything?" "What can I produce?" were important
questions, and no less important was, "What of all
earthly pursuits is the most important?" Helvetius gave
the answer, "Legislation"; for the legislator had the
possibility of being both moralist and educator—in his
power was the determination of the conditions under
which man should live, and the consequent determination of what the plastic mind of the babe should develop into. "And have I indeed a genius for legislation? I
gave myself the answer, fearfully and tremblingly—
Yes!"

Bentham determined to do for human society what
Newton had done for natural science. If one could apply to legislation scientific principles, and discover for
social engineering a mathematical calculus, he could
look for no less a change in human relations and the
structure of society than physics had wrought on the
face of the world.

Bentham followed Helvetius further still. In *De l'esprit* Helvetius had written: "Everyone, if I may say so,

has for teachers both the form of government under which he lives, and his friends and his mistresses, and the people about him, and the books he reads, and finally chance, that is to say an infinite number of things, events whose connection and causes we are unable through ignorance, to perceive." The legislator is therefore a teacher, a moralist; morality and legislation are, he says, "one and the same science." It is by means of good laws alone that virtuous men can be made; the art of the legislator consists in forcing men in their own self-interest to be just to one another. Bentham accepted this view wholeheartedly, and agreed with Helvetius that the great moral problem of the world was the conflict of interests. His own function, then, he took to be that of making an artificial identification of private interest and the good of all, or at least the "greatest happiness of the greatest number." The problem of how to keep the selfish individual from pursuing his own interest at the expense of society Bentham solved by placing a definite pain, a punishment, at the entrance to each of these antisocial goods.

As has been said, Jeremy was far from being an ungrateful son, and he tried time and again to convince his father of the magnitude and importance of the work he had in mind, even sending him parts of what he was writing for criticism:

> I have sent you a few passages from my Book which I have got Mr. Clarke's clerk to transcribe— the remainder of the Chapter of Offences principal and accessory he has with him in Town and has probably finished by this time—that of Theft I have not yet revised.

"Offences principal and accessory"—No, decidedly, that would not do.

Jeremiah Bentham, who had been a lawyer himself, really respected only the kind of learning calculated to gain one respect and honor in his profession. He complained that Jeremy's work was too abstruse, by which he meant probably that it was attempting to reach fundamental principles instead of studying specific cases and precedents, and concluded by urging his son to devote himself to practice, to seek the solid honors given to those who confine themselves to "Law as it is."

Bentham was somewhat hurt by this criticism of abstruseness, for, of all qualities of style, he most valued that of clearness, and he could not take as guide the platitudes and worldly common sense of his father, however kindly meant. In his answer to his father, he found it necessary to make his declaration of independence, and with great tact and courtesy, but unmistakable firmness, he replied:

It gives me great satisfaction to find that the specimen which you have as yet seen of what I have in hand has met with your approbation: that being the case, one great end of it is answered. Having occasion to say something to the Public on the subject of the abstruseness of which you take notice and which I see must, from the causes you mention, to a certain degree remain after all my efforts to clear it away, I will not anticipate anything on that behalf at present —In the meantime, excuse the liberty I take in supposing that with regard to some parts that abstruseness may possibly appear greater to you in common with others of your former profession than to men at large, as, besides having a new language to acquire, you have the old one to unlearn. As to myself, if I had waited until I had been immersed in the depths of practice, I am satisfied, I should never have had ability, even if I had had inclination, to engage in the design. . . . Others, I believe, there will not be wanting which may find easier access to popular apprehension—With others this may be a point of prudency. With me it is a matter of necessity—I cannot rest till I feel myself everywhere at the bottom—I cannot go on with what is *before* me, while I have anything behind me unexplored—I feel myself to have acquired to a considerable degree that pleasing and uncommunicable sensation—Thus only can one hope to keep clear of those inconsistencies, into which I see my predecessors (as far as I have predecessors) humble servants for the most part to authority and to one another, falling evermore. Forgive me, Sir, if I declare simply, and once for all, that till this great business is disposed of I feel myself unable to think of any other. The *Will* is here out of the question. Whatever may be the case with others, I find it impossible with me to bring the powers of invention to a mechanical obedience to the good pleasure of that Faculty—The sense of *necessity* which may set them to work in some, strikes me motionless—I am in this respect like David, I can "give no melody in my heaviness." In the track I am in, I march up with alacrity and hope: in any other I should crawl on with despondency and reluctance. If I am not likely to succeed in a pursuit in which I am engaged with affection and with strong presentments of success: much less am I where both are wanting.

Having made this declaration of independence, Bentham went back to his reading, experimenting, and thinking. As he thought, he wrote. Every day he covered ten or fifteen pages with the careful analysis of offences and punishments that was not to see the light of day until 40 years later, when Dumont of Geneva published it as the *Théorie des peines*. As far as relatives or acquaintances could see, Bentham was already, at the age of twenty-four, one of those solitary eccentrics, who, cursed by temperament and perhaps by an odd and twisted sort of genius, simply fail to fit into the scheme of life. He had no close friends, his open dislike for "Law as it is" kept him from the shoptalk of his fellow barristers in Lincoln's Inn, and his small income as well as his natural tastes kept him out of the middle-class circles that his father and stepmother tried to believe was the world of fashion.

In point of fact, he was neither solitary nor eccentric, though his pleasures were not those of Queen

Square Place. He was passionately fond of music, possessed both harpsichord and violin, and played well on either. He loved the theatre, as well he might at a time when Garrick was at the height of his powers, when Mrs. Cibber was just going off the stage, and Mrs. Siddons beginning her career.

But Bentham's chief interest, apart from the study of legislation, from 1772 to 1775 was the education of his young brother Samuel. Samuel had gone on to "improve in polite literature" as rapidly as Jeremy had done in his childhood, and he had been sent to Westminster School in his turn, in spite of Jeremy's protest. In 1770, when he was thirteen, a choice of a career had had to be made for him, and at that time Jeremy had been more successful in getting his way. He wanted Samuel to become a scientist, and had managed to secure his father's consent to apprenticing the boy to a ship builder at Woolwich dock yard, in the expectation that he would become a naval architect. The responsibility for Samuel's education in science and mathematics Jeremy took on himself. The boy proved an apt pupil, and the relation between the brothers was a close and sympathetic one.

Bentham's interest in natural science, and particularly in chemistry, had not diminished on account of his work on legislation, and Samuel shared to the full this interest. Together they filled many pages with the solutions of mechanical and physical problems, in the process staining their fingers and tea cups with chemical reagents in a happy intimacy.

It was not easy to keep one's self supplied with books, paper, chemicals, and linen of a gentleman on £103 a year. Even his leisure-time experimenting was beginning to prove too costly for Bentham when an opportune legacy of £100 not only enabled him to bring himself even with the world, but left about £10 over, which he proceeded to lay out on materials and apparatus. Though Samuel must have been pretty fully occupied with his work in the dock yard, with the attempts he was making to improve the old boat he had been allowed to use, and with the severe regimen of study his brother had laid out for him, he entered willingly into the spirit of research. He proposed to spend some of his own money in fitting up the alembics, flasks, and athanors necessary to the experiments. Perhaps his willingness was greater than his leisure, for Jeremy wrote to remind him:

What we were last upon was the air experiments—the apparatus was to have been proceeded upon forthwith, specimens were to have been fitted up, and your most obsequious elder brother and humble servant to command was to have been commanded down by the time all was ready—a letter after a considerable time has come from your honor, and in the said letter concerning the said apparatus or concerning his said proposed-to-be-commanded journey your said humble servant has heard nothing.——To confess the truth, your said humble servant, being then, as at all times a little upon the lazy order, is not very sorry for the pretence——But you, Sir, may it please your proprietorship, where is your consistency, your steadiness, your resolution? Where are the fruits of your gold that you melted into glass? Is the glass to be melted into Pitch again to caulk your Boat with? You who blew so cold, do you now blow colder as the weather, Sir, blows warmer? Think, and if you regard not an epigram of Martial, hear a text of Scripture, "These things ought ye to have done and not to have left the others undone."

To Samuel's protest that he had been unable to get the joiners to prepare certain wooden apparatus, Bentham rallied him with the spirit of a chemist who had carried on experiments with his tableware, and who had prepared his own phosphorus from urine.

Pish—Troughs—What signify the Troughs? The Joiners are not to cut the corks to the Phials—are

they? are they to fit on the Athanors? Paltry excuses
—anything may do for a trough for an experiment or
two to try how things fare—take your Hat—or what
should hinder your borrowing a wash-tub? Pray Mr.
Boatbuilder, how goes on Euclid? Is it the Joiners
who are to translate Euclid for you, or do you leave
him to translate himself?

Then emotional difficulties upset both chemistry and
law. Jeremy Bentham, a briefless barrister of twenty-six,
had fallen in love with Miss Mary Dunkly, a friend of
his friends, the Linds. The Linds both approved of the
match, for they were concerned about Jeremy's solitary
life, but there was real reason for anxiety, since the
young woman had no money, and Bentham only £100
a year. The chief hope, in which Bentham was encour-
aged by Lind, was in making a living by the pen, but
whether such a career could combine both livelihood
and the reform of the law was a question sufficiently
dubious to throw Bentham into a state of agitation.

Jeremiah Bentham, now thirty years removed from
his own imprudent romance, was solidly opposed to the
marriage. He had been disappointed by Jeremy's refusal to practice law, and saw no reason for countenancing
an act so rash, so "criminal" as this proposed "suicide."
Jeremy was thus in a difficult situation. He could not
bring himself to the practice of law, and unless he did
that, what source of income could he look to that would
support a family? His £100 a year, though insufficient
for London, would have given him a start in the colonies,
and he seems to have considered emigration to East
Florida as a possibility. Lind knew that Bentham was
an able and effective writer, and believed his future assured if he could be induced to publish. If Bentham
were married and dependent on his pen, he would be
compelled to write, and each publication would raise
his income as well as increase his reputation. At all
events it was Lind's plan for living by the pen that
seemed most feasible to Benham, and he wrote to his
brother:

May 23, 1775

Ah my dear Sam, how shall I set down to write to thee or now I have set down, how shall I know when to leave off? Yes, bad success indeed, that is the reason of my long silence. Tis impossible for me to think of giving the particulars by letter. This, however, thou canst not know too soon—that my Mother has been my zealous and (for any just ground that I can possibly form to myself of suspicion to the contary) my sincere advocate. I believe, if I had gone all lengths, I might have extorted my Father's consent, but it would have made him supremely wretched, and would have put an end to your Gallic expedition. I could not bear that my Mother should be so early and severe a sufferer for her generosity to me. She had given me such proofs and under her own hand of her encouraging me to persist, as would ruin any scheme if she had formed one, of recommending herself by means of it to my prejudice. My present plan is in few words this. I believe I shall spend the next half year at Mr. Lind's. My Father, (when will miracles cease?) knows it and tolerates it, Mr. Lind will assist me in rummaging over the Statute-books for materials and heads etc. for a Digest. In the intervals of that employment which will be many I shall go on with my Comment on the Commentaries [Blackstone's *Commentaries on the Laws of England*]. I hope still to have completed it in 3 months or 4 at the furthest.

Tis on this rests my sole dependence now for the accomplishment of my marriage Scheme. I find that according to the course of the Market £120 may not unreasonably be expected from a Bookseller for a handsome octavo volume. If the reception that my first scheme meets with is such as entitles me to think I can have alacrity enough to produce one every year, I shall trust to that, and take the desperate leap, trusting to the chapter of accidents and my mother's good offices, for reconciling my Father. At present we are all the best friends imaginable. He certainly does love you and me next to his money. . . . But I must not enter into details or reflections. Mr. Lind offered me his house as an asylum if I would venture immediately upon marriage, but I declined (you may imagine with what gratitude) for the reasons I have above intimated and because I could not justify it to myself the hazarding of everything upon the uncertainty of his affairs. From the Contract Scheme, I doubt nothing is to be expected.

I expect today an answer from a gentleman who has seen my chambers and seems to be inclined to take them. If so, I shall migrate to Mr. Lind's and there if Fortune should smile upon me, shall be in readiness to receive my Polly. I now know her age exactly. She is not 18 till December next. The affair of Browning Hill is uncertain. If that should not succeed my wish would be to find out some snug parsonage or something in that stile near you at Chatham. East Florida will not do. None of our fruits will grow there according to De Brahm.

I am now hard at work with Mr. Lind revising his book. . . . Adieu—that is all, my dear Sam, I can give you for the present.

But before these plans could be carried out, it was necessary to finish the *Comment on the Commentaries* and to find a publisher for it. The work, involving as it did a careful analysis of the fundamental conception and principles of law, was too difficult and important to be rushed, and it went forward slowly. Bentham probably found occasionally irksome the necessity for explaining to a girl of seventeen why it was that prudence and common sense forbade a hasty marriage. In spite of the tone of his letter to Sam, the truth was that he was very hesitant about cutting himself off entirely from his father, hoping rather that in time Jeremiah Bentham could be won over to consent to the marriage and to make a proper settlement.

By the end of the year, the marriage scheme had apparently fallen through, not only because Jeremiah

Bentham was still set as firmly as ever against it, but also because the girl of seventeen was offended at Bentham's attitude.

The *Comment* being almost finished, Bentham went back to consider a point that Blackstone, copying Burlamaqui, had inserted in his discussion of municipal law. This had to do with the nature of sovereignty, and as Bentham considered that it had little to do with the treatment of municipal law, he had at first passed it over with brief notice. He now examined it more closely. "I sat down," he says, "to give what I intended should be a very slight and general survey of it. The farther, however, I proceeded in examining it, the more confused and unsatisfactory it appeared to me: and the greater difficulty I found in knowing what to make of it, the more words it cost me, I found, to say so." In short, having completed the criticism of Blackstone's introduction, Bentham entered upon a digression that he treated at length and that became the *Fragment on Government*.

> When it was nearly completed [he explains in the Preface to that work], it occured to me, that as the digression itself which I was examining was perfectly distinct from, and unconnected with the text from which it starts, so was, or so at least might be, the *critique* on that digression, from the *critique* on the text. The former was by much too large to be engrafted into the latter: and since if it accompanied it at all, it could only be in the shape of an appendix, there seemed no reason why the same publication should include them both. To the former, therefore, as being the least, I determined to give that finish which I was able, and which I thought was necessary: and to publish it in this detached manner, as the first, if not the only part of a work, the principal and remaining part of which may possibly see the light some time or other, under such title as that of "A COMMENT on the COMMENTARIES."

On a loose sheet at the end of the manuscript of the *Comment on the Commentaries,* he wrote: "Advertisement/Upon the Anvil/By a hand concerned in the present publication/*The Elements of Critical Jurisprudence*/Commencing with the Penal Branch of it."

But for all this advertisement, neither the *Comment on the Commentaries* nor *The Elements of Critical Jurisprudence* ever appeared until the twentieth century. One of the major problems concerning the life of Bentham is the reason for his slowness to publish. His theory of punishments was, in its main outlines, complete at this time. Why did it have to wait 40 years for Dumont of Geneva to translate and publish it from the mss? *The Comment on the Commentaries* was not only not published, but Bentham never referred to it again. *The Critical Elements of Jurisprudence* was never published, though Dumont was to use part of it later. We can only say that it was so because Bentham was Bentham and that it was so he worked. His very abilities often seemed to work against his success. On one side, his mind was that of a medieval school-man, a belated Abélard or William of Paris. This analytical power, and his control of logic, served him well in attacking smooth generalizations. His dialectic was formidable because he pushed his opponent back to his assumptions and premises, and then showed the assumptions to be ridiculous historically or rationally, and the premises unworthy of acceptance. This ability often led him into controversy, though he felt controversy to be far less important than construction. The other side of Bentham's mind and, as he thought, the most important was the systematic. He had the ability to conceive great systems and to organize the most intricate of plans. These he saw first as an organic whole, and then down to their most minute articulations. This ability might have ranked him with Descartes or Locke had it not been for his self-criticism. To him the great work of synthesis was never complete, however satisfactory it might seem to his friends. The outlines were not enough; he must push some phase to completion. Then, seeing the disparity between that treatment of a relatively insignificant part and a number of more important parts, he would set himself to the years of careful work necessary for completion of the whole. Resolutely refusing to publish the mere sketch or design, he would set himself to the great task.

And then another complication arose. Bentham was no closet philosopher; he was an intelligent and sensitive human being, living in a world where the sufferings of his fellowmen, from the anomalies and absurdities of an antiquated legal system, were every day before his eyes. He was no more ready to tolerate the complacency of "everything-as-it-should-be Blackstone" than Priestley was, and he was capable of an honest and absorbing wrath at what seemed to him the stupidity or chicanery of men in power. He knew his own ability at controversy, and when some great judge or statesman pronounced a declamation on the excellence of the common law or the state of the poor law, Bentham would lay aside the great work and turn to a pamphlet. The pamphlet issued after some months' work, before he had taken up his original plan again, some other phase of immediate law reform, some legal decision at odds with the principle of utility, or a newspaper paragraph reporting that hundreds of men were being hanged yearly for forging bank notes, would set him analyzing a new field of law, working for the revision of a statute, or inventing bank notes that could not be forged —in the manner of the reformer rather than that of the philosopher.

To the observer, such a method of working could only seem doomed to failure. His friend George Wilson, a successful lawyer, after watching him for ten years, was to express the commonsense view when he wrote in 1787:

> I am still persuaded, my dear Bentham, that you have, for some years, been throwing away your time; and that the way in which you are most likely to benefit the world and yourself is, by establishing, in the first place, a great literary reputation in your lan-

guage, and in this country, which you despise.

It is not because Trail and I disapproved, that you abandoned your Introduction, your Code, your Punishments, etc. The cause lies in your constitution. With one-tenth part of your genius, and a common degree of steadiness, both Sam and you would long since have risen to great eminence. But your history, since I have known you, has been to be always running from a good scheme to a better, In the meantime, life passes away and nothing is completed.*

"A common degree of steadiness"! Even the close friend failed to understand Bentham's problem or the nature of his genius. Bentham's was a most uncommon degree of steadiness, a steadiness that in the pursuance of one great plan, the reform of law, kept him for five and fifty years piling high his close-written folios, working habitually from six in the morning till ten at night. Had he been content with the half good, with the almost complete, his friends and the public might have been better pleased.

But this is to look back on the Bentham of 1781 with more knowledge than a man of thirty-three could have of himself. Fortunately, in that year someone called to Lord Shelburne's attention the five-year-old *Fragment on Government* and mentioned Bentham as the author. Shelburne detested Blackstone at this time and, as leader of the Opposition, was on the lookout for able writers to attack the administration. Having read the *Fragment,* he thought he saw in Bentham an effective propagandist. Remembering the way in which Bentham had refused his offered patronage a year before, he decided to visit the unusual young lawyer who could be contemptuous of Blackstone and seemed to want nothing for himself. Accordingly, he called in person on Bentham, in July, 1781, in his chambers in Lincoln's Inn. He was struck by Bentham's personality and ability, and gave

*Jeremy Bentham, *Works,* edited by John Bowring (11 Vols. Edinburgh: Tait, 1838–43), Vol. X, p. 171.

him an invitation to his country seat at Bowood in Wiltshire, so courteously expressed that Bentham was delighted to accept. Thus began a friendship that was to last for 25 years and was to give Bentham a sense of his own value that he could have had in no other way.

Lord Shelburne himself was an enigma to his contemporaries. He was the eleventh Earl of Kerry and could look on most of the Whig aristocracy as upstarts; he was enormously wealthy, and not compelled to sell himself for political purposes. So little understood were his ways of thinking that, to his contemporaries, he was the symbol of deceit and trickery, nicknamed "Malagrida," the archetype of the Jesuit. A radical Tory, a Tory democrat, he antedated Disraeli by a century, and it was appropriately Disraeli who was the first to understand and appreciate him.

Lord Shelburne [says Disraeli] seems to have been of a reserved and somewhat astute disposition: deep and adroit, he was however brave and firm. His knowledge was extensive and even profound. He was a great linguist; he pursued both literary and scientific investigations; his house was frequented by men of letters, especially those distinguished by their political abilities or economical attainments. He maintained the most extensive private correspondence of any public man of his time. The earliest and most authentic information reached him from all courts and quarters of Europe; and it was a common phrase, that the minister of the day sent to him often for the important information which the cabinet could not itself command. Lord Shelburne was the first great minister who comprehended the rising importance of the middle class; and foresaw in its future power a bulwark for the throne against "the Great Revolution families." Of his qualities in council we have no record; there is reason to believe that his administrative ability was conspicuous; his speeches prove that, if not supreme, he was eminent, in the art of parliamentary disputation, while they show on all the questions discussed a richness and variety of information with which the speeches of no statesman of that age except Mr. Burke can compare.

It was a new world that Bentham was entering, and he noted with interest the differences in manner. Perhaps the greatest difference was in the women. The mixture of reserve and gentle courtesy in their manners impressed him, but the most surprising thing was that their opinions on literature and ideas seemed to be valued by Shelburne. Bentham had been much attached to Mrs. Lind, but, when he invited the Linds to visit him at Leatherhead, he had suggested that the two men would need to be by themselves "when you and I in our profound wisdoms are sitting in council over the affairs of state." In this new world, things were otherwise. Chatham at the height of his power had given almost as much weight to the opinions of his sister as to those of Frederick the Great. Shelburne was in the habit of entertaining the ladies of his family by reading aloud to them the more important sermons and pamphlets published. Bentham was now to find that the mark of his having been recognized as an important thinker and writer was the fact that Shelburne should acquaint the ladies with his work. The Introduction to the Code under the title of *An Introduction to the Principles of Morals and Legislation* had been printed before Bentham went to Bowood, and he took along the proof sheets to show Shelburne that he was capable of something more than the *Fragment*. Describing his life, he wrote to his father:

I am as much at my ease as I ever was in any house in my life: one point excepted, the being obliged by *bienséance* to dress twice a-day. I do what I please, and have what I please. I ride and read with my lord, walk with the dog, stroke the leopard, draw little Henry out in his coach, and play at chess and billiards with the ladies. My Lord's custom is to read to them after tea, when they are at work; and now nothing will serve him, but in spite of everything I can say, he will make them hear my driest of all dry metaphysics. He takes the advantage of my being here to read it in my presence, that I may explain things. This has gone on for several evenings. I must cut short; for while I am writing this in my dressing-room above stairs, they are waiting for me half-a-mile off in the library below stairs.

At the end of the week, Bentham made the acquaintance of a young man of two-and-twenty, as yet distinguished only for three eloquent speeches in parliament, but destined to be perhaps the greatest minister England ever had. Had the French Revolution never occurred, Bentham might have found in William Pitt the man of affairs who could have made, and might have been disposed to make for England, a matchless constitution in reality. But Bentham saw in Pitt only a raw youth; Pitt found in Bentham only a master at chess; and Napoleon was to furnish other business than making or mending constitutions.

Various other figures of political and legal importance appeared as guests at Bowood, of whom the most important was Lord Camden, late chief justice and lord chancellor. Shelburne pushed Bentham's *Introduction to the Principles of Morals and Legislation* on his notice, but with no result.

I had not been long in London [Bentham wrote] on my return from Bowood when I received a visit from Lord Shelburne. "I will deal plainly with you," said he; "I told you I should put your book in the hands of Lord Camden and Mr. Dunning [later Lord Ashburton]. I have done so. Lord Camden acknowledged its merits in the character of a theoretical work; but he confessed he had found some difficulty in comprehending it, and if such is the case with me (said he), I leave you to imagine how it may be with the generality of readers." . . . Of Dunning's opinion I recollect not any particulars: it was but too plainly of the same cast.

Faced by this kind of disappointment, Bentham's interest turned more and more to Russia and the possibility of creating a Code for Catherine the Great. He noted her exact words:

"There can be but two cases," says the Empress of Russia (Instructions, art. VI, #35–36) "in which an act ought to be forbidden: where the tendency of it is pernicious to such and such individuals in particular, and where it is pernicious to the community in general. For the end, the only proper end and object of the law is the greatest possible happiness of those who live under its protection. It cannot have another."
Here then the supremacy of the principle of utility stands confessed: a fuller and more explicit recognition of it language cannot frame.

What more appropriate place than Russia, then, for the philosopher of legislation? Utility not "dangerous," as Dunning had called it, but taken for granted. Untold resources of raw materials to be utilized by the scientist and economist; a virgin soil for the legislator.

At least, the path seemed open, for Samuel Bentham was already at work in Russia and was well placed. The young master shipwright, trained in the sciences and mathematics by his elder brother, had set out on his Russian expedition in 1779. Armed with letters furnished by Lord Shelburne, he had been welcomed at the court of Catherine. There his handsome person and quiet address had first made him popular, and then had nearly ruined him. There had been a case of love at first sight between the handsome Englishman and a maid of honor at the court. She was about sixteen years of age, and was daughter to a proud house, ranking by wealth and station hardly below the empress. Naïvely enough, Samuel had expected to marry the girl. When the affair became known, the parents were furious and swept the weeping daughter off into retirement. Samuel's standing at court was no longer satisfactory, and even his commission in the army was in danger for a time. He might at least have done Catherine the honor of falling in love with her first.

Fortunately, he was allowed to leave the court for the field of action. He was favorably known to Prince Potemkin, who though discarded as a lover by the empress in 1774, still remained on good terms with her as minister. Potemkin had in mind two great projects in which he could use Samuel. In the first place, he proposed to construct a navy in the Black Sea to be used against the Turks. Samuel's fitness for such a task was obvious. In the second place, Potemkin proposed no less grandiose a scheme than to bridge the gap between feudal Russia and industrial England. This was to be done by the colonization of a great area in the steppes, not as a primitive agricultural community, but as a completely organized industrial unit. By securing from England the technology of modern agriculture and industry, and by applying almost unlimited capital, Potemkin would make the wastes of the steppes into modern farms on the English plan. With his scientific and chemical training, Samuel found this project no less interesting than shipbuilding and entered on it with enthusiasm. He soon found that his training was far from adequate. He called on his elder brother for assistance, and Jeremy got together for him all the treatises on agriculture, commerce, and manufacturing that he could lay hands on. Scarcely anything could come amiss, for Samuel was engaged, as he wrote, "as Jack-of-all-trades —building ships, like Harlequin, of odds and ends—a rope-maker—a sail-maker, a distiller, brewer, maltster, tanner, glass-maker, glass-grinder, potter, hemp-spinner, smith, and copper smith."

So useful was Jeremy Bentham's work of information that Potemkin wrote asking him to select men as well as books. He needed two experienced dairy-women and a "clever man" to supervise a huge model dairy. Besides acting as general manager of the dairy, the man must possess considerable botanical knowledge. A remittance of £500 was enclosed to pay the expenses of the three. The prospect of helping to establish a model civilization interested Bentham enough so that he finally proposed to accompany the persons selected, at his own expense.

In addition to the desirability of seeing the particular country for which he was to legislate, he may have felt that his experience of humanity needed rounding out, by travel and observation of men in different climates and different types of society. At any rate, if he was to learn more about men from observing them, travel was almost necessary, for he had observed intensively in his native country for 30 years. He had seen Westminster School and Queen's College; he had gone through the emotional storm and stress of youth in the London of Dr. Johnson and of Buckmaster the tailor, "shot through and through with a pair of black eyes" one day, and discovering Gibbon the next; he had lived on a footing of intimacy with the men who ruled England, who made and unmade public opinion; he had seen manners and manner in the English social world from the fustian of Queen Square Place and the tawdry magnificence of the carpet-knight Mackreth to the quiet beauty and poise of the Foxes and the Vernons.

The journey, which he made by way of Constantinople and as round about as possible, he found entertaining and amusing, but it taught him little that was new about mankind. On the whole, it tended to confirm his view that, *for the legislator,* the similarities of men are more numerous and important than their differences. He saw palm trees and seedless grapes; he sent Angora goats to England for introduction on the Bowood estates; but he found no two-headed men, nor did he find any who were not "under the governance of two sovereign masters, pain and pleasure."

In the middle of January, after a great deal of discomfort and some danger, Bentham arrived at Kremenchug in the Ukraine, Potemkin's headquarters. He crossed the river on the ice and was hospitably received by the governor, in Potemkin's absence.

A full measure of disillusion was to come when Bentham saw the ideal community in operation. In February, he removed to his brother's house at Zadobras, near Crichoff, and found that the Russian Utopia was little better than a madhouse. Samuel Bentham was in charge, but Samuel Bentham was several hundred miles off, following Potemkin in one of his wild journeys.

Samuel Bentham was kept traveling round with Potemkin, who would talk business only in the intervals when cards were being dealt, even in his carriage.

The final aim of the journey (for which Bentham's uncle had furnished the funds)—to meet the empress and to prepare for her the all-comprehensive code to govern all of Russia—seems to have been postponed until the translation of the penal code was finished. In truth, the success of such a scheme was dependent on Bentham's pushing himself forward, no less in Russia than in England. He had refused, whether through a sense of his own dignity or through indolence and shyness, to follow such a course in England, and he was no more willing, when put to the test, to follow it at the court of Catherine.

He could justify his action, of course, on the ground that the Code was not yet in a form to present to the empress. He was not merely translating the *Introduction to the Principles of Morals and Legislation* into French, but, in characteristic fashion, was expanding such parts as required it, and there were few with which he was satisfied as they stood. Moreover, he was not even putting his whole attention on translation. He was interested in some of Samuel's inventions, one of them a new architectural plan for a prison. In this prison, which he called a "Panopticon," the novelty consisted in the fact that the prison was made of tiers of cells arranged in a circle around an observation platform in the center, whence the governor could see, without moving, all that went on in the prison. Bentham himself was also engaged in writing an essay attacking laws against usury, on the ground that they tended to hamper invention by preventing capital's being attracted to new and therefore speculative enterprises.

His friend George Wilson, an able Scottish barrister, urged Bentham to return to England in the letter previously quoted in part:

> You have now made a reasonable visit to your brother [he wrote 26 February 1787] and on your own account you are doing nothing there which may not be done at least as well here. . . . It is not because Trail and I disapproved, that you abandoned your Introduction, your Code, and your Punishments, etc. The cause lies in your constitution. . . . I don't know why I talk thus, unless, because at this distance I may do it with safety; for, except the satisfaction of discharging so much spleen, I expect no good effect from it.

Wilson also objected to the use of the French language, feeling, as he had said, that Bentham's real work lay in England rather than among foreigners. "Not being a citizen of the world," he remarked, "I hear of the miscarriage of improvements in France with great philosophy."

He was right in his view that no "good effect" would be produced by his criticism. Bentham answered the charge of lack of steadiness only by sending along, two months later, a new work.

> My dear Wilson [he wrote], I send for your edification, a Defence of Usury and some other enormities. Abuse it and keep it, or abuse it and print it, as to your wisdom may seem meet. Don't let Trail see it or hear it (the blasphemous 14th letter I mean) till he has submitted to have his hands tied behind him, for fear of mischief. . . . You may call this confined subject, flying at small game: but with submission, I don't think such a confined subject stands, as such, a worse chance for being read than a great system. As for the form of letters, it was written

in this form before the law against letter writing was promulgated; and the Defence of Projectors could not have been conducted in any other way with near so much advantage. If you do print it, don't let it linger; but send it to the press quickly, that it may begin to lay in a little stock of reputation for me against I get home.*

Wilson, when he received the manuscript, approved of the content, but put off sending it to the press, presumably because he, also, thought it was "small game" and certainly because he wanted Bentham to come back to England. Finally Old Jeremiah Bentham got wind of the work, and for various reasons decided to put it through the press himself, and did so.

The most important part of the *Defence of Usury* was the letter to Adam Smith in defence of Projectors. In the *Wealth of Nations* Adam Smith had criticized any prohibition of lending at interest on the ground that such a prohibition had for its effect simply a raising of the rate of interest, since the lender must insure himself against legal penalties by exorbitant rates. He pointed out that, in countries where lending at interest is authorized, the law, with a view to preventing the extortion of usury, ordinarily fixes the maximum rate that can be taken without legal punishment. Bentham's attack on the *Wealth of Nations* was really based on the fact that Adam Smith made no attempt to inquire as to whether such a fixation is good or bad or useless, but had simply contented himself with asserting that this rate should always be a little above the lowest current price, or at the price commonly paid for the use of money by those who can give the soundest security. If the legal rate be made lower than the current rate, the law is really a prohibition and will be violated. If the rate be fixed much above the current rate, at eight or ten percent for example, then the law favors, not wise and prudent men, but those who alone are willing to pay so high a rate—the "borrowers," prodigals, projectors, inventors, and speculators.

The implication here, that projectors and inventors were to be set off against "wise and prudent" men, had enough personal application to the Crichoff projectors to start Bentham off. In answer to Adam Smith, he proposed to extend to money Smith's own central principle of free trade, and to demonstrate that no man of mature age, acting freely and with his eyes open, should be prevented from making any bargain to obtain money that seems proper to him. Consequently, no one should be prevented from furnishing him with money on any condition to which he sees fit to assent.

To arrive at this conclusion, Bentham went into a characteristic analysis of the prevailing opinions about usury. He found two inveterate prejudices that seemed to him to account historically for the refusal to accept the idea of free trade in money. One of these prejudices was religious and was based on asceticism; the other was philosophic and was based on Aristotle. Ascetic morality condemned not merely usury, but the whole idea of the acquisition of wealth, and was reinforced by the medieval prejudice against the Jews. Trade in money was therefore held to be culpable because it was necessary to commerce and to luxury and was largely carried on by Jews. To a country that accepted commerce, wealth, and luxury as desirable, no further attack on this prejudice should be necessary than pointing out its historical origins.

Philosophically, the objection to usury went back to Aristotle's statement that money is naturally sterile. Two *darics* (gold coins) left together will not beget another *daric*. To this Bentham answered, in dry contempt of authority, Aristotle's or not:

A consideration that did not happen to present itself to that great philosopher, but which had it happened to present itself, might not have been altogether unworthy of his notice, is that though a *daric* would not beget another daric, any more than it would a ram, or an ewe, yet for a daric which a man borrowed, he might get a ram and a couple of ewes; and that the ewes, were the ram left with them for a certain time, would probably not be barren. That then, at the end of the year, he would find himself master of his three sheep, together with two, if not three lambs; and that, if he sold his sheep again to pay back his daric, and gave one of the lambs for the use of it in the meantime, he would be two lambs, or at least one lamb, richer than if he had made no such bargain.

As to money being diverted from legitimate business by the borrowings of prodigals, Bentham simply appealed to common sense and observation. What a prodigal wants is the things money will buy. It is always easier for him to secure such goods on credit than it is to borrow cash, no matter what the rate of interest, since no restriction is placed on the price that the shopkeeper is allowed to add to the cost of his wares. Actually, of course, a very high rate of interest is charged on the capital employed by merchants who cater to prodigals, though this is disguised under the high price charged for the goods.

As for the argument that indigence must be protected from extortion, or simplemindedness from imposture, Adam Smith himself had argued that each individual is the best judge of his own interests. Furthermore, extortion and imposture in themselves are torts, against which the law offers a remedy. Fraud is fraud, whether in selling goods or lending money.

The *Defence of Usury* caused some little stir on its appearance, and it did begin to "lay in a little stock of reputation" for the absent Bentham, though it was many years before the repeal of the Usury Laws took place. The *Monthly Review* for May, 1788, called the book "a gem of the finest water," and Adam Smith himself commented to Anderson, "The work is one of a superior man. He has given me some hard knocks, but in so handsome manner that I cannot complain."

Bentham's work on prison discipline was not so fortunate. The central idea, that of the Panopticon, or Inspection House, was developed at Crichoff from an architectural plan sketched by Samuel Bentham. The subject of prison reform had a logical interest for the reformer of penal law, and Bentham had been concerned with it for many years.

The first analysis of prison discipline had been published in 1777 by the great philanthropist, John Howard, under the title of *The State of the Prisons in England and Wales, with Preliminary Observations, and an Account of some Foreign Prisons*. His account of the state of affairs stirred up even the complacency of the eighteenth century. The prisons were as bad as possible. There was little or no ventilation, drainage hardly existed; foul smells, filth, overcrowding, and contagious diseases were commonplaces. Even water was supplied only in the scantiest amounts, and for food the wretched inmates were dependent on charity and the caprice of the jailers. The only bedding was rotten straw. All were heavily ironed, whether felons or accused awaiting trial. As if the rapacity of the jailers were not enough, there was extortion and oppression from the more hardened prisoners, in particular "garnish," the tax paid by each individual into the common fund to be spent by the whole body, generally for drink. Idleness and drunkenness, squalor and cruelty led naturally enough to vicious intercourse, sickness, and madness. At the best, English prisons were in a state of culpable neglect; at the worst, they were scenes of unbelievable injustice and oppression.

The Hard Labour Act of 1778, which was largely the result of Howard's report, had been intended to remedy some of these abuses, but it had produced little more than a statement of good intentions. The overcrowding had been brought about by the loss of American colonies to which prisoners could be transported. The operation of the Act was postponed by the discoveries of Captain Cook in the South Seas, described in the *Voyages,* published in 1777 and 1784. There was at least a strong current of public opinion to the effect that the loss of America might be balanced by the colonies in the Pacific, and the idea of transporting convicts to these new lands appealed both to humanitarians and to imperialists. In consequence, the building of the prisons provided for in the Act was put off from time to time. It is important to note, however, that the Act was never repealed, so that Bentham's plan was far from absurd. By the law there must be constructed a penitentiary house to carry out the express stipulations of the Act. The Panopticon was a penitentiary house calculated to the last detail to answer the purposes of the Act. No more practical application of the energies of a reformer could have been conceived.

To the architectural features of the plan—central inspection, central heating, running water, and cleanliness —Bentham added certain principles of management, not specified in the Act, but easily reconcilable with it. The first of these was the Contract Principle, according to which the governor of the prison undertook to feed and care for each prisoner for a fixed sum, smaller in amount than the cost of transportation or imprisonment on the old plan. In return, he was to have whatever profit he could make from the labor of the prisoners. The prisoners were to receive a percentage of what they produced in the form of wages. Abuses were guarded against by having the prison open to inspection at all times, both by the commission and by the general public. Another principle, that of insurance, was called in to make certain of the governor's interest in the well-being of the prisoners. A normal death rate was to be agreed upon between the government and the contractor-governor, the rate to be lower than that actually existing in the old prisons. The contractor then insured the lives of the prisoners, so that he faced heavy penalties if the death rate rose. Thus his profits would depend on his keeping the men in good health and at productive work.

On the Panopticon, a single detail of penal law, a concrete, specific, and practical application of the principle of utility, Bentham, who had been condemned as "always running from a good scheme to a better," centered his attention for over 20 years. To it he gave up his time, his more ambitious works, and his fortune, which after Jeremiah Bentham's death in 1792 amounted to about £700 a year.

The result was failure, though with an ironical twist. Bentham's attempts to apply his principles to existing institutions were all failures. If applied at all, they were to be applied in places remote in time and space from Bentham's world. Joliet Penitentiary in the state of Illinois, U.S.A., constructed in 1920, is an exact replica of the architectural plan of the Panopticon, even to the central heating and water supplied to each cell. In Central America the imposing name of Panopticon is given to even the humblest one-roomed jail, though none of them bears any relation to Bentham's plan beyond the use of the name. But in England neither name nor architecture has been used, yet Bentham threw away the best part of 20 years of his life in advocating the scheme. Wilberforce, in 1793, described "poor Bentham . . . dying of sickness of hope deferred." "Never was anyone worse used than Bentham," he wrote later. "I have seen the tears run down the cheeks of that strong-minded man, through vexation at the pressing importunity of creditors and the insolence of official underlings, when, day after day, he was begging at the Treasury for what was, indeed, a mere matter of right." The government had given him enough in the way of promises to justify his buying a tract of land and starting construction. At last, in 1812, the government finally refused to carry out the plan, but acknowledged Bentham's claim to recompense, and came down with a settlement of £23,000 in cash. Bentham was not to be allowed to benefit his country, but he was to receive money enough to triple his income. Small wonder if he said afterwards, "I cannot look among Panopticon papers, it is like opening a drawer where devils are locked up," and wryly noted that he was "condemned to join the Baal Peor of bloodsuckers."

Thus, the whole story of the Panopticon, though it takes us beyond the proper limits of this study, is interesting as a study in common sense. "Take up one thing and stick to it," says the commonsense friend. "All your life you have been running from a good scheme to a better. In the meantime life passes away and nothing is completed." As a boy of nineteen Bentham had a truer intuition of his powers. "Have I a genius for legislation?" he had asked himself, and had dared to answer, "Yes!" At the age of forty, he had turned aside from the promptings of his own genius to follow the course of common sense. The Panopticon was already acknowledged by the world as ingenious and useful, it was already legislated for, but it ended in flat failure. Its effect might easily have been to turn Bentham into a morose and cynical "projector." That it did not do so was due to the masses of manuscript that had been piling up in his study during the years he had "wasted" between the ages of twenty and forty. Chance was to justify his faith in his own genius during those years.

In 1784, before the journey to Russia, Bentham had made the acquaintance of an intelligent but obscure young barrister, Samuel Romilly, a friend of George Wilson's. Romilly was a great admirer of the *Fragment on Government,* and he and Bentham soon became friends. "Our love for pusses," Bentham explained gravely long afterwards to Bowring, "our mutual respect for animals—was a bond of union. For pusses and mouses we had both of us great kindness." He was now, in 1788, happy in meeting Romilly again at a dinner at Lansdowne House. There was also present at the dinner a Swiss writer and former clergyman, an old friend of Romilly's, by name Étienne Dumont. The meeting between Bentham and Dumont was of the highest significance for both. It marked the beginning of Dumont's career as disciple and editor to Bentham; for Bentham it was the beginning of that reputation on the continent and in the Americas which was to bring him in his old age the title of *El legislador del mundo.* If the visit to Bowood seven years before had ended in disappointment, the dinner at Lansdowne House was to make amends. Romilly learned that Bentham was slowly turning his *Code* into French, and, securing some of the mss. a few days later, he sent them along to Dumont. As Romilly probably expected, Dumont was struck by the power and originality of the passages shown him, and, with the comment that the author was worthy of serving the cause of liberty, he offered to superintend the publication himself. Bentham was happy to accept the offer, and proceeded to turn over to Dumont his papers on punishment and penal law. Relieved of the necessity of going to Paris, he was once more unengaged, except for the Panopticon scheme.

Now, Dumont had met, in the busy days of 1788, through Lord Shelburne also, the other man of genius who was to make use of his talent and industry: the Comte de Mirabeau. And Mirabeau, with his facility for appropriating the brains and energy of all about him, had at once put Dumont to work. Mirabeau's paper was the *Courrier de Provence*. Dumont was to edit that journal. And among the first contributions of the new editor to the journal were long extracts from the mss. of Jeremy Bentham. Mirabeau was an effective and moving orator, ready to take and use any ideas that seemed calculated to produce the results he wanted. Dumont he found to be a fruitful source of material, and more and more, the voice of Mirabeau expressed the thoughts of Dumont. And as Dumont, the soul of candor and generosity, explained, the ideas were taken direct from the mss. of the powerful but little-known English philosopher, Jeremy Bentham.

Bentham's most important work, which he had had printed in 1780, had long lain neglected. "A great quarto volume of metaphysics, upon Morals and Legislation," he described it in a letter to Lord Wycombe, "which had been lying imperfect at the printer's ever since I have had the honour of knowing you. . . . The edition was very small, and half of that devoured by the rats." This work, coldly received by the lawyers at Bowood in 1781, Bentham chanced to show to Wilson in

November, 1788, and Wilson, with unusual enthusiasm
for him, urged Bentham to publish it at once.

Bentham's Abstract Doctrine in 1789 II

By 1789, the date of the publication of the *Principles of
Morals and Legislation,* the main outlines of the Benthamic philosophic and legal doctrines were clearly
enough stated to be worth considering in some detail at
this point. We shall do well to consider the system as an
abstract whole, beginning with the felicific calculus as
found in the text of the *Principles* (see p. 113).

The question is, of course, whether an attempt to
classify, to analyze, and to measure human pleasures
and pains is possible at all, even for the fairly crude
purposes of the legislator. It is the intent of this volume
to make clear what Bentham's thought was, rather than
condescendingly to put him straight where he was
wrong. Anyone who disagrees with him can do that,
though most of those who have done it in print have begun by misrepresenting him. The representation of Bentham's systematic thought is extremely important if one
is to understand the events of his life. More than almost
any other thinker who dealt with political matters,
Bentham's work was his life. Time and again he entered
the arena of practical politics, but by the time all the
necessary compromises were made, Benthamism had
almost evaporated. Eventually he faced the stern necessity of writing for an age to come into being a
hundred years after he was dead. Since we are that age,
we should perhaps look at him not as historians, but as
human beings to whom legislation and morals are important in themselves.

THE FELICIFIC CALCULUS

Most writers who have discussed Bentham's felicific

calculus, from John Stuart Mill on, have been in such haste to get to its weaknesses and shortcomings that they have not been much interested in giving a straightforward exposition of the scheme. Let us then, for a moment, make Bentham's assumptions with him, at least until we see what are the actual logical consequences of his analysis. Since most of the hostile criticism turns on the idea that some human satisfactions are so much higher than others that the distance between them is immeasurable, let us begin with the observation that Bentham too has a hierarchy of values, not strikingly dissimilar from that of his critics. The difference comes in his belief that, if any act, thing, or person is *compared,* favorably or unfavorably, with another, a scale of measurement can be created to describe the judgment made, for by making a comparison, *any* comparison, a scale of differences is implied.

It may well be that by classifying Bentham's 14 pleasures into groupings of our own more conventionally accepted in the Western tradition, we shall be able better to understand his calculations.

Let us divide his 14 pleasures, then, into two main groups, which we shall call "privative pleasures" and "expansive pleasures." Privative pleasures might also be called "engrossing pleasures"—their characteristic mark is that, in general, the more I have of such pleasures the less other people have. In the list of privative pleasures we have four out of Bentham's list of 14: (1) sense, (2) wealth, (3) power, (4) malevolence. They are very real pleasures, all of them, and from some writers one would suppose that they comprised the Bentham's entire list, rather than the demonstrably lowest and least valuable.

The expansive pleasures are opposite to the privative in that, in general, the more I have of such pleasures, the more pleasures others have created for them, directly or indirectly. We may divide these expansive pleasures into three classes: the social pleasures, the pleasures of art and science, and the pleasures of religion. The social pleasures in Bentham's list would be three:

(1) amity, (2) good name, and (3) benevolence, all tending to be centered around the emotions, as the privative are around desires. The pleasures of art and science, or the intellectual group, speaking roughly, are linked up with discipline, that is to say with man's ability to stamp his mind and will on the recalcitrant materials of nature and of thought. If it were not for these pleasures, man would sheer away from the arduous toil involved in all disciplined activity. It is because these pleasures are rich, rare, and delightful that anyone who has known them prefers them to the privative pleasures valued by slaves and undeveloped persons. They are, of course, the pleasures (1) of skill, (2) of memory, (3) of imagination, (4) of association, (5) of expectation, and (6) of relief. They are demonstrably and measurably superior to the privative pleasures. One pleasure remains of the fourteen: the pleasure of piety. Bentham was not religious himself, but he defined these pleasures as those "that accompany the persuasion of a man's being in the acquisition or in possession of the goodwill or favour of the Supreme Being: and as a fruit of it, of his being in a way of enjoying pleasures to be received by God's special appointment, either in this life or in a life to come." Now considering that pleasures are usually complex, that is to say, composed of combinations of these 14 simple pleasures, it would seem that the pleasures of piety accompanied by those of power, of memory, of association, of expectation, and of imagination, if not full enough to satisfy a religious mystic convinced that the present world is dust and illusion, would at least suggest that the religious life could be rich in pleasure and in better pleasures, demonstrably and measurably, than those of sense and of wealth. Sometimes, of course, the pleasures of piety are allied to those of malevolence, but this is a rather poverty-stricken set of pleasures compared to those mentioned.

What does one mean by "lowest and least valuable, by measurement" in referring to pleasures? The answer lies in the fact that a pleasure is measured in relationship to its seven *dimensions:* certainty, propinquity, purity, intensity, duration, fecundity, and extent. These have been arranged in a somewhat different order from that used by Bentham, in order to achieve a simple mathematical approach. As here arranged, the first three —certainty, propinquity, and purity—can be expressed only as fractions, that is, they approach the figure *one* as their limit. Few pleasures are completely pure, or, to say it in another way, most pleasures have something in the way of pain either accompanying them or resulting from them. "Stay awhile, thou art so fair," we cry to the golden moment of happiness, but it will not stay with us. Certainty also only becomes complete when the thing has happened. Anything less than that can only be expressed by a fraction. Propinquity is fractional, in the same way, because the goal to be reached is the limit set. *Very near, almost, approximation* are the fractional expressions. So too are *very distant, tending toward,* n^{-10}. On the whole, life being what it is, one may say that each of these dimensions of a pleasure tends to be *subtractive* of the sum arrived at by consideration of the other four dimensions, i.e., intensity, duration, fecundity, and extent, all of which are to be expressed by whole numbers. The unit of intensity is the smallest amount that can be perceived. The unit of duration is the shortest time that can be perceived and registered in terms of the pleasure. Of all the seven dimensions, it is clear that the most powerful, mathematically speaking, are fecundity and extent. Fecundity is the power of giving birth to other pleasures, and extent is the number of persons affected.

Dimensions are multiplied by each other, and pleasures of different values are added to each other.

The limited dimensions of certainty and propinquity are most important in balancing the exchange of present pain against future pleasure. If men are to labor hard, they usually wish to be certain of their pay, both as to amount and as to time of payment. Farmers and mining prospectors seem to undervalue so much these elements of the calculus of pleasure that one is forced to conclude either that their rational powers are feeble, or that there are other pleasures, stronger than those of wealth, to be found in a gambler's or in a farmer's way of life—pleasures of power, perhaps, for the ability to refuse to work for money is one of the most striking kinds of power. Pleasures of skill, of association, of imagination, and of expectation, at least, might go far in making up the defect in the pleasure of wealth, but the certainty of amount of wealth might be counted on to motivate larger numbers of people.

Bentham probably tended to stress these limitative factors chiefly because he began his work in terms of legislation. The legislator's stock consists mainly of pains. If offences are to be prevented, the pains annexed to correcting them must be dealt out quickly and surely. If not, then about all the legislator can do is to increase the intensity of the punishment and hope for results. The eighteenth-century legislator was a good example of this process. There were 160 offences punishable by death, but there was no police force worth mentioning, and crime flourished.

If we are to consider the great, the magnificent, the noble pleasures, however, we must go to the opposite pole from the legislator's concern with crime. Let us consider instead the relationship of genius and of great art to the idea of pleasure. Is great art great because of its contribution to man's pleasure, or is it something so inherently different from everything else, and different in a way that defies analysis, that measurement is absurd? If we take the first answer to be true rather than the second, it seems clear that our demonstration must rest largely on the dimensions of fecundity and extent. Let us, half playfully, see what can be done in measuring things as absurdly different as a good dinner and a Mozart opera.

Let us begin with the dinner considered as a work of art in order to be just to civilized man. The Masai tribesman opens a vein of one of his cattle and drinks blood when he wishes a meal, and in doing so he undoubtedly enjoys the pleasures of sense, of wealth, and of relief. Still the total value of the pleasure adds up to a pretty small sum, even if we assign to intensity a figure of ten or twenty times the minimum of one. Privative pleasures can't go very high. A civilized dinner almost inevitably starts by considering something more than the pleasures of sense. The wine I drink may have a delicate aroma and marked taste, complementing or supplementing the fish, fowl, roast, sweet, sour, bitter or salt of other elements in the repast. But most of all, since I am a man and not a pig, it will evoke memories of other times and of other persons, of shared experiences, of Burgundian hillsides or claret in Cambridge college halls. A good dinner, in other words, is a considerable work of art, full of the pleasures of skill, of power, of amity, of memory, carried to a very considerable pitch of intensity. The person who has made such a thing and presented it to his guests may well feel some of the pleasure of benevolence as well as all the others, *including sense.*

Let us say we give our Masai warrior's gulped-down ration of blood a composite value of 150, i.e., certainty = 1 x proximity = 1 x purity = 1 x intensity = 10 x duration = 5 x fecundity = 0 x extent = 1 = 50 for each of the pleasures.

$$sense = 50$$
$$wealth = 50$$
$$relief = 50$$

Added, the total is 150. We can see that the more numerous group participating in the civilized dinner will increase the dimensions of extent to, say, eight and the dimension of duration to at least ten or a value of 800 for each pleasure, and we have added four more pleasures, making seven in all: 7 x 800 = 5,600. The proportion, 5,600 to 150, seems a reasonable one to anyone who has known both situations. The state of nature *is* "poor, nasty, short, and brutish" whether one draws the conclusion from his own interior divine revelation, from observation, or from a calculus of pleasures. Even a dinner, we see, is valuable in proportion to what is added to the pleasure of the senses.

A dinner, however, is weak in one of its dimensions—fecundity. Fecundity is the power of giving birth to other pleasures, and it is in this dimension, as well as that of extent, that art has so powerful a multiplier that many have mistaken it for infinitude. There are and have been a great many men but not an infinite number. The distance to the farthest perceptible star is very great, but is not infinite. We may measure that distance by light-years rather than by a foot rule, but we do measure it.

Fecundity and extent are ideas so important in shaping our thinking, they show themselves in so many different ways, and at times they are so difficult to detect that a few examples taken from technology may throw some light on the nature of pleasure produced by art. Take an electrical generator, then. Its most familiar form is to be found mounted on the engine of an automobile: 20 pounds or so of iron and copper and carbon and fiberglass insulation, charging a battery to supply light and start the engine, run the radio, or even, as we get weaker and weaker, to open and close windows for us. It is a most ingenious device, but in this form, it has very little *extent,* since it serves only three or four people. It has no *fecundity,* being incapable of reproducing even itself. If we go to any modern powerhouse, we find a generator, also composed of iron and copper and carbon and fiberglass insulation, but larger in size, weighing many tons instead of a few pounds; still nothing more than a rotor spinning quietly in its bearings, with an electric current flowing through its terminals. Its difference from our automobile generator is not simply one of size, though it may well put out a hundred thousand times as much current. Its extent is consequently considerable, since it may light up a city of a hundred thousand people. Its real difference lies in its fecundity, for it *can* reproduce itself. That is to say, it can smelt metals, make fiberglass from stone, purify carbon, wind coils, and run lathes. Its fecundity is so great that a simple observer from another planet might be forgiven if he insisted that it was a living thing or animal, while the automobile generator was obviously a machine; that the two were so different as to be absolutely incommensurable.

Now, in the world of human pleasure, there is some such difference as this between the pleasures grouped around a good dinner and those accompanying or generated by a great work of art. Probably the experience furthest removed from what most of us are capable of would be, say, Mozart at the height of his powers at work on *The Magic Flute*. (Anyone unfortunate enough not to admire *The Magic Flute* may use *Don Giovanni* instead.) The compound structure of immediate pleasure to Mozart must have been high in value, even after all the pain and frustration inevitable in so complex a task—pleasures of power, of skill, of association, of imagination, and of memory especially. The Greeks knew, as every artist knows, that memory is the mother of the Muses. There was the pleasure of benevolence, witness Sarastro, and there was even the pleasure of piety, for to Mozart the enlightenment and the Masonic theme of light after darkness can hardly be called anything but religious feeling. All these pleasures have been generated and have been felt by Mozart when we finally get the text of the opera committed to paper, before horsehair and sheep-gut and vibrating reeds have so much as entered the picture, except in Mozart's mind and memory.

Mozart is dust, and ten generations of composers and violinists and singers and conductors and oboists have followed him. Today it is probable, given the thousands of record copies of the opera, that there is no hour of the day or night but finds this music heard by someone. What figure shall we assign to the dimension of extent, or number of persons affected? It is a large number, but any competent statistician or social historian could give us a figure sufficiently exact to enable us to compare it to the number of dinner guests in our first example so that the enormous disproportion stated as a mathematical ratio would be acceptable to most of us.

Fecundity is less easily measurable, for its increase is geometrical rather than arithmetical. To use a physical metaphor, extent is like a stone dropped in a pond or a meteorite hitting the sea. The waves move out in an ever-increasing circle until the energy is absorbed entirely. Fecundity is more like a nuclear chain-reaction, with increasing amounts of energy released as we proceed from the starting point. How much of the pleasure we experience in hearing Beethoven or Strauss or Verdi may have been originally engendered in the work of Mozart would be difficult to estimate and not worth examining into for any purpose beyond our immediate one of trying to see whether Bentham's dimensions give us the significant data we need for assigning a mathematical value to pleasure.

Perhaps here is the best place to discuss one of the most frequently quoted of Bentham's remarks: "Pleasure for pleasure, pushpin is as good as poetry." Even if one took the remark as literal and complete, without qualification or limitation, it could be answered by saying that, since Bentham in other places says more significant and truer things about the nature of pleasure, one may ignore this. As he himself puts it in one place: "Not having the honour to be Pope, I have no pretensions to infallibility; having never had the honour to belong to any party, I am under no promise never to become wiser."* Probably the difficulty lies in the phrase "as good as," for there *is* an apparent antinomy or contradiction between two positions in the utilitarian doctrine. The first says, "One pleasure is as good as another, since both represent a clear balance of pleasure over pain in order for the word pleasure to mean anything at all." The second statement says, "Pleasure for pleasure, one pleasure is almost always measurably better than another, since its dimensions are demonstrably greater." We can see that the two are not really contradictory if

*Mss. U.C., Port. III, p. 225.

we change the word *pleasure* to the word *life*. Life for life, a mouse is as good as an elephant, since both are highly complex organisms, well adjusted to the environment. On the other hand, life for life, a mouse is *not* so good as an elephant in terms of utility to man, of money value, of size, or of length of life. There is nothing mysterious or mystical about the differences. They are measurable. It may be said with some truth that all life is one, as all energy is one. Having said as much, Western man, at least, proceeds to consider the differences in the forms in which life manifests itself, e.g., the variations in levels of energy. And one way of considering them is to measure them, however crudely.

Fecundity has certain important relations to the privative pleasures. It is not ordinarily of much significance to the pleasures of sense, since these generally tend to resent the presence even of any other pleasure in their vicinity. When the cult of sensual pleasure was at its peak in England in the 1890's—art for art's sake, burning with a hard gemlike flame—some of its high priests tried to cultivate all the senses simultaneously, the exquisite linen, luxurious decor, perfumes on the air, and music blended with the truffles. They found that the music had to be pretty bad to be tolerated as an accompaniment to food; that wine, women, and song, in short, were almost mutually exclusive if one really cared anything for wine or women or song. The pleasures of amity and of association are moderately fecund, to be sure, and since civilized people seldom indulge the pleasures of sense in a form so poverty-stricken as to be separated from the better pleasures, sense itself in recollection makes memory fruitful by bringing in all the associated pleasures.

Perhaps the major differences between the legislator's attitude toward pleasures and pains and that of the artist is this, that the legislator should always be conscious of what he is doing and prepared to defend his course rationally. He is engaged in liberally dispensing pains on every hand, whether as taxes or coercions.

There is nothing else he can dispense—except permissions or licenses letting my neighbor do something I am forbidden to do. The artist, on the other hand, works slowly and painfully toward an end of which he is not quite certain. Dr. Johnson put it bluntly when he said that only a fool ever wrote for anything except money, yet how little even of Johnson's work had more than the slightest possible relation to money it is easy to see. He may have written the *Vanity of Human Wishes* to pay his mother's funeral expenses, and Milton may have paid bills with the £10 he secured for *Paradise Lost,* but the complex of pleasures that have grown out of Johnson's work and of Milton's have little to do with the pleasures of sense or of wealth. Their extent is longer, their fecundity tremendous.

THE FOUR ENDS OF GOVERNMENT

In making use of calculation as to pleasures and pains, the legislator will have considered his specific measure with respect to the four ends of government: subsistence, abundance, security, and equality. Only in this way can he be certain of what he is doing. All legislators and sovereigns have had something of an intuitive awareness of how these matters operate, but it seems probable that a rational awareness of ends aimed at and the means best calculated to bring about those ends would enable the legislator to work more surely and more effectively.

In his statement and exposition of these ends of government, Bentham was always a political realist, concerned mainly with ascertaining how men do act in given situations, and prepared to deal with such actions. The most difficult thing in any government is how to deal with the strong man. Bentham knew that wealth would always be able to make itself felt in any form of government, and his way of recognizing the fact was not to abolish wealth, but to make sure that its operation should be in the open rather than underground. The wealthy man would hate the controls that touched on his "freedom," but Bentham knew that property was the creation of law, and he was not afraid of phrases like "freedom" or "natural rights." " 'Natural rights' is nonsense," he said; " 'inalienable and imprescriptible rights' is merely nonsense on stilts." For in his view rights are constructed by law, and without law there is only the right of the strongest to take what he wishes and of the possessor to keep what he can hold onto. As for property, he showed what a highly metaphysical and legal construction that is by pointing out that it has nothing to do with possession, with contiguity, or with habitual use. When you are challenged as to your ownership of anything, only one answer is adequate—the magistrate's announcement that you are allowed to act in a certain way toward a certain object while everyone else in the world is coerced from so acting—if necessary with the help of the entire army and navy. Your freedom is the coercion, actual or implied, of everyone else. Even so, Bentham thought property to be the greatest force tending to the production of abundance, one of his four ends of government.

The ends of government in Bentham's system are subsistence, abundance, security, and equality. Property trenched on equality. How much it should be allowed to do so would depend on the relative values assigned abundance and equality. As to subsistence, Bentham approached the matter in an analytical fashion. Of any ten persons chosen at random, we shall find some incapable of providing their own subsistence. The infant, the aged, the feebleminded or insane must be subtracted at once as a dead load on the remainder. Many more are capable of producing something toward their own subsistence but less than the necessary minimum. Since, even in India, the population is increasing, it must be true that a good many men are gifted with *extra* ability. Consequently, the mark of a good society is the way in which this extra ability is made use of. One can, of course, kill off the aged and helpless, and exposed the unwanted infants, and there have been societies that answered the problem in that way. One can make slaves of the stupid, the irresponsible, or say, the physical and mental inferiors, in order to make sure that what they can do they shall be made to do, and even more societies have settled the matter in that fashion. Bentham thought it possible to have a better society, that is to say, a society with greater happiness and less pain, if one were willing to take seriously the relationship between subsistence and abundance.

In thinking of the legislator, Bentham thought always as a calculator, an economist. What is the *balance* as between pleasures and pains after the legislator has acted? Insofar as the balance is in the black ink of pleasures rather than in the red ink of pains, he has acted properly. If he has done so, the society has moved that far away from poverty and toward abundance. Since there will always be a huge load of unproductive persons riding on the shoulders of the producer—the aged, the infant (and man's infancy lasts for many years before he can support himself), the helpless, the tax collector, the policeman, the insane, any criminal not put to death—it is surely the legislator's task to smooth the path for the producer rather than to badger or interfere with him, *unless* the balance of pleasures can be demonstrably increased by so doing. Civilization, in short, in Bentham's view, rests on abundance, a quite different concept from that, not unknown in our own time, of an equitably shared poverty. Poverty, he insists, is the normal, the *natural* state of society. This must be true since less than half the population is capable even of providing for its own subsistence. Only in a complex society with good laws and a good constitution can any considerable abundance exist, and that abundance will be proportional to the merit of the laws and of the constitution.

Abundance is really Bentham's major aim, for if even subsistence is something that cannot be taken for granted, abundance can come into being only in a complex society with good laws. The two other ends of government that he sets up are means to the production of abundance as well as good in themselves. They are security and equality, linked in a reciprocal way to each other. Security there must be in order for extra ability to reap the fruit of its labor and be protected in the peaceful enjoyment of it. Absolute equality there cannot be, given the various endowments of men, but there should be as close an approximation as is consistent with security and abundance. And by equality, Bentham means primarily economic equality.

THE METHOD OF PERIPHRASIS*

Aware as we are of this sympathetic perception of the complex range of pleasures and pains felt by men, by actual human beings capable of feeling deeply, of anticipating the future and remembering the past—as students of law and of man in society we must move to the other extreme of knowing the language of abstraction. What is the meaning of such terms as *power, right, liberty, protection, privilege, immunity, exemption,* and *property?* To give the answer in full would be to reproduce some hundreds of thousands of the words Bentham wrote and published. We shall not go far wrong, however, if, in considering such terms, we insist that they maintain a constant reciprocal relationship with actual pains and pleasures, even though our analysis may begin with a largely formal structure.

It is hardly too much to say that we *think* by means of "fictitious entities," to use Bentham's term. In his earliest work, the *Comment on the Commentaries,* Bentham explained his method of "periphrasis" for making clear whatever meaning is tied up in the complex bundle of a fictitious entity. This should not be confused with a legal fiction, which is a deliberate or unconscious attempt to conceal reality, to mislead the reader. It is true that the method of periphrasis will also bring to

---

*I am deeply indebted for much of this material on periphrasis to an unpublished doctoral dissertation, *Bentham and the Method of Periphrasis,* by Christopher Wright, now Associate Director of the Columbia University Council for Atomic Age Studies.

light the true nature of a legal fiction, and that is always worth doing, but it is a relatively negative activity. Bentham used the term "fictitious entities" rather than "abstractions," its nearest synonym, in order to deal with a large number of ideas not always recognized as abstractions. In particular, the idea of property needed, he felt, the most careful kind of analysis, yet to many a man his property is the most concrete thing he can think of. He can touch it, handle it, use it. If it has no relation to his pains and pleasures, what has? The very bread he puts into his mouth is by virtue of its being his property. To find out what makes the bread his property, however, involving as it does the pains and services of dozens of other men from the ploughman to the delivery boy, means that we must deal with numerous fictitious entities such as law, magistracy, and coercion. For property is the creation of law, a fictitious entity itself.

The great constructive activity of linking up actuality with language is what man does whenever he can be said to be thinking. Too much attention has probably been paid to Bentham's later work on Fictions, first published by Dumont in 1814 and so much simplified that Bentham angrily said that Dumont had *never* understood him. It was this later work which most interested C. K. Ogden because it was close to his own theories of the nature of language and did not have the close linking to ideas about law and about property in Bentham's early work. *The Limits of Jurisprudence Defined*, though written in 1780, was not available for study until after 1945, and it is in *Limits* that the method of periphrasis is used with the brilliance and energy of youth. Bentham used the method to study such fictitious entities as property, obligation, rights, services, permission, command, and prohibition. Fictitious though these entities are, they are the only way by which we can describe the complex relationships between man and man; they are the key to analysis of how these entities are defined, and the way in which they come to bear on the final actualities of pain and pleasure. The term "jural relationships" is used by some modern students of jurisprudence to describe certain aspects of this same web.

Bentham's use of periphrasis is meant to be dynamic rather than static. Conventional definition by *genus* and *differentiam* is based on a static idea of classification. Such questions as "To what group does this object belong?" and "In what way does it differ from other members of the group?" may be a useful, brief way of pigeonholing an object, but life is a very complex business not well suited to pigeonholing. Pigeonholing may tell us what conventional opinion is with regard to the thing defined—it can seldom tell us what are its potentialities. For that the mind must be able to walk all around the thing, to feel its way through at least a significant number of threadlike connections with fictitious entities on its own level or on other levels, and to observe the connections with pain and pleasure. If none can be found with pain and pleasure, either one hasn't looked hard enough, or the fictitious entity, though conceivable, is empty of significant meaning.

It cannot be insisted too often how far Bentham was ahead of his time in his approach to thinking about the nature of language, so far indeed that he seems still far ahead of the point reached by Ogden and Richards 30 years ago. Semantics, or the proper way of communicating what one thinks, is an important subject matter and far from easy to be sure of, but *what* it is one thinks is even more important. Most conventional opinion seems to regard the thinker as a man with a somewhat wider range of view than the rest of us. He has climbed to the first or second ridge of the mountain range surrounding the valley where we live. He sees more, he sees more widely, he sees farther. Implicit in this concept of experience, however, is the presumption that any one of us, placed at the same elevation, would see as much. This whole concept suffers mainly from the defect that it is in its nature static. One must *know* in order to *see*, and knowing is a dynamic process. If the man who climbs remains the same man, the higher he climbs the less he understands of what his eyes look at. If he were a true Benthamite, he would spend a year on the lower slopes in study, so that when he looked at a forest he would see the ecological relations of oak and beech and ash and thorn and bracken and mold and mushroom and soil chemistry and water flow; on the next ridge, the same for pine and juniper and the alpine plants. On the next ridge above the treeline, he would spend another year, until rocks ceased to be rock and became the beds of ancient seas mixed with liquid fire and upheaved, twisted, bent, and shaved smooth by ice in an infinitely long period of time, all revealing itself to his eye as clearly as the hands of the clock tell the hour. Our Benthamite might be said to *see* the expanded view he gazes upon. The ordinary climber is like the tourist seeing Europe from the air.

Yet the greatest irony of all the ironies with respect to Bentham, and they are many, is that to most minds he is primarily interested in classifying—in pigeonholing. Leslie Stephen even uses that word: "Things thus present themselves to Bentham's mind as already prepared to fit into pigeonholes."

Let us return to our periphrasis, not as a semantic process, but as a way of thinking. As has been said, Bentham thought that there were several levels of fictitious entities more or less removed in distance from the foundation in (what may be called for convenience) the actuality of pains and pleasures. If we examine a fictitious entity such as power, by this method, we see how we are led on inevitably from point to point. A power, for example, may be said to be either over things or over persons. If over things, it may be either the type of power a badger has in excavating his burrow, or a power over things may imply a rather elaborate set of powers over persons, that is to say, a right to their services. Man is a social being and a tool user as soon in history as we have any evidence of his existence at all. Cro-Magnon man was a mighty hunter and his power over animals was considerable, but as a man he set up many claims to services by others even if the killing of the deer was a solitary enterprise. The cave paintings and graffiti suggest that the first thing he did in hunting was to make use of ritual. The artist created the image of the deer, the priest struck through the image with the ritual weapon, and *then* the hunter went out to exercise a power over nature. It would seem probable that the process also tended to create a special kind of *right* to the slain deer beyond the mere physical ability to hold possession of it against anyone weaker than oneself. The right would be to ask for the help of all proper members of the clan against some burly thug who proposed to take the deer away from the hunter. In other words, a power over things has been created by a *right* to services. In a similar way, a power over persons in its crudest form may rest on individual physical strength, but in any important form it will imply social action, either of restraint, of constraint, or of forbearance, action approved of by the group. Where these things exist, we have society and we have law. Where they do not, we have neither. *Liberty,* for example, means very little if all it means is the liberty to hide my slain deer away until some heavyweight twists my arm to make me reveal the hiding place. Liberty necessarily involves the *coercion* of anyone who would interfere with me in the exercise of that liberty. How far my liberty should extend is a question that will be decided for me by the society in which I reside. Far from being a *right,* it is a legal creation of great delicacy and complexity. But what is a *right?*

Bentham would say that the word *right* is meaningless until the law has spoken. If I have a right, it is because the magistrate has announced that he will enforce it. There must have been certain "investive" and "collative" events occurring to provide evidence that the *right* is mine. I have inherited a farm on the death of my father, not because I have a natural right to the inheritance, but because the sovereign has announced that the death of an owner of real estate shall be one of the collative events investing the eldest son with that right.

It would be equally "natural" for the investiture to take place on the eldest daughter or on a sister of the owner, if the law so chose. A will—that is to say, a witnessed document in a certain form prepared and signed by the testator to come into effect after his death—is not valid because such documents create rights, but because the sovereign has announced that he will adopt as his own determination the desires of testators that follow certain prescribed formal patterns. If he had announced that all real estate should become state property on the death of the present holders, the rights of the heirs would not be worth talking about.

Rights, then, are what law is about. "In direct legislation," says Bentham, "it is the business of the civil branch to distribute proprietary and other rights, of the penal to provide punishment for the violation of those rights: of the constitutional to distribute rights to be exercised for the benefit of the community at large."*

But what is this *property* we have been talking about? It is not based on possession, for wrongful possession or acceptance is a frequent cause of controversy in any legal system. Act of using, act of handling, none of these will do for Bentham. To him property is a set of *expectations* based on experience. Property, that is, is a *grounded* expectation of being allowed to act in a particular way with respect to something while at the same time everybody else in the world is coerced from so acting except with your permission. This is indeed to occupy a highly privileged position, a position that can be justified on the ground of the greatest happiness to the greatest number only if the legislator keeps clearly in mind the relationship between the pains of labor and the creation of wealth.

This is indeed the main purpose of the involved treatise on language dealt with under the term *periphrasis*—to help the legislator. Since all he has to work with is pain, since my reward is your taxation, my freedom your coercion, let him think first about his edicts in

*Mss. U.C., Port. 99, p. 118.

terms of their immediate consequences in pain. Let him think what *rights* are, what *property* is, about what *law* is. In considering these concepts, the method of periphrasis will be helpful. If he does think in this manner, the final result of his actions may well be the triumph of good over evil, a balance of pleasure over pain.

1792 to 1808   III

The year 1792 marks a dividing line in the life of Bentham for several reasons. He was forty-four years old, but in one sense he was only a promising young man, running from a good scheme to a better one. For 20 years he had lived on the £103 a year left him from his mother's inheritance, writing books no one could read except for a few experts. At forty-four he came into his inheritance on his father's death, amounting to something like £700 a year, and he could at last go on with his Panopticon project. As has been said, the result was a failure, though it took 20 years for the government to acknowledge that Bentham must in justice be paid £23,000, a great part of which he had already spent on plans and land.

The year 1792 marks also the death of his French admirers, le Comte de Mirabeau and le duc de la Rochefoucauld, and the beginning of the Terror in France.

His acquaintance with Dumont was to continue, however, with really important results. As a consequence of their partnership, the *Traités* appeared in 1802, to be followed by the *Théorie des peines et des récompenses* in 1811, *Tactique des assemblées législatives* in 1816; *Traité des preuves judiciaires* in 1823; and *De l'organization judiciaire et de la codification* in 1829. Dumont died in 1830, aged seventy, but he had given Bentham worldwide fame in their 37 years of collaboration. Even as early as 1816, Dumont had written to Bentham from Geneva, "Mme. de Staël has been reading in society the *Book of Fallacies,* and with great success."

Apart from his relationships with Dumont, Bentham continued to write ten or fifteen pages a day on Evidence, on Procedure, on the wickedness of the British government, as well as some thousands of letters yearly about the Panopticon scheme.

COLQUHOUN AND THE THAMES POLICE BILL

Aside from Panopticon, the most important event in Bentham's political activity in this period was his co-operation with Patrick Colquhoun in 1798 on the Thames Police Bill. He drew up for Colquhoun, a London magistrate, a bill for the organization of the Thames police so carefully adjusted to the actual needs of London that all its main provisions were in operation 50 years later, though by that time both Bentham and Colquhoun were dead. In 1798, however, the political system was so entrenched in habit and in special privilege that nothing could be done. To read the history of any reform in England at our distance of a century and a half is to find a world of Alice in Wonderland, a spectacle that only the comic genius of a Dickens could represent.

The Thames Police Bill proposed by Colquhoun seems to cover a rather limited subject, a few miles of tidal stream with the quays adjoining. Actually, however, one had in the river a large number of the problems of constitutional law beautifully exemplified—vague and overlapping jurisdictions: Parliament, the Corporation of the City of London, the parishes and the magistrates. Wherever one looked, and Colquhoun insisted on looking, there was confusion, waste, and crime. Entrenched special interests were well repreresented in Parliament—the new sources of wealth and commerce were not. Professor Radzinowicz has given a documented picture of the corruption of officials that almost passes belief.* Parliament played its part. Select committee after select committee was appointed—1796, 1799, 1800—and each made its recommendations for improvement. "The implementation of their proposals was impeded by quay owners and others who had vested interests in the area."

On account of silting up of the channels (though "silt" is a polite name for the materials), vessels sometimes had to wait a week before they could reach the Pool, where they anchored at random, sometimes as many as 775 in a space designed for a maximum of 545. About 2,000 barges and lighters took off the cargoes eventually, though ships and cargoes sometimes had to wait as long as six weeks. The goods, or some of them, were landed at the quays from the lighters, where they were examined by the customs. Few of the quays were roofed. With no light capable of illuminating anything over 20 feet away from it, one can see why rum and sugar and spices at least tended to shrink in transit. Apart from the ordinary night plunderers, mud larks, and river pirates, the most interesting groups were the light-horsemen, composed of gangs of watermen, lumpers (longshoremen), and coopers. These would purchase a license to plunder a ship from the mate and the revenue officer at from 20 to 30 guineas a night to each officer. Colquhoun estimated that, of the 1,400 revenue officers, 700 were delinquents, though of the 3,444 mates, only 500 were false to their trust. Six out of seven of the lumpers, however, were thieves. Accompanied then by a revenue officer, the light-horsemen would board a ship, the lumpers would bring up the barrels, the coopers would open them, and the black bags known as "black straps" would be filled, the barrels reheaded and stowed back in the hold, and the lighter's

*Leon Radzinowicz, *A History of English Criminal Law and Its Administration from 1750* (3 vols., London: Macmillan & Co., 1956), Vol. II, pp. 349–404. "A Venture in Preventive Police" gives the full story with an account of the part Bentham played in Colquhoun's Thames Police Bill.

cargo delivered to the waiting receivers down the river. If by ill chance a revenue sloop was encountered, the revenue officer would announce the cargo as confiscated goods under his possession. The West India merchants alone estimated their losses at nearly £300,000 per annum.

Despite these facts, the Lord Mayor and the Court of Common Council objected to Colquhoun's well thought-out bill for the policing of the river as "an infringement of the privileges of the merchants of the City and an improper and unnecessary interference with their jurisdiction." Colquhoun kept on, however. He wrote to the Home Secretary, the Duke of Portland, that he had "laboured for the last three months . . . fixing a system of Legislation applicable to River offences in all their ramifications" in which he has been assisted "by a friend of great legal knowledge." (The legal friend, as Radzinowicz points out, was Bentham, and a summary view of the bill was reprinted in the *Collected Works,* Vol. X, pp. 330–33.) Long negotiations took place, and at one point it seemed likely Colquhoun would be superseded by some Shadwell justice who knew nothing of the matter. Bentham wrote the Speaker of the House: "Whatever intentions may have been entertained by somebody or other, of doing something or other, at some time or other, he is, in point of fact, the creator, and the sole creator of everything what has been done. His services have been gratuitous. . . . He has toiled at it, days and weeks together; he has sitten to be shot at, and has been shot at and seen a man put to death by his side."*

The Thames Police Force came into being in some what modified form in 1800, so that when Sir Robert Peel created the London police force in 1829, he had a quarter of a century's experience to call upon in the precedents of the Thames Police Force. One-fourth of

---

*Jeremy Bentham, *Works,* edited by John Bowring (11 vols., London, 1843), Vol. X, p. 335.

an inch in political reform had been gained, but by 1829 Bentham was no longer interested in the whimsicality of Parliament. He was constructing the Constitutional Code.

For many years before he began the Constitutional Code, Bentham had been deeply engaged in working out a great plan for the solution of the problem of unemployment, attempting to link up the architectural plan of the Panopticon (a structure where the workmen would be at all times under the eye of an inspector at a central point) with a kind of garden village. Wives and children would help the economy by gardening, and the children would be properly educated.

Education was at all times so interesting to Bentham that it is rather surprising to find that the Ministry of Education occupies so little space in the Constitutional Code, a page and half compared to 105 for the defensive force. Partly this was due to the fact that Bentham had written extensively on education in other places, particularly in the *Chrestomathia,* which had been published in two volumes in 1816 and 1817, 15 years before the first volume of the Code was published (the only part seen through the press by Bentham). His whole work is essentially centered on education, and in his plan it is only where education fails that the legislator steps in as a sterner schoolmaster, measuring out pains and coercion to accomplish the socially desirable end. If, as Bentham believed, education is the art of showing people where true happiness lies, if intelligence exists so that we may know what the order of nature is on which our pleasures and our pains depend, and so that we may choose the best means of realizing our desired ends, then to ask whether all people ought to receive an education is quite simply to ask the question whether they ought to be happy or miserable. He was, however, an Englishman, living in the first quarter of the nineteenth century, when such official education as did exist was under the aegis of the Church of England. What Bentham meant by education was neither indoctrination in a creed nor even the spending of years in becoming acquainted with the great classical works in Latin and Greek. He himself had had such an education, and his tremendously complex nomenclature is almost entirely coined from Greek metal.

His system of education was severely utilitarian, so much so that Benthamism came to have for some people the reputation of being crude, rough, and mechanical. This was not because Bentham himself was unaware of the importance of education in the fields of imaginative art, especially of music. Any discipline implies a long and slow process, however rich the eventual award in pleasures. Probably on the whole, in his opinion, the legislator had better keep clear of any attempt to foster the arts, except by education. Why produce undoubted pain by taxation, for a doubtful result? The amount of pain produced by taxation is quite simple to estimate.

Pleasure, [he says, is] all destructible by law—what [i.e., it is] not producible [by it]. All pleasures whatever it is within the Law's power to prevent: of the most refined and delicate pleasures the production is not within its power. It may with certainty prevent a man from any pleasure he would have in seeing a good Tragedy—by preventing him from seeing any Tragedies. But it can not with anything near to equal certainty cause him to have any of that pleasure which some men feel at seeing a good Tragedy. It cannot give him that disposition of mind which qualifies him for relishing a good Tragedy. What is more it cannot by any means be sure (though it may do a great deal towards it) of letting him have good Tragedies to see. It may, by its commands on the persons who are to pay, furnish the instruments of all sorts that are requisite for the exhibition of Tragedies. It may pay authors, hire actors, and furnish scenery and music. But whether those authors shall write well, those actors perform well, the scenery be well painted and well shifted, and the music well performed is more than it can make sure of. In point of pleasure it may furnish the means, but it cannot ensure the application.

As to the business of producing pleasures it can operate only by the indirect, the slow, the distant, the precarious way of Education.

The only place in relation to education where Bentham allowed his imagination to run riot (and for all his spurns and fleers at poetry, imagination was his strongest point) was in his Panopticon scheme. We have seen that he began with the idea of a prison for malefactors (and only relinquished that when political opposition blocked it as a practical possibility), but the plan grew to include the whole problem of unemployment and the unemployable. Indigence was no crime, and even for crimes no more pain should be produced than was necessary to insure obedience to the law. The poor law was bad because it was irregular and uncertain in its operation. Bentham considered helplessness and inability to conquer in a competitive world sufficiently painful in themselves not to need the penalty of death to reenforce them. He began then to sketch out a great scheme in which society would take over the care and, necessarily, the governance of all those who could not support themselves, either temporarily or permanently. It led him into the necessity for constructing a world for them where at least they should not be a dead weight of expense to those who *were* gainfully employed. Housing would be of the utmost simplicity, but in the interests of health and efficiency it would include central heating and running water in every apartment, facilities at that time unknown to the aristocracy, except perhaps to a few eccentrics. There are thousands of pages of manuscript of the most elaborate detail as to how the economy could function. Food was the major expense, of course, and the earth was ready to supply a great part of that. Gardens and fruit trees could be cultivated to some extent by the feeblest even of women and children. There is an improved *ptenotrophium,* or hen-and-egg factory, to make use of waste (what waste? one wonders) and of spoiled grain bought in quantity and stored in scientifically controlled magazines. There is a *frigidarium,* or underground ice house. Bentham spent hundreds of pounds in constructing such an edifice in his garden, storing meat bought at low prices in seasons of a glutted market, and he kept accurate records over more than a year as to how long perishable foods could be stored without decay. Unemployed craftsmen would be employed in a kind of state factory—not wastefully exercising the tenth of a horsepower a strong man can develop, but using water power, steam, and other prime movers. (There are at least a dozen pages of manuscript and drawings on the idea of developing a "flash engine" using gunpowder or any other substance producing expanding gases to drive a piston and turn a wheel.) His two governing principles were "No more expense than can be justified by results" and "No unnecessary pain." He was even willing to trench slightly on the first in favor of a certain number of inexpensive musical instruments to each hundred of his Panopticon population, since the production of music was a very pure source of pleasure, as he knew from his own ability to play the violin and the organ. It was in the educational plans for the children of indigents that he really let his imagination expand. In point of fact, if his scheme had been economically possible, the children of the unemployed would have had more of scientific and technological training furnished them than the most privileged youth of England could have purchased anywhere outside of Germany.

Now the right to exist and even the right to work had been conceded by English law for generations. That is to say, the community accepted its responsibility for the care of its members who were either helpless or unable to work through no fault of their own. The poor law enabled the parish Justices of the Peace to levy a poor rate on the inhabitants, to make an official list of the able unemployed, and to appoint overseers to superintend work furnished them. The poor laws of 1562, of 1572, and of 1601 were extended in 1722 to include the setting up of a workhouse in every parish, implying that any able-bodied man unwilling to accept workhouse conditions and discipline was to be considered a rogue or vagabond unworthy of any assistance. And the general consensus of historians seems to be that the workhouse system succeeded in a considerable measure, at least in reducing the poor rate, and that the poor suffered less than in the system of whimsical personal charity in use on the Continent. By the end of the century, sentiment in England had greatly extended outdoor relief, so that by 1797 Pitt even proposed to regularize by law not only outdoor relief but wage allowances of the Speenhamland type in addition; that is to say that, where the actual wage was below the "normal wage," public assistance should make up the difference.

As far as one can see, Bentham's poor-relief scheme would have broken down all competitors. Slave labor is not particularly efficient, but his slaves might leave at any time, and while they were in the Panopticon they would have more nearly a just share of what they produced than would the free laborers in Britain. With machinery and technology used to the full, their output would also be far greater, no matter what was made— shirts, wheeled vehicles, furniture or tools. Nothing could have been more alien to the British tradition of hand craftsmanship, long apprenticeship, and conventional management. Every unemployed worker used by Bentham would produce twice as much as his traditional employed competitor. Then there would be two more umemployed workers for Bentham to use, until at last there would be something rather like state capitalism on the Russian model. That is to say, something of the sort would happen if laisser faire were allowed free working. Actually, of course, the entrepreneurs would have resorted to political action at once, and since they and the landlords *were* Parliament, no government of the time could have dreamed of putting the scheme into operation.

SIR SAMUEL BENTHAM
AND THE GREAT EXPERIMENT

The whole career of Bentham's brother, Sir Samuel Bentham (the title was given him by the Empress Catherine of Russia), shows that *any* projector who is ahead of his time, in engineering as well as in political economy, will be refused recognition. Sir Samuel's wife quotes an official letter* written in 1813 which shows that the brothers Bentham were really dangerous innovators from the point of view of officialdom or of any accepted order of things. Sir Samuel said:

For my part, I had, whilst in Russia, made some progress in contriving such machinery for shaping wood as should secure accuracy and save manual labour; which contrivances, soon after my return to this country [1791] I had occasion to carry to a much greater extent, with a view to the affording beneficial employment to some thousands of untaught hands in a public establishment; with this view I analyzed the several operations requisite for working in various materials, more particularly in wood; and finding the artificial, but common classification of works according to the trades or handicrafts for which they are used, was productive of a variety of inconveniences, and even mischiefs, I classed the several operations that have place in the working materials of every description, according to the nature of the operations themselves: and in regard to wood particularly, I contrived machines or engines for performing most of those operations, whereby the need of skill and dexterity in the workman was done away with. These machines or engines, being capable of being brought into action by the simple process of

---

*See the book by Maria Bentham: *First Introduction of steam engines into naval arsenals; and machinery set in motion thereby* (London, 1847). She lists 105 principal inventions with their dates, and they include such matters as "Moveable Steam Engines—1801."

turning an axis, were consequently capable of being
worked by a steam engine, or any other inanimate
force. In regard to the application of this machinery
for working in wood, besides the general operations
of planning, rebating, morticing, sawing in curved,
winding, and transverse directions, I had completed
in the way of example an apparatus for preparing all
the parts of a highly finished window sash; another
for every part of the more complicated article, an or-
namented carriage wheel; so as that no dexterity or
skill remaining necessary in the cutting out, shaping
or smoothing the several parts completely, the whole
of those operations were capable of being performed
as well by a steam engine as by manual labour; and
nothing remained for finishing the work of the joiner
or the wheelwright but the putting the several com-
ponent parts together. In the year 1794, it having become generally known that I had at my brother's residence in Queen Square Place these and other machines in a working state,

various members of government boards visited the
place and seem to have been frightened by what they
found, not wholly without reason. Of course their objections were self-contradictory, being to the effect that
machinery was inefficient and uneconomical, and at the
same time that it would put all the skilled laborers out
of jobs. There were, says Sir Samuel,

a variety of objections, such as apprehension of the
derangement of established practice; doubts of the
efficiency or economy of machinery as applied to naval purposes; dread of danger of fire from the use of
steam engines, and of risings of the artificers at the
introduction of machinery to diminish the need of
their skill as well as their labour.

It may well be that Samuel Bentham's appointment
as Inspector-General of Naval Works in 1796 and his
experience in that office until 1805, had much to do

with Jeremy Bentham's decision to turn his attention to a Constitutional Code completely developed. For the Inspector-General had found that wastefulness in money, in time, and in labor was a built-in part of what government existed for, under the British Constitution. *Any* proposal for reform ran into the concrete fact that someone was making money or making a living out of the wastefulness. A mast-pond could be built for £17,525, by Samuel Bentham's estimate, with more abundant water supply and storage than in the one officially estimated at £189,000. The £189,000 one was built. (Actually the cost, counting proper interest on the money over the 31 years allowed for completion of the project would have amounted to £458,000, according to Samuel Bentham's figures.) He proposed, for example, as another small matter, that the carrying out of chips from the Portsmouth dockyard be prohibited. One of the minor officers, who tried to administer this rule, had to be supplied with a guard on his way to and from the dockyard. England was at war with Napoleon, but priceless oak timbers and oak planks were being cut up into "chips," a chip being any piece under three feet in length. In consequence, stairs in new Portsmouth houses were just under three feet wide; doors, shutters, cupboards were formed of wood in pieces just under three feet long. They were solidly built, however, of good material—oak.

He discovered the important fact that a government can be corrupt, even though most of its members are personally honest. A reform requires something like unanimity of opinion and willingness to act; abuses need only one or two men determined to maintain their privileges and profits to be at the right place to block or *postpone* action. At the lowest level, sabotage of steam engines and new types of ships was a commonplace; at the highest level, Lord Spencer, Mr. Nepean, and the Lords of the Admiralty could be convinced, if they could find time to witness a test supervised by Samuel Bentham himself. No intermediary board could be trusted, however honorable most of its members might be. Machinery is extremely easy to sabotage in a way that will convince an honest man who doesn't know much about machinery that the projector is making grandiose claims for an untested novelty. In Jeremy Bentham's words, "a board is a screen."

It was found easier at first to send Samuel Bentham off to Russia to build ships there in order to get rid of an annoyance. To be sure, his dredge, a chain of iron buckets driven by a steam engine, could work to a depth of 28 feet and raise soil at a cost of less than a penny a ton, allowing for capital cost and depreciation —but what of all the honest contractors and laborers deprived of a livelihood?

In the end, both of the brothers were "condemned to join the Baal-peor of bloodsuckers." Samuel was forced out of the naval establishment in 1806 as a really necessary alternative to a complete overhaul of naval building practice. He was given a pension of £1250 a year on the grounds of ill health and distinguished service. He did not wish to retire, and it was really the Admiralty that was suffering from ill health after ten years of Samuel Bentham as Inspector-General. President Madison of the United States should have voted the thanks of the nation to Lord Spencer for the satisfactory outcome of the War of 1812. Judging by the tests in 1804 of Samuel Bentham's sloop-of-war, the *Dart,* armed with 24 32-pounders, which sailed past the entire home fleet under full sail in the channel, American frigates would have had a difficult time in 1812, had a dozen more *Darts* been constructed. By that time, however, Samuel Bentham had been enjoying his pension for six years, and British naval construction had gone back to "sound principles."

Having been convinced by Samuel Bentham's experience that "practical" reform was hopeless, at least as far as the Benthams were concerned, Jeremy turned his main attention to the making of an ideal Constitutional Code, not for the England of his day but for future generations. He did not accept the necessity without a certain amount of personal bitterness. There are semi-humorous passages in his unpublished manuscripts where he insists that there are in Britain only two actual parties, alternating in their control of the country. These are the Oppressionists and the Depredationists. The Oppressionists hate the mass of people so much that they will oppose any measure, even one that would put money into their own pockets, if it would in any way improve the position of the poor. The other party, the Depredationists, are more liberal. To be sure, they are mainly concerned with measures that will bring them money, but they will even allow the condition of the poor to be improved if they themselves profit sufficiently from the measure.

1808 to 1832   IV

Bentham was reenforced in this radical view of the political world by a new group of young men whom he encountered in 1808. In fact, we may say that the year marks a transition in Bentham's life hardly less significant than the year 1792. At the age of sixty he was to find for the first time a number of able and eager young Englishmen prepared to act on his principles and, in some instances, to help spread his ideas.

The most important of these men was James Mill, aged thirty-five. He had turned away from the vocation of clergyman, for which he had been trained at the University of Edinburgh, had made his way in Scotland and in London by the power of his reviews in the great quarterlies, and had come to admire the work of Bentham before he had met him. In 1809 he helped Bentham edit the *Elements of the Art of Packing as Applied to Special Juries,* a work that struck directly at the governmental trick of using juries to achieve the desires of the central government, but Bentham's old friend, Sir Samuel Romilly, persuaded Bentham not to publish the pamphlet, which he was certain would invite prosecution. (It was published twelve years later, in 1821.) In 1810, Major Cartwright, one of the radicals who proposed both universal suffrage and the secret ballot, joined the group. Henry Brougham (later Lord Brougham) who had known Mill at Edinburgh, shared some of their ideas, and was beginning to make his way in the political and legal world. Sir Frances Burdett in Parliament forwarded measures agreed on by such other members of Mill's acquaintance as Henry Bickerstith (later Lord Langdale) and Francis Place. Place was the radical tailor of Charing Cross, and he was in some ways the ablest political manager of them all. (It was Place, 20 years later, who defeated the Duke of Wellington on the Reform Bill by posting placards that said: "To stop the Duke, go for gold." A run on the Bank of England neither Whigs nor Tories could face, and the Reform Bill passed.)

James Mill also prepared for Bentham the *Introductory View of the Rationale of Evidence* in 1812. In Bentham's view, the technical rules with respect to evidence gave employment to a good many lawyers, but had little value apart from that. Hearsay evidence might not be worth much, but there was no reason why it should not be weighed. In short, the general view was that court-martial procedure let fewer guilty persons escape, no matter how much money they could spend for lawyers. And the purpose of a trial is that the *guilty* should be convicted.

Mill and Bentham worked together happily for a number of years. Bentham's property at Queen Square Place, near Westminster Abbey, had in the garden a house where Milton had lived, and this was arranged for the Mills. Bentham was also fortunate in leasing at an absurdly low figure a magnificent residence in a corner of Devonshire, called Ford Abbey, and here he and the Mills spent six months or more of each year from 1814 to 1819, hard at work in the great rooms, where there are still to be seen the organ, the library, and the drawing room with the famous blue tapestries woven from Raphael's cartoons, for which the Russian Czar is said to have offered £200,000 in 1910. Much hard work was done, but circumstances became more and more pleasant for Bentham. In 1817 the Masters of the Bench of Lincoln's Inn elected Bentham to be one of them. Since the Masters include many of the justices of the highest courts, this is an honor seldom given to any but lawyers of political eminence or to those who are widely known in legal practice. Probably not one of the Masters would have agreed with Bentham, but they honored him.

The last great assistance to Bentham came from the son of James Mill, John Stuart Mill. In 1825, at the age of nineteen, he took on the responsibility of editing the full text of Bentham's work on *Evidence*. This was no *Introductory View,* such as his father had done, running to some fifty thousand words, but the complete work, some twenty times that amount. J. S. Mill had an official position in the India House, so it was in what might be called his leisure that he completed and made into a single consecutive work the thousands of pages of Bentham's manuscripts. That John Stuart Mill should break down, as his autobiography records, on finishing the work in one year, is reasonable enough. Most professional editors would have been dead. A million words of text, from sources with not more than 50 pages of consecutive manuscript, considering Bentham's crabbed handwriting, would have required years even to read for anyone but a young man of genius. But the work was done, and done magnificently.

Fortunate, then, in his association with Mill and his friends and talented son, fortunate too in having all he had spent on Panopticon returned in a lump sum of £23,000, Bentham could turn to his real center of interest, the construction of the Constitutional Code. He used the money to found the *Westminster Review,* in order to give the Radicals a forum, and then went to work for the rest of his life on the Code. Since this was his greatest work, in the opinion of men as different from each other as Graham Wallas and Harold Laski, and since it was the major concern of his last 15 years, a serious examination of it may well be made. It might be amusing to go over the squabbles among Bentham's secretaries and the various editors of the *Westminster Review,* or to show the vanity of an old man under the honors and correspondence from abroad, but the old man was doing important work, and important things should come first. The story of the way John Bowring, one of his secretaries, bored from within to separate Bentham from every one of his old friends who had a mind of his own (Dumont, the Mills, and Francis Place in particular) is a sad one and some day may be told in full. At any rate, when Bentham died in 1832, Bowring was left as executor, and he did bring out in 1843 the last of the 11 volumes known as *Bentham's Works.* Even in that, he reprinted the five volumes of J. S. Mill's *Evidence* without mentioning Mill's name.

THE CONSTITUTIONAL CODE

When Bentham constructed his ideal code, he used the experience of three nations. He tried to make use of the best features of the French system, with its logical distribution of authority and function, of the American, with its many sublegislatures in the various states, and of the British system as far as the parish or township unit was concerned—what he was to call the "tris-sub-legislature." He did not adopt the New England town-meeting concept, but rather the English Justice of the Peace, or what he called the "local headman."

The Constitutional Code resembles the French system in that the central government is a logical structure, with fourteen ministers whose names suggest their functions. There is an election minister, a legislation minister, an army minister, a navy minister, a preventive-service minister, an interior-communication minister, an indigence-relief minister, an education minister, a domain minister, a health minister, a foreign-relations minister, a trade minister, and a finance minister. These are all appointed by the Prime Minister from a carefully screened list of eligibles. The fourteenth minister, the minister of justice, is elected by the legislature. This legislature is an omnicompetent body, elected by the supreme Constitutive, which is the Sovereign. This supreme Constitutive, consisting of all sane adults, elects annually a single chamber of deputies. These deputies elect the Prime Minister and the minister of justice, and the Prime Minister appoints all other ministers. So far we seem to have sovereignty very neatly centralized and ready to operate in an omnicompetent fashion, issuing orders and edicts to subordinates out on the periphery of the realm. At this point, however, Bentham introduced a new element based on American practice. He had been struck, during the long walks and talks he and John Quincy Adams had had together when Adams was U.S. Minister in London, with the value of the separate governments of the American states in acting as experimental laboratories for testing out political ideas inexpensively. If Massachusetts wanted a free public-school system at the taxpayer's expense, it was not necessary to win Georgia to approval of the idea. If the scheme proved satisfactory, Georgia might adopt it. If it failed, only Massachusetts had lost. Accordingly, Bentham began dividing his sovereignty, taking part of it away from the central government and giving it to a sublegislature.

So much for the distribution of sovereignty at the second level, in what Bentham would have called the "bis-sublegislature." He was to go one step further in geography and in subordination. At this level he made use of an English model and of English experience in the organization of the parish. Bentham had followed with great interest the open vestry elections in his own parish of Westminster, and had learned something of local government in observing the complexity of the problems dealt with in so large a parish. Accordingly, at the third level, Bentham retained the eighteenth-century justice of the peace as seen in the best examples he had known. To be sure, Bentham gave him a most un-English name—he called him the "local headman."

For, whether in Wiltshire or in France, in Turkey or Bulgaria or Russia or in Poland, Bentham had observed one phenomenon that was constant. There always *was* a local headman, someone who accepted responsibility, who settled disputes, who took command in flood or earthquake or famine. Why not call him what he is?

We are now getting down to the level at which actual human beings are affected by government, and to Bentham government is always to be thought of in terms of persons suffering pains and pleasures. The legislator is a pain-dispenser—let him take care. And the corollary is, information—exact information—must flow continuously from the parish to the central government so that no unnecessary pains will be produced by action there. Thus it is that we find at the side of our yearly elected headman a local registrar who serves as the memory and record of the parish, and hence of the state. This registrar is a high-class civil servant on permanent tenure. His functions include registering not merely the whole group of vital statistics, but also a simplified system of property recording, so that a glance will show the exact nature of the ownership of all real property, together with all recognized contracts, whether of transfer, conveyance, or covenant. From the registrar's records, a yearly statistical digest will be made for the benefit of the legislature and sublegislatures.

In one direction Bentham has something of the imaginative power one finds in a great poet—he can feel the impact or the pressure on individual senses of the pain or pleasure produced by a general act. In Shelley's phrase—he makes the pleasures or the pains of the species his own. "A man to be greatly good," says Shelley, "must imagine intensely and comprehensively; he must put himself in the place of another and of many others; the pains and pleasures of the species must become his own. The great instrument of moral good is the imagination."

With this sensitivity to the pains of others always in operation, Bentham starts in with the family and the village, works out the amount of local responsibility required and the points at which it may fall short of adequacy so that the larger community may be expected to act, if only in disaster or emergency. What are the proper means of communication between the local community and the center? Where is the proper responsibility for action? What are the proper assurances against incompetence and dishonesty in this relationship? What is the proper permanent representation of the country to the central government—that is to say, how do we choose suitable representatives through a proper nominating system, the most important part of any electoral pattern? Having obtained our central parliament and government, we must then observe that, in one sense, a good government is an impossibility, presenting us with a class war rather than a center of beneficence. For there are only two classes in Bentham's world, the governors and the governed. When a governing class is created, it must be kept under control either by constant vigilance or in some other way. Now constant vigilance on the part of an entire electorate is simple nonsense. If people can live in the shadow of a volcano and come to ignore it, they certainly are not going to spend a good part of their time vigilantly observing their governmental officials for possible mistakes or even for dishonesty. Moreover, dishonest people are notoriously plausible. "Confidence men" are so called because they elicit confidence. No, there must be a system with all kinds of built-in safety devices—fuses to blow, bells to ring, meters with red lines and flashing lamps. That is what a constitutional code is for.

In Bentham's system, every official, elective or appointive, lives in a pitiless glare of light. His office hours are posted, and he is paid daily, as he meets them. The rights of suitors are posted outside his office, as well as the obligations of suitors. Possibly such conditions of office would seem intolerable to any gentleman of high principles and a sensitive sense of honor. Bentham had known many high-principled and honorable gentlemen in office, but too many of them lacked what he called "appropriate aptitude" for their posts, and too many others tended to confuse the interests of the public with their own personal interests without even knowing they were doing so. It would be the business of a code to make them aware of the difference between the nation and its government.

For the most part the battle has been won with respect to "maximizing official aptitude." At least there are examinations upon examinations for permanent officials in the civil service, and the programs associated with the names of Chadwick, Shaftesbury, and later with the Fabians are now a part of our lives. The civil service is, on the whole, intelligent; it is, on the whole, efficient with respect to carrying out its responsibilities. But whether all minor officialdom really feels itself to be the servant of the public rather than its governor (or even sometimes a rather dictatorial nursemaid) let anyone answer who has encountered it, whether in Timbuktu or Oshkosh.

Bentham was very much aware, as his passages on private deontology show, that tyranny is one of the most natural and widespread activities of the human race, whether in the family, in the shop or factory, or in any place where marked superiority and inferiority— physical, intellectual or moral—are found to exist. As he says, a mere question from a person in a superior position to an inferior may be a tyrannical exercise of power. The civil servant of the highest intellectual qualification may be precisely the one who needs the greatest curbs put upon him, for to the power that goes with his official status he adds that of his own ability.

It was because he looked forward to a time when the state should be democratically organized that Bentham tried so hard to invent constitutional devices to prevent tyranny and oppression then. He did not expect men of the future to be any better or more public-spirited than the men he knew under George IV. That is not to say that he was cynical about mankind. "In all human minds," he says, "in howsoever widely different proportions, self-regard, and sympathy for others, or say extra-regard, have place. . . . To give increase to the influence of sympathy at the expense of self-regard . . . is the constant and arduous task, as of every moralist, so of every legislator who deserves to be so." He felt that the constitution-maker must solve the problem of how to minimize confidence without withholding power. An official must have power if he is to be held responsible for his operations, and Bentham's governor is responsible as no official before or since has ever been. He is responsible whether he acts or not. He is dislocable, in Bentham's phrase, either by his superordinate, for reason given, or by the people, for no reason whatever. If one-fourth the voters in any one district will sign a petition of recall, his name must be voted on in a general election, under two captions: *dislocate him: retain him.* Even so, that is not enough. Bentham's government is a positive government, not a negative one. It touches man at all points from the cradle to the grave; it is responsible to the local needs of the parish, and makes available to the parish supplies of goods and persons not otherwise available to it. And all the more must the official be kept aware at every moment that he is a servant. The deputy, the judge, the administrator are paid daily and publicly when they enter on the day's duties. A code of conduct for the minister hangs on one wall of the office; a code of conduct for the suitor on the other. A deputy must always be ready if a principal is ill. The year contains three hundred working days. The legislator's work is as important as a physician's. And always there is the pitiless record open to public inspection, and to having the worst possible construction put upon one's acts in the Press. No longer will the newspaper man be dependent on the official handouts of the public-relations man, or the even less trustworthy account furnished by a disgruntled official who lost in the struggle for power. There is nothing absurd about the Public Opinion Tribunal as set up by Bentham. It is a picture to horrify any dignified official who thinks himself superior to his employers. But good work, too, goes on the record, and it may well be that some men of solid parts would come out better than the showy administrator who believes in leaving detail—and work—to people who are made for that sort of thing. At any rate, Bentham trusted the press, for under democracy it was the only thing one could trust. Left to himself, an administrator tends to relax into unthinking routine, or if ambitious, to turn one secretary into three, a dozen, into a department.

THE POLICE POWER: THE PREVENTIVE SERVICE MINISTER

Bentham usually stated his views forcefully as to major generalizations. The qualifying and modifying discourse may fill a volume, whereas the generalization is brief and may be easily quoted and remembered. Added to this is the fact that, as time went on, he wrote more and more for himself and for persons not committed to the habits and anomalies of the British constitution, but interested rather in constructing a system for which a rational defense could be made. Take for example his handling of the police power of the state. Observe, first, that he does not call it that, nor does it operate under the ministry of justice. Considering what so-called ministries of justice have come to mean in some modern states, and the fear and loathing justifiably associated with the term, perhaps it is just as well that he does not. No, it is to the Preventive Service Minister that, in his language, "it belongs to give, under the Prime Minister, execution and effect to all ordinances of the legislature, insofar as they have for their object the prevention of calamity; or of delinquency, otherwise than by exercise of the functions belonging to the judiciary." The prevention of calamity and of delinquency is a large order, and it is not surprising to find that the means for accomplishing the object are on a scale to worry any nineteenth-century believer in laissez-faire. We begin with a corps of engineers and inspectors not only concerned with preventing the kind of jerry-building the short-term speculative builder prefers, but also devoted to the construction of vast public works, though their functions are implicit in the list of examples he gives rather than provided for in detail.

Examples of arrangements for the prevention or mitigation of calamity . . .; against collapse, of earth, in hilly or mountainous situations, precautionary surveys: of edifices, particularly in towns, precautionary surveys: for reparation, or demolition of ruinous ones; also precautionary arrangements in the construction of new ones.

Against inundation—surveys of bridges, dykes and embankments; also arrangements for the draining of lands. Against conflagration—precautionary construction of edifices.

Neither does Bentham consider disease and pestilence, any more than bad food and drink or impure drugs, a matter to which the state is indifferent. There must be lazarettes for contagious diseases, under the direction of the Preventive Minister. There must be "arrangements for preventing the vent . . . of articles of food or drink in a state regarded as dangerous to health." Regarded by whom? Certainly not by the vendor. Obviously by inspectors in the Preventive Service Ministry. The engineers, too, will need to act in such a manner as to protect the community from disease "from putrid water, naturally accumulated, [by providing] drainage in enclosed tunnels."

The Preventive Service Ministry is even charged with the responsibility for seeing to it that no unusual scarcity of the ordinary articles of daily use should occur; in his words, against extraordinary scarcity of necessaries —"precautionary supplies, insofar as freedom of trade is inadequate to the purpose." And as means to this end, he lists government magazines, vehicles, and draft animals.

It is, moreover, in the provision made for a police force as such that we begin to sense what a vast force is at the disposal of the ministry not merely, in Bentham's language, for the procurative, custoditive, reparative, transformative, and eliminative functions but also the "statistic, recordative, publicative, and officially informative." The reason the Preventive Service Minister can make only occasional use of the permanent army forces is that they are lacking in "local knowledge, including that of the characters, family circumstances, abodes and haunts of individual delinquents, and persons most in danger of falling into delinquency." This local knowledge necessary for proper *preventive* police action includes not only the "moral circumstances: disposition of the several inhabitants, as resulting from habitual sources of livelihood and other occupations, but also an exact knowledge of the region and its topography—plains, hills, mountains—rivers, lakes and seas —whether sandy, clayey, chalky, gravelly, rocky, etc.— ground weedy, or woodless." The preventive police force is also the natural source of statistical information for the election minister. Since virtually universal suffrage exists, the registration for voting will be a part of the preventive-service records. Other statistics will be kept, including "sites of the several habitations, thence abodes of the respective house-holders, with their inmates of both sexes and all ages."

There are times when Bentham almost impresses one as the grandfather of bureaucracy itself, so intent is he on "recordation" and on the duplication of copies. It should be noted, however, that he had no interest in archives for the sake of archives, or in multiplication of copies in order to keep secretaries occupied. The importance of his insights into the nature of statistics and a genuine bookkeeping has attracted the interest of professional statisticians in the last few years only, and they have found that his inventiveness and ingenuity anticipated many of the techniques devised a century after his death.* He was interested in records as related

---

*See particularly Louis Goldberg, "Jeremy Bentham, Critic of Accounting Method," *Account-Research,* Vol. 8, No. 3 (July, 1957), pp. 218–45. See also conclusion page.

to the present moment or to future forecasts. He was interested in statistics again as a matter of the moment, so that one could, *at any time,* find out how much had been done in relation to a current program, what the costs were, and whether unnecessary expense was building up, in time to correct it.

To achieve this end, a new and different language was necessary, in his view. For businessmen, no less than lawyers, were committed to a series of fictions. Rice could owe tea, stone could owe shipping, and labor could owe interest. In fact only men could owe other men, and things will in the end work better if facts are not only faced but kept in mind by the use of language continually linked to fact. No man used *abstractions* more skillfully than Bentham, but he distinguished between an abstraction and a fiction. An abstraction generalizes facts—that is to say, if you push it back to its origins, they refer to the impact something has made on the senses and perceptions of a man. A fiction when so pushed back, *turns out to be actually contrary* to fact, and is usually devised to get around an awkward situation, whether it involves a small boy explaining the jam stains to his mother, or the lawyer devising ways of avoiding the challenge of common-sense views of equity.

One can be somewhat sympathetic to the general opposition to that most un-English institution, a police force. France had one (composed largely of ex-convicts) and the very word brought to mind the 150,000 *lettres de cachet* of Louis XV, the secret police, the *visites domicilières,* the *mouchards* or spies. Louis XV was said to have enjoyed the perusal of the "moral bulletins" sent him daily by the police.

His Highness, the Prince of Conti, who keeps Mlle Lemierne, one of the leading actresses at the opera, . . . has sold her several times, so they say. . . . M. de Chateaurenard has gained a footing by means of 15 louis a month with Mlle Dorney, an understudy at the opera, who was abandoned some time ago by the

Baron de Wangen. . . . Last year Mlle Dalbigny lived with the Abbé Ranoud, who was arrested at her house in the midst of a debauch. As a matter of fact she really lives, more discreetly, with his Grace the Abbé de Brillac, at the rue Saint Audie-des-arts, at the Hotel Bretagne.

D'Argenson, the Keeper of the Seals, would have no mistresses other than nuns, and died in a convent which he had changed into a harem.*

One might have thought all this only adolescent fantasy, but for the fact that the best informed of foreigners usually found the Paris police even better informed.

Whether true or not, such stories were believed in England. "Police" meant a central register of 20,000 names of charlatans, swindlers, chorus girls, kept women, their lovers, libertines and homosexuals, clients of gaming houses; and the police had a very special interest in any one of standing, whether priest, humanitarian, or man of letters, found in their vicinity. "Police" meant a register of all hotels and lodging houses, with detailed information concerning their residents. For private houses, it meant the police right to enter on the slightest pretext, during the day or night, to interrogate the occupants, to remove papers and to make arrests.

Englishmen did not like the French idea of police, whether under the former regime or under the post-revolutionary governments. As long as possible, they held to their own system of watchmen. During the Gordon Riots of 1780, when the mob burned and looted for days, the constabulary went on its customary rounds with staff and bell and lantern. The mob saw no reason to attack the elderly pensioners who offered it no interference, so the bells rang out and the familiar cry "Ten o'clock and all's well" could be heard across the way from the crashing shop fronts. It would be clear to any

*Leon Radzinowicz, *A History of English Criminal Law and Its Administration from 1750* (3 vols., London: Macmillan & Co., 1956), Vol. III, Appendix ("Political Aspects of the Police of France"), pp. 548 n., 551 n.

sensible watchman, mainly elderly and feeble anyway, that the less one had to do with such aggressive and dishonest people as made up the mob, the better. It seems reasonable to suppose that Bentham's acquaintance with Colquhoun in the 1790's had much to do with the revolutionary proposals of *Bentham's Constitutional Code* in 1830.

THE JUDICIARY

To the judiciary Bentham gave over a very large part of the Constitutional Code in the form we have it. Partly this was because it was always a labor of love with him to explain how fantastically unjustified Blackstone and Lord Eldon were in admiring the current English legal system. It should be observed, however, that, whatever the defects of Bentham's code, it is not guilty of one charge that lawyers who ought to know better sometimes bring against him. Because he is severe on what he calls "judge-made law," one should not suppose him guilty of thinking that any code can be made that will cover all cases without judicial interpretation. On that subject Bentham had written in 1782:

> I mean, of course, what has been distinguished by the name of *liberal* interpretation: that delicate and important branch of judiciary power, the concession of which is dangerous, the denial ruinous. . . . Human reason does not seem to be yet far enough advanced to warrant our laying the discretionary mode of interpretation under an absolute prohibition in all cases whatever.

There may be times, in other words, when the judge will have to think because the legislator has failed to foresee events. Bentham would have the judge admit or rather declare his having so acted. He is then supposed either to amend the faulty law or to draw up *in terminis* a legal mandate to cover the case. This new or amended law he submits to the government advocate and to the eleemosynary advocate of his court, and they record upon it their approval or disapproval. It is then forwarded through the minister of justice, who records the hour received, his own approval or disapproval, and the hour at which he has transmitted it to the legislature. In seven calendar days from that time it becomes law unless the legislature votes its disapproval.

It cannot be emphasized too strongly that, in regard to all the details of the Constitutional Code, Bentham made full use of expert specialized knowledge before he began the organization of any immediate function. When a young barrister, Edwin Chadwick, showed, in an article in the *Westminster Review* ("The Means of Insurance against Accidents") that by simple administrative measures of hygiene and sanitation many of the causes of poverty, dissipation, crime, and disease could be removed, it was clear that he had read Bentham's work on punishment to good effect. A year later Chadwick followed this article up with another powerful essay in the *London Review,* called "Preventive Police." James Mill and Francis Place were enthusiastic about this article. Henry Bickerstith, later Lord Langdale, a distinguished K.C., was helping Bentham with the Constitutional Code at the time, and he brought the essay to Bentham's attention. Bentham had never met Chadwick, but "within a few weeks he had engaged him as secretary, with the special duty of writing for the Code the sections dealing with the Minister of Police and the Minister of Health. Thus began that fast friendship broken only by Bentham's death."* Yet though Chadwick had made himself so authoritative a writer on these subjects that Peel's Committee, in 1828, had asked him first to give evidence and then to draw up an extensive memorandum on the subject, the Ministry of Police covers only two pages in the Constitutional Code and the Ministry of Health another two and a half pages. A careful look at the Minis-

*Samuel E. Finer, *The Life and Times of Sir Edwin Chadwick* (New York: British Book Center, 1954), p. 31.

try of Health will show, however, that here is the plan, explicit and detailed, for which Edwin Chadwick was to spend the next 60 years of his long life fighting: vestries, water companies, physicians, the *Lancet,* the *Times,* and all respectable and right-thinking people who found references to sewage far more intolerable than the thing itself. Chadwick lived to be ninety, and thanks to the assistance of three major cholera epidemics, each of which came just at the right time to put the official views of the medicine men and the cabinet in the wrong, Chadwick expanded his two and a half pages into many volumes of statutes and administrative regulations. It was not necessary to change the views expressed in the two and a half pages—the whole world accepts them now.

To see how weighty, how dense, and how solid a great deal of the Code is, it may be useful to look at the 22 articles in Chapter XI: Ministers Severally, Section X, Health Minister. It is a relatively short section, that of the Health Minister, running, as has been said, only two and a half pages (Vol IX, pp. 443–45), and an examination of it will serve to indicate the techniques used throughout the Code, as well as to define the terms used by Bentham.

Article 1 places the Health Minister under the Prime Minister in carrying out the will of the legislature in regard to the national health.

Article 2 is almost the same for the Health Minister as for all other Ministers: "under the direction of the Prime Minister, it belongs to him to exercise,—in relation to all persons . . . under him, the locative, suppletive, directive and dislocative functions." This is to say that the Minister is responsible for hiring his subordinates; he is responsible for making sure that there is an adequate supply of trained persons to be hired; he is responsible for their direction while employed; and it is he who decides when to transfer, promote, suspend, or discharge the employee, though as will be seen, other persons, such as the Prime Minister, may also possess the "dislocative" power. Article 2 goes on, "as to his own office, the self-suppletive function"; that is, he must have a competent deputy ready to fill his own place in event of illness or absence or his own "dislocation" for cause. "As to things," the article continues, "[it belongs to him to exercise,] insofar as thus employed, but in concert with the Finance Minister, the procurative, custoditive, applicative, reparative, transformative, and eliminative functions." These seem fairly obvious in meaning, and it is only necessary to note that procuring things needed at a proper price and at a proper time, and in eliminating things not needed without waste of money, of space, or of time involves an elaborate and continuous bookkeeping, referred to later. "As to persons and things" the Minister exercises the "inspective function."

This particular activity of Ministers is described at length in Chapter IX, Section IX of Book II. The most important aspects of inspection have to do with making sure that bookkeeping is in proper order, that functionaries are suited to the work they are doing, that complaints for "obviating oppression" shall be heard, and that extraordinary merit shall be recognized. In addition to "progresses," "circuits" and regularly scheduled inspection visits, there should be also visits determined by casting lots, so that chance inspections will be anticipated without their time being known. Article 2 goes on: "as to persons, things, and occurrences thereto belonging, the statistic, recordative, publicative, and officially informative" functions are performed by the Minister. The "recordative" is historical, so that one can know who did what, and when, and why. The statistic is concerned primarily with the present moment, so that one can know how much of anything is now in store, how far along any piece of work is, and what it has cost in money and labor and supplies up to this time. "Publicative" activity is that which informs the general public, or, as Bentham never forgets to call it, "The Supreme Constitutive," as to what a department is doing or is falling short of doing. The "officially informative" is the passing up and down the chain of command the properly detailed information necessary to the department's efficient operation. This is not something to be taken for granted, but the thing on which the very life of an organization depends. Only one more item remains: "as to states of things, ordinances, and arrangements, the melioration-suggestive" responsibility of the Minister is a very real one in Bentham's system. It is hardly too much to say that "extraordinary merit" can be more easily demonstrated by this means than by any other. Merit does the job properly as it is presented to one, with diligence and competence clearly in evidence. But extraordinary merit says, "Do we really need to do this job at all? Why make 50 measurements to drill 20 holes and repeat the process indefinitely? Why not set up a jig with all the holes pre-drilled at the right points and make a dozen wagon beds at a time?" "But that would throw a dozen men out of work," says the routine mind. "Splendid," says Bentham, "unnecessary work is waste. Never call it anything else. If everyone is attempting to present melioration-suggestive ideas, we'll find something *useful* for these men to do."

So far we can go in the analysis of article 2, which in itself consists of exactly one hundred words. Yet lazy readers are sometimes heard to complain that Bentham seems to them long-winded.

Actually, Bentham's language has the qualities of any proper technical language: it is repellent to the casual reader, whether the subject matter be law, medicine, electronics, or music, for it looks like the English language at first sight but with many repetitions of key words, because the same word is always used for the same thing; and since it aims at precision and exactness of statement, it needs close attention in the reading. Its awkwardness and ugliness are usually concealed from its users by the fact that considerable numbers of the profession use it for communicating with each other. Bentham uses his technical language to communicate with future nations, or with devoted students of political institutions.

Article 3 of the Health Minister section provides that

the Minister shall exercise the "inspective, the statistic, and the melioration-suggestive" functions with regard to all institutions, private or public, designed for public use, whether constructed or run by various sublegislatures or not, so long as the public health is affected. A crowd in a theatre, a railway train, or a school may be only a matter for statistical information in relation to plague or water supply, but it may be producing a situation with which the legislature must deal.

Article 4 gives the Minister control of all medical functionaries in the army, control involving the "locative, suppletive, directive, dislocative and suspensive" powers. Exception is made for certain suspensive powers inherent in the position of army commander. Once more we feel the strength of the adjective *suppletive,* for the responsibility for supplying something means that you must be given the means of creating the thing if it does not exist in sufficient quantity or of proper quality. If physicians are needed, you *may* have to create them.

Article 5 makes similar provision for the Navy, and Article 6 brings the Health Minister into relationship with the police force, or as it is called, the *preventive service* department. Article 7 gives the Minister responsibility for the "locative, suppletive, directive, dislocative and suspensive" functions of medical functionaries serving in the Indigence Relief Ministry, and again the powerful word is *suppletive.* It is quite inconceivable that the elaborate health functions of all these various departments could be supplied by hiring casual surgeons and physicians not able to find profitable practice for themselves. The Minister is *responsible* for an adequate supply of medical men for the purposes of the state envisaged in the Code, a state having very little similarity to the England of 1830.

Articles 8 to 22 have to do with explicit institutions to come into being under the Health Minister's aegis, institutions for the most part existing only in the most embryonic form in Bentham's time. Article 8 provides that hospitals, lazarettes, and laboratories as things immovable with associated movable things shall belong to the Minister, acting together with the Finance Minister, as to the "procurative, custoditive, applicative, reparative and eliminative" functions.

Article 9 puts prisons, madhouses, "edifices, with their appurtenances, belonging to the field of service of the Indigence Relief Minister," and "edifices with their appurtenances, belonging to the field of service of the Education Minister" under the *inspection* of the Minister of Health. Articles 10, 11, and 12 provide that the Minister shall inspect shops and storehouses where drugs are distributed, as well as shops and storehouses where surgical instruments are kept for sale, and Article 13 brings in the statistic and recordative function as well as the melioration-suggestive, with respect to all these matters.

It is only with article 14, however, that we find the powers of the Minister of Health operating *explicitly* in novel ways, so that government interference with the right of the individual to make money in any way that seems good to him is sharply increased. If the inspector of the Ministry finds a shop where medicaments have been rendered unfit for use, he either destroys such drugs or materials or renders them incapable of use for medical purposes.

It should be said that to avoid oppression in all of these activities of the Ministry, an appeal may be made to the Judge Immediate, whose office is open 24 hours a day so that he may be roused from his sleep as easily as a physician for emergency purposes, and a Judge Immediate has a great deal more power than any justice of the peace. No individual in the state is to be more than 20 miles from a Judge Immediate, to be reached at the worst extreme by eight hours travel on foot.

In article 15 we deal with the Minister's "Aqua-procurative, or say Water-supply-securing function." Here we see Edwin Chadwick's hand rather clearly, for Chadwick had already taken for his special subject the supply of water to London and its relation to the sewage-disposal problem, and Chadwick had been Bentham's secretary. One must read Professor Finer's book on the life of Chadwick to get the full documented horror of what nineteenth-century laissez-faire meant to a great city like London. For of course London was not a city—that would have meant centralized government, most un-English. It was a collection of three hundred parishes, acting under 250 local Acts of Parliament. Even that does not suggest the chaos and complexity. The parish of St. Pancras alone had no fewer than 16 paving boards (controlling matters of sewage and waste disposal), and those boards acted under 29 separate Acts of Parliament. Perhaps one touch can illustrate the malodorous consequences. Evidence was given that one of the companies supplying drinking water to London took the supply from the Thames where, at low water, each gallon of water contained one quart of untreated sewage. The Code reduces the concrete circumstances to abstraction in what seems almost an ironical manner, considering how constantly Bentham stresses elsewhere the reality of sense impressions: "He will include in his observation the quantity, quality, and proportionability of distribution of the subject-matter of this supply."

Article 16 charges the Minister with a "Malaria-obviating, or anti-malarial function." Bentham takes malaria in its original meaning, of course, of bad air, but the activities of the Ministry would promote public health even if they did not affect the malaria plasmodium, for they deal with accumulations of stagnant water, with gases from mines, common sewers, and drains, with places of interment, public assemblies, and any manufacturing establishment likely to "deteriorate the air."

Article 17 deals with the Health-regarding-evidence-elicitive-and-recordative function of the Minister. Bills of mortality from each bis-subdistrict registrar will be demanded by the ministry, giving record of births, of deaths, of attaining voting age, and of insanity. From the Army Minister, the Navy Minister, the Preventive Service Minister, the Indigence Relief Minister, and the Education Minister, reports will be demanded covering disease and mortality rates in the establishments and hospitals under their control. From these services, also, registers of the weather will be requested.

Articles 18 and 19 provide for the Minister's having custody of all governmental medical museums—institutions that provide a proper source of teaching materials: anatomical preparations, surgical instruments, *materia medica,* herbaries, medical libraries and graphical collections, human-body models in health and in pathological distortions.

Article 20 governs the aptitude-securing function of the Minister. All applicants for medical posts will be given a probationary examination presided over by the Minister with three to five assessors elected by the body of persons who have previously passed satisfactory examinations as to technical skill, with due attention paid to the sinister corrupting effects of love of ease as a motive for applying for the post.

Article 21 sets the Minister in direct opposition to the claims of the Medical profession to regulate its own division of labor, rate of payment, or terms or modes of attendance. He will need to act jointly with the Prime Minister *and* the Public Opinion Tribunal in the public interest in this Professional-Confederacy-checking function.

Article 22 points out that the way in which all these functions can be carried out best is by relying on what Bentham calls the "appropriate-publication function." Sinister interest seeks darkness; the Health Minister must make use of the "utmost publicity."

And how is this "utmost publicity" to be attained? Once more, there is no "royal road" to accomplishment of the end or even to an understanding of Bentham's machinery. He himself went so far as to say at one time that the 68 pages on *statistics* in the 1830 edition of the *Code* would furnish in themselves the key to good government. The machinery is, quite simply, bookkeeping. The 43 books to be found in every minister's office, in every subordinate office, in every bis-subordinate office, and in every tris-subordinate office, were to be there for two purposes. The first was to act as a crutch for a newly appointed official. For him, a few days study of the books, identical in structure and content with those in any other government department, would make him familiar with the history of the office, its current inventories and commitments, the stage reached by every project under way, and an elaborate dossier on every person employed.

The second purpose was to make available to the general public, "the Supreme Constitutive," under its aspect as a Public Opinion Tribunal, exactly the same information. One need not be an expert accountant or a lawyer to understand *these* books. Their complexity comes in the originality required for setting them up in the first place, discarding Italian double entry as misleading to anyone except the expert accountant. These must be self-revelatory to anyone who can read at a journalist's level, for their chief claim to existence is the hope that the journalists will find them worth reading.

Some discussion of the general theory may be useful. We have then two general categories: (1) service books having to do with operations, and (2) loss books. It is the second category that is really novel and capable of being made extraordinarily useful. In one sense we may say that, since these books all deal with governmental activities, most of what they will treat is loss. For a government to spend, it must tax, and taxation is pain. Let its taxation, then, exist only for the creation of a greater happiness than the inevitable pain. Above all, *minimize expense* by cutting out needless or useless expenditure. These loss books will show quite clearly how to identify such expenditures. This whole process of minimizing expense is no penny-pinching process. A penny may be wasted and so may a million pounds. A penny may be profitably spent and so may a million pounds. Bentham's loss-preventive system is even better designed to avoid the great waste than the small one, since its purpose is to keep everyone in the department and a good many outside *thinking about the matter*, and that not occasionally but habitually and every day.

Thinking about possible waste and loss is the surest path to recognition, to promotion, and to honor in *this* system. This is not a negative idea, for the best possible way of preventing loss in any operation is to do away with it altogether—that is to say to find a better (and cheaper) way of achieving the same ends.

Given the almost universal human tendency to settle comfortably and happily into routines and habits, Bentham seems at first glance to be insisting on too much initiative and individual judgment. His own intent is quite different: it is to make the formation of good habits easy—to set up procedures where the response to a wasteful situation is as nearly automatic as the operator of a sailboat keeping the sails full rather than spilling the wind wastefully.

Our bookkeeping deals primarily with money, of course, since money is our basic accounting device. It relates persons, immovable objects, and movable objects to each other in a pattern governed by time, for action takes place in time. We must know when action begins, the nature of the action (its *use*), and when the action ceases. If we know who and what the persons are, their relationship to each other, the manner of their dealing with things movable and immovable, together with the flow of money in these relationships, we may be said to have a satisfactory picture of actuality—past, present, and to come.

The Italian bookkeeping may operate fairly well for a merchant desperately concerned that no penny of his is wasted or diverted to anyone else, willing to examine the books almost from day to day to make certain that his interest is being served. Government will have no person in it with an *equal* determination that the taxpayers' money shall not be so wasted or directed. The government official will be honest and trustworthy as to his responsibility. No one will steal directly from the funds trusted to his care. He will *not,* however, have the passionate defence of the wild animal protecting his jugular vein, *his* money. The trustee needs a different kind of bookkeeping than does the trader.

We begin by noting that the observed world consists either of *persons* or *things*. Our books must then deal with these in an intelligible manner. *Things* seem to need a triple classification: (1) *immovables,* that is to say land, with its edifices and appurtenances, its waters and subterranean structures; (2) *movables;* and (3) *money*. These four categories then: persons, immovables, movables, and money, will appear in all our books.

There are three great groups of books: inventories, journals, and loss books. Naturally, the inventories, or outset books, are of two kinds, the original inventory, and the periodical inventory each January 1st. Even more important than money, movables, or immovables in this analysis of assets is the catalogue of persons. It includes not merely all the data as to how the person came to be employed and the various examinations passed, but a personal-merit register for each employee.

It is here that the inventory comes alive by virtue of its human relationship to the loss books. Any employee who discovers actual or potential loss as he goes about his daily business is trained to make a report to that effect, *not to his superior officer,* but by entering his report in the proper loss book. The matter must then be inquired into by his superiors. If his judgment is not borne out by investigation, a signed statement to that effect is made opposite the entry by the responsible minister or his deputy. In that event, *no* entry is made in the personal-merit register. If the opinion is validated by investigation, a signed statement is made in the loss book as to how the situation had been corrected, and a notation *is* entered in the employee's personal-merit register crediting him with putting a stop to loss or losses. Entries in the books are not to be changed or deleted by any authority, for one of their reasons for existence is that the general public may know what goes on and who is responsible for what happens.

All of this design to have the business of a governmental department open to the eyes of the meddling journalist or the merely curious general public one may be sure will never be brought into being by an actual administrator. He has headaches enough already. Considering how many of Bentham's "preposterous" notions have been adopted since his death, however, it may be possible that, in another generation, the administrator and the administrative law he makes will come under the sort of scrutiny Bentham advocates. Administrative lawmaking has gone far and fast in our time. In the Congressional Directory the mere listing of names of administrative bureaus takes up twice as much space as does the whole of the judicial system. It is an administrator, not an elected Congressman, who decides what taxes one shall pay, whether one may hunt, marry, or borrow money. From the disposal of sewage to national security, one is under his direction, and there are very few checks upon his decisions. One *can* fight it through the courts. If Bentham was right in thinking that the only real class struggle is between the governors and the governed, we should be prepared to admit that the governed seem to have lost in the struggle at the present time.

It is sometimes advanced as a criticism of Bentham's realism that he failed to foresee the development of party politics, or at least that he does not deal with the problems the party system brings into being. It could be argued that, in the *Book of Fallacies,* Bentham covered pretty satisfactorily under the heads "Fallacies of the Ins" and "Fallacies of the Outs" most of the points and most of the maneuvering to be found under the party system, but in the *Constitutional Code* he ignores the party system for much the same reason that Hamilton and Madison ignored it in the *Federalist Papers.* The party system is only one form of allowing interests to express themselves with respect to government. Whatever the form of government, interests will tend to get themselves recognized and represented. It may almost be said that, under the party system, nothing else gets adequately recognized except by chance. Wise provision for the future is not an interest capable of electing anybody; even a reasonable conservation of national resources or of health seldom finds a satisfactory way of paying the campaign expenses of a candidate for public office under the party system.

Accordingly, Bentham makes no provision for parties. They will be there in any case. His main concern is one of special relevancy to all the new states and nations coming into being in our time. It is the establishment of what M. Bertrand de Jouvenel* characterizes as "majesty," that is to say the relationship between the government and the citizens in which the rulers believe they are governing for the whole society, and the citizens believe in both the moral concern for the public good and in the competence of their rulers.

Now it is very easy for rulers to believe that they are governing for the whole society, or at least for all right-thinking members of it, even if they have had to obliterate a considerable number of "wrong-thinking" and perverse individuals. However sure rulers may be of their own good faith, foresightedness, and relative disinterestedness, it is not too much to say that there is little belief in the general populace that either the competence of their rulers or their moral integrity meets reasonable expectations. However slight the degree of actual corruption in government in the nations operating under the party system, there is enough *belief* in such corruption, among the governed to discredit most government, whether municipal, state, or national, to the extent that all but a minority withhold from it their affection and loyalty. They will obey its laws and pay its taxes, but they do not believe the laws to be just as between themselves and a great corporation or public utility, for example, nor do many of them think they get value received for their taxes.

Observe that, as far as the idea of "majesty" is concerned, the truth or falsehood of the belief does not matter. The flow of loyalty and affection depends upon *belief*.

The relevancy of all this to Bentham is that his pri-

*Encounter, March, 1959, p. 35.

mary concern is, of course, that the government shall be worthy of confidence. But almost as important is the attempt to set up a system where this competence and integrity is continually *dramatized*. To be sure, the devices used will tend to throw into strong relief against a brilliant light any genuine rascality or stupidity, and consequently to make rascals and incompetents seek a kindlier climate. But the main thing is that quite simple people will be able to feel secure and to trust their governors.

CONCLUSION

The *Constitutional Code* thus rounds out and ends the great work begun 52 years before with the *Introduction to the Principles of Morals and Legislation*. Both concern themselves with the operations of the "logic of the will," as Bentham calls it, of which the most important application is the science of law. "It is," says Bentham, "to the art of legislation, what the science of anatomy is to the art of medicine . . . nor is the body politic less in danger from a want of acquaintance with the one science, than the body natural from ignorance in the other. . . . Such then . . . the difficulties: . . . —an unexampled work to achieve, and then a new science to create: a new branch to add to one of the most abstruse of sciences. . . . Are enterprises like these achievable?"* asked the young author who had been told that he was too abstruse even for the professional lawyers. "He knows not. This only he knows, that they have been undertaken, proceeded in, and some progress has been made in all of them." He could have said no more at the age of eighty-four, when he was still writing page after page of the *Constitutional Code* a month before his death, and with the *Code* largely unfinished. Still, it had been "undertaken, proceeded in, and some progress made."

*Preface to the *Introduction to the Principles of Morals and Legislation*.

To the end, the advocate of happiness rationally achieved found his own greatest happiness in productive work. In February of 1832 he wrote to that most extraordinary diplomat and man of affairs, Talleyrand, the man who had served and survived the Church, the French Revolution, Napoleon, and the return of the Bourbons, inviting him to dinner, since Talleyrand had asked to see him. In a gay and witty letter* he says apologetically, "I give my mornings to nobody. I have so much to do, and so short a time to live, that I cannot abridge my working hours."

In what remains the most authoritative estimate of Bentham's work, Professor H. A. Hollond's bicentenary essay in the *Cambridge Law Journal* (No. 1, 1948), the distinguished jurist sums up the life in these terms:

> Death came peacefully to Bentham the day before the great Reform Bill received the Royal Assent . . . There could hardly be an epitaph more appropriate to Bentham than a quip of his old friend Talleyrand, who visited him shortly before his death. Bowring remarked that from no modern writer had so much been stolen without acknowledgement. Talleyrand assented, adding, "et pillé par tout le monde, il est toujours riche."†

Talleyrand's remark shows a better appreciation of Bentham's philosophy than does Bowring's. The man of genius shares his pleasures of skill, of memory, and of power with the whole world, and he has more pleasure after doing so than before.

---

*Jeremy Bentham, *Works,* edited by John Bowring (11 vols., London, 1843), Vol. XI, p. 75.

†*Cambridge Law Journal* (Vol. X, London: Stevens and Son, 1948), p. 43.

SELECTIONS
FROM THE
part 2 # MAJOR WORKS
OF BENTHAM

INTRODUCTION TO THE PRINCIPLES OF MORALS AND LEGISLATION*

I. OF THE PRINCIPLE OF UTILITY

I. Nature has placed mankind under the governance of two sovereign masters, *pain* and *pleasure*. It is for them alone to point out what we ought to do, as well as to determine what we shall do. On the one hand the standard of right and wrong, on the other the chain of causes and effects, are fastened to their throne. They govern us in all we do, in all we say, in all we think: every effort we can make to throw off our subjection, will serve but to demonstrate and confirm it. In words a man may pretend to abjure their empire: but in reality he will remain subject to it all the while. The *principle of utility* recognizes this subjection, and assumes it for the foundation of that system, the object of which is to rear the fabric of felicity by the hands of reason and of law. Systems which attempt to question it, deal in sounds instead of sense, in caprice instead of reason, in darkness instead of light.

But enough of metaphor and declamation: it is not by such means that moral science is to be improved.

II. The principle of utility is the foundation of the present work: it will be proper therefore at the outset to give an explicit and determinate account of what is meant by it. By the principle of utility is meant that principle which approves or disapproves of every action whatsoever, according to the tendency which it appears to have to augment or diminish the happiness of the party whose interest is in question: or, what is the same thing in other words, to promote or to oppose that happiness. I say of every action whatsoever; and therefore

*First published by Bentham in 1789; reprinted in *Works* (1843), Vol. I, pp. 1ff. The first five chapters are given complete; the remaining chapters are given only in Bentham's outline.

not only of every action of a private individual, but of every measure of government.

III. By utility is meant that property in any object, whereby it tends to produce benefit, advantage, pleasure, good, or happiness, (all this in the present case comes to the same thing) or (what comes again to the same thing) to prevent the happening of mischief, pain, evil, or unhappiness to the party whose interest is considered: if that party be the community in general, then the happiness of the community: if a particular individual, then the happiness of that individual.

IV. The interest of the community is one of the most general expressions that can occur in the phraseology of morals: no wonder that the meaning is often lost. When it has a meaning, it is this. The community is a fictitious *body,* composed of the individual persons who are considered as constituting as it were its *members.* The interest of the community then is, what?—the sum of the interests of the several members who compose it.

V. It is in vain to talk of the interest of the community, without understanding what is the interest of the individual. A thing is said to promote the interest, or to be *for* the interest, of an individual, when it tends to add to the sum total of his pleasures: or, what comes to the same thing, to diminish the sum total of his pains.

VI. An action then may be said to be conformable to the principle of utility, or, for shortness sake, to utility, (meaning with respect to the community at large) when the tendency it has to augment the happiness of the community is greater than any it has to diminish it.

VII. A measure of government (which is but a particular kind of action, performed by a particular person or persons) may be said to be conformable to or dictated by the principle of utility, when in like manner the tendency which it has to augment the happiness of the community is greater than any which it has to diminish it.

VIII. When an action, or in particular a measure of

government, is supposed by a man to be conformable to the principle of utility, it may be convenient, for the purposes of discourse, to imagine a kind of law or dictate, called a law or dictate of utility: and to speak of the action in question, as being conformable to such law or dictate.

IX. A man may be said to be a partisan of the principle of utility, when the approbation or disapprobation he annexes to any action, or to any measure, is determined by and proportioned to the tendency which he conceives it to have to augment or to diminish the happiness of the community: or in other words, to its conformity or unconformity to the laws or dictates of utility.

X. Of an action that is conformable to the principle of utility one may always say either that it is one that ought to be done, or at least that it is not one that ought to be done. One may say also, that it is right it should be done; at least that it is not wrong it should be done; that it is a right action; at least that it is not a wrong action. When thus interpreted, the words *ought,* and *right* and *wrong,* and others of that stamp, have a meaning, when otherwise, they have none.

XI. Has the rectitude of this principle been ever formally contested? It should seem that it had, by those who have not known what they have been meaning. Is it susceptible of any direct proof? It should seem not: for that which is used to prove every thing else, cannot itself be proved: a chain of proofs must have their commencement somewhere. To give such proof is as impossible as it is needless.

XII. Not that there is or ever has been that human creature breathing, however stupid or perverse, who has not on many, perhaps on most occasions of his life, deferred to it. By the natural constitution of the human frame, on most occasions of their lives men in general embrace this principle, without thinking of it: if not for the ordering of their own actions, yet for the trying of their own actions, as well as of those of other men. There have been, at the same time, not many, perhaps, even of the most intelligent, who have been disposed to embrace it purely and without reserve. There are even few who have not taken some occasion or other to quarrel with it, either on account of their not understanding always how to apply it, or on account of some prejudice or other which they were afraid to examine into, or could not bear to part with. For such is the stuff that man is made of: in principle and in practice, in a right track and in a wrong one, the rarest of all human qualities is consistency.

XIII. When a man attempts to combat the principle of utility, it is with reasons drawn, without his being aware of it, from that very principle itself. His arguments, if they prove any thing, prove not that the principle is *wrong,* but that, according to the applications he supposes to be made of it, it is *misapplied.* Is it possible for a man to move the earth? Yes; but he must first find out another earth to stand upon.

XIV. To disprove the propriety of it by argument is impossible; but, from the causes that have been mentioned, or from some confused or partial view of it, a man may happen to be disposed not to relish it. Where this is the case, if he thinks the settling of his opinions on such a subject worth the trouble, let him take the following steps, and at length, perhaps, he may come to reconcile himself to it.

1. Let him settle with himself, whether he would wish to discard this principle altogether; if so, let him consider what it is that all his reasonings (in matters of politics especially) can amount to?

2. If he would, let him settle with himself, whether he would judge and act without any principle, or whether there is any other he would judge and act by?

3. If there be, let him examine and satisfy himself whether the principle he thinks he has found is really any separate intelligible principle; or whether it be not a mere principle in words, a kind of phrase, which at bottom expresses neither more nor less than the mere averment of his own unfounded sentiments; that is, what in another person he might be apt to call caprice?

4. If he is inclined to think that his own approbation or disapprobation, annexed to the idea of an act, without any regard to its consequences, is a sufficient foundation for him to judge and act upon, let him ask himself whether his sentiment is to be a standard of right and wrong, with the respect to every other man, or whether every man's sentiment has the same privilege of being a standard to itself?

5. In the first case, let him ask himself whether his principle is not despotical, and hostile to all the rest of the human race?

6. In the second case, whether it is not anarchical, and whether at this rate there are not as many different standards of right and wrong as there are men? and whether even to the same man, the same thing, which is right to-day, may not (without the least change in its nature) be wrong to-morrow? and whether the same thing is not right and wrong in the same place at the same time? and in either case, whether all argument is not at an end? and whether, when two men have said, "I like this," and "I don't like it," they can (upon such a principle) have any thing more to say?

7. If he should have said to himself, No: for that the sentiment which he proposes as a standard must be grounded on reflection, let him say on what particulars the reflection is to turn? if on particulars having relation to the utility of the act, then let him say whether this is not deserting his own principle, and borrowing assistance from that very one in opposition to which he sets it up: or if not on these particulars, on what other particulars?

8. If he should be for compounding the matter, and adopting his own principle in part, and the principle of utility in part, let him say how far he will adopt it?

9. When he has settled with himself where he will stop, then let him ask himself how he justifies to himself the adopting it so far? and why he will not adopt it any farther?

10. Admitting any other principle than the principle of utility to be a right principle, a principle that it is

right for a man to pursue; admitting (what is not true) that the word *right* can have a meaning without reference to utility, let him say whether there is any such thing as a *motive* that a man can have to pursue the dictates of it: if there is, let him say what that motive is, and how it is to be distinguished from those which enforce the dictates of utility: if not, then lastly let him say what it is this other principle can be good for?

II. OF PRINCIPLES ADVERSE TO THAT OF UTILITY

I. If the principle of utility be a right principle to be governed by, and that in all cases, it follows from what has been just observed, that whatever principle differs from it in any case must necessarily be a wrong one. To prove any other principle, therefore, to be a wrong one, there needs no more than just to show it to be what it is, a principle of which the dictates are in some point or other different from those of the principle of utility: to state it is to confute it.

II. A principle may be different from that of utility in two ways: 1. By being constantly opposed to it: this is the case with a principle which may be termed the principle of *asceticism*. Ascetic is a term that has been sometimes applied to Monks. It comes from a Greek word which signifies *exercise*. The practices by which Monks sought to distinguish themselves from other men were called their Exercises. These exercises consisted in so many contrivances they had for tormenting themselves. By this they thought to ingratiate themselves with the Deity. For the Deity, said they, is a Being of infinite benevolence: now a Being of the most ordinary benevolence is pleased to see others make themselves as happy as they can; therefore to make ourselves as unhappy as we can is the way to please the Deity. If any body asked them what motive they could find for doing all this? Oh! said they, you are not to imagine we are punishing ourselves for nothing: we know very well what we are about. You are to know, that for every grain of pain it costs us now, we are to have a hundred grains of pleasure by and by. The case is, that God loves to see us torment ourselves at present: indeed he has as good as told us to. But this is done only to try us, in order just to see how we should behave: which it is plain he could not know, without making the experiment. Now then, from the satisfaction it gives him to see us make ourselves as unhappy as we can make ourselves in this present life, we have a sure proof of the satisfaction it will give him to see us as happy as he can make us in a life to come. 2. By being sometimes opposed to it, and sometimes not, as it may happen: this is the case with another, which may be termed the principle of *sympathy* and *antipathy*.

III. By the principle of asceticism I mean that principle, which, like the principle of utility, approves or disapproves of any action, according to the tendency which it appears to have to augment or diminish the happiness of the party whose interest is in question; but in an inverse manner: approving of actions in as far as they tend to diminish his happiness; disapproving of them in as far as they tend to augment it.

IV. It is evident that any one who reprobates any the least particle of pleasure, as such, from whatever source derived, is *pro tanto* a partizan of the principle of asceticism. It is only upon that principle, and not from the principle of utility, that the most abominable pleasure which the vilest of malefactors ever reaped from his crime would be to be reprobated, if it stood alone. The case is, that it never does stand alone; but is necessarily followed by such a quantity of pain (or, what comes to the same thing, such a chance for a certain quantity of pain) that the pleasure in comparison of it, is as nothing: and this is the true and sole, but perfectly sufficient, reason for making it a ground for punishment.

V. There are two classes of men of very different complexions, by whom the principle of asceticism appears to have been embraced; the one a set of moralists, the other a set of religionists. Different accordingly have been the motives which appear to have recommended it to the notice of these different parties. Hope, that is the prospect of pleasure, seems to have animated the former: hope, the aliment of philosophic pride: the hope of honour and reputation at the hands of men. Fear, that is the prospect of pain, the latter: fear, the offspring of superstitious fancy: the fear of future punishment at the hands of a splenetic and revengeful Deity. I say in this case fear: for of the invisible future, fear is more powerful than hope. These circumstances characterize the two different parties among the partizans of the principle of asceticism; the parties and their motives different, the principle the same.

VI. The religious party, however, appear to have carried it further than the philosophical: they have acted more consistently and less wisely. The philosophical party have scarcely gone farther than to reprobate pleasure: the religious party have frequently gone so far as to make it a matter of merit and of duty to court pain. The philosophical party have hardly gone farther than the making pain a matter of indifference. It is no evil, they have said: they have not said, it is a good. They have not so much as reprobated all pleasure in the lump. They have discarded only what they have called the gross; that is, such as are organical, or of which the origin is easily traced up to such as are organical: they have even cherished and magnified the refined. Yet this, however, not under the name of pleasure: to cleanse itself from the sordes of its impure original, it was necessary it should change its name: the honourable, the glorious, the reputable, the becoming, the *honestum,* the *decorum,* it was to be called: in short, any thing but pleasure.

VII. From these two sources have flowed the doctrines from which the sentiments of the bulk of mankind have all along received a tincture of this principle; some from the philosophical, some from the religious, some from both. Men of education more frequently from the philosophical, as more suited to the elevation of their sentiments: the vulgar more frequently from the superstitious, as more suited to the narrowness of their intellect, undilated by knowledge: and to the abjectness of their condition, continually open to the attacks of fear. The tinctures, however, derived from the two sources, would naturally intermingle, insomuch that a man would not always know by which of them he was most influenced: and they would often serve to corroborate and enliven one another. It was this conformity that made a kind of alliance between parties of a complexion otherwise so dissimilar: and disposed them to unite upon various occasions against the common enemy, the partizan of the principle of utility, whom they joined in branding with the odious name of Epicurean.

VIII. The principle of asceticism, however, with whatever warmth it may have been embraced by its partizans as a rule of private conduct, seems not to have been carried to any considerable length, when applied to the business of government. In a few instances it has been carried a little way by the philosophical party: witness the Spartan regimen. Though then, perhaps, it may be considered as having been a measure of security: and an application, though a precipitate and perverse application, of the principle of utility. Scarcely in any instances, to any considerable length, by the religious: for the various monastic orders, and the Societies of the Quakers, Dumplers, Moravians, and other religionists, have been free societies, whose regimen no man has been astricted to without the intervention of his own consent. Whatever merit a man may have thought there would be in making himself miserable, no such notion seems ever to have occured to any of them, that it may be a merit, much less a duty, to make others miserable: although it should seem, that if a certain quantity of misery were a thing so desirable, it would not matter much whether it were brought by each man upon himself, or by one man upon another. It is true, that from the same source from whence, among the religionists, the attachment to the principle of asceticism took its rise, flowed other doctrines and practices, from which misery in abundance was produced in one man by the instrumentality of another: witness the holy wars, and the persecutions for religion. But the passion for producing misery in these cases proceeded upon some special ground: the exercise of it was confined to persons of particular descriptions: they were tormented, not as men, but as heretics and infidels. To have inflicted the same miseries on their fellow-believers and fellow-sectaries, would have been as blameable in the eyes even of these religionists, as in those of a partizan of the principle of utility. For a man to give himself a certain number of stripes was indeed meritorious; but to give the same number of stripes to another man, not consenting, would have been a sin. We read of saints, who for the good of their souls, and the mortification of their bodies, have voluntarily yielded themselves a prey to vermin: but though many persons of this class have wielded the reins of empire, we read of none who have set themselves to work, and made laws on purpose, with a view of stocking the body politic with the breed of highwaymen, housebreakers, or incendiaries. If at any time they have suffered the nation to be preyed upon by swarms of idle pensioners, or useless placement, it has rather been from negligence and imbecility, than from any settled plan for oppressing and plundering of the people. If at any time they have sapped the sources of national wealth, by cramping commerce, and driving the inhabitants into emigration, it has been with other views and in pursuit of other ends. If they have declaimed against the pursuit of pleasure, and the use of wealth, they have commonly stopped at declamation: they have not, like Lycurgus, made express ordinances for the purpose of banishing the precious metals. If they have established idleness by a law, it has been not because idleness, the mother of vice and misery, is itself a virtue but because idleness (say they) is the road to holiness. If under the notion of fasting, they have joined in the plan of confining their subjects to a diet, thought by some to be of the most nourishing and prolific nature, it has been not for the sake of making them tributaries to the nations by whom that diet was to be supplied, but for the sake of manifesting their own power, and exercising the obedience of the people. If they have established, or suffered to be established, punishments for the breach of celibacy, they have done no more than comply with the petitions of those deluded rigorists, who, dupes to the ambitious and deep-laid policy of their rulers, first laid themselves under that idle obligation by a vow.

IX. The principle of asceticism seems originally to have been the reverie of certain hasty speculators, who having perceived, or fancied, that certain pleasures, when reaped in certain circumstances, have, at the long run, been attended with pains more than equivalent to them, took occasion to quarrel with every thing that offered itself under the name of pleasure. Having then got thus far, and having forgot the point which they set out from, they pushed on, and went so much further as to think it meritorious to fall in love with pain. Even this, we see, is at bottom but the principle of utility misapplied.

X. The principle of utility is capable of being consistently pursued; and it is but tautology to say, that the more consistently it is pursued, the better it must ever be for humankind. The principle of asceticism never may, nor ever can be, consistently pursued by any living creature. Let but one tenth part of the inhabitants of this earth pursue it consistently, and in a day's time they will have turned it into a hell.

XI. Among principles adverse to that of utility, that which at this day seems to have most influence in matters of government, is what may be called the principle of sympathy and antipathy. By the principle of sympathy and antipathy, I mean that principle which approves or disapproves of certain actions, not on account of their tending to augment the happiness, nor yet on account of their tending to diminish the happiness of the party whose interest is in question, but merely because a man finds himself disposed to approve or disapprove of them: holding up that approbation or disapprobation as a sufficient reason for itself, and disclaiming the necessity of looking out for any extrinsic ground. Thus far in the general department of morals: and in the particular department of politics, measuring out the quantum (as well as determining the ground) of punishment, by the degree of the disapprobation.

XII. It is manifest, that this is rather a principle in name than in reality: it is not a positive principle of itself, so much as a term employed to signify the negation of all principle. What one expects to find in a principle is something that points out some external consideration, as a means of warranting and guiding the internal sentiments of approbation and disapprobation: this expectation is but ill fulfilled by a proposition, which does neither more nor less than hold up each of those sentiments as a ground and standard for itself.

XIII. In looking over the catalogue of human actions (says a partizan of this principle) in order to determine which of them are to be marked with the seal of disapprobation, you need but to take counsel of your own feelings: whatever you find in yourself a propensity to condemn, is wrong for that very reason. For the same reason it is also meet for punishment; in what proportion it is adverse to utility, or whether it be adverse to utility at all, is a matter that makes no difference. In that same *proportion* also is it meet for punishment: if you hate much, punish much: if you hate little, punish little: punish as you hate. If you hate not at all, punish not at all: the fine feelings of the soul are not to be overborne and tyrannized by the harsh and rugged dictates of political utility.

XIV. The various systems that have been formed concerning the standard of right and wrong, may all be reduced to the principle of sympathy and antipathy. One account may serve for all of them. They consist all of them in so many contrivances for avoiding the obligation of appealing to any external standard, and for prevailing upon the reader to accept of the author's sentiment or opinion as a reason for itself. The phrases different, but the principle the same. It is curious enough to observe the variety of inventions men have hit upon, and the variety of phrases they have brought forward, in order to conceal from the world, and, if possible, from themselves, this very general and therefore very pardonable self-sufficiency.

1. One man says, he has a thing made on purpose to tell him what is right and what is wrong; and that it is called a *moral sense* and then he goes to work at his ease, and says, such a thing is right, and such a thing is wrong—why? "because my moral sense tells me it is."

2. Another man comes and alters the phrase: leaving out *moral,* and putting in *common,* in the room of it. He then tells you, that his common sense teaches him what is right and wrong, as surely as the other's moral sense did: meaning by common sense, a sense of some kind or other, which, he says, is possessed by all mankind: the sense of those, whose sense is not the same as the author's, being struck out of the account as not worth taking. This contrivance does better than the other; for a moral sense, being a new thing, a man may feel about him a good while without being able to find it out: but common sense is as old as the creation; and there is no man but would be ashamed to be thought not to have as much of it as his neighbours. It has another great advantage: by appearing to share power, it lessens envy: for when a man gets up upon this ground, in order to anathematize those who differ from him, it is not by a *sic volo sic jubeo* [so I wish, so I arrange], but by a *velitis jubeatis* [as you wish it shall be ordered].

3. Another man comes, and says, that as to a moral sense indeed, he cannot find that he has any such thing: that however he has an *understanding,* which will do quite as well. This understanding, he says, is the standard of right and wrong: it tells him so and so. All good and wise men understand as he does: if other men's understandings differ in any point from his, so much the worse for them: it is a sure sign they are either defective or corrupt.

4. Another man says, that there is an eternal and immutable Rule of Right: that that rule of right dictates so and so: and then he begins giving you his sentiments upon any thing that comes uppermost: and these senti-

ments (you are to take for granted) are so many branches of the eternal rule of right.

5. Another man, or perhaps the same man (it's no matter) says, that there are certain practices conformable, and others repugnant, to the Fitness of Things; and then he tells you, at his leisure, what practices are conformable and what repugnant: just as he happens to like a practice or dislike it.

6. A great multitude of people are continually talking of the Law of Nature; and then they go on giving you their sentiments about what is right and what is wrong: and these sentiments, you are to understand, are so many chapters and sections of the Law of Nature.

7. Instead of the phrase, Law of Nature, you have sometimes, Law of Reason, Right Reason, Natural Justice, Natural Equity, Good Order. Any of them will do equally well. This latter is most used in politics. The three last are much more tolerable than the others, because they do not very explicitly claim to be any thing more than phrases: they insist but feebly upon the being looked upon as so many positive standards of themselves, and seem content to be taken, upon occasion, for phrases expressive of the conformity of the thing in question to the proper standard, whatever that may be. On most occasions, however, it will be better to say *utility: utility* is clearer, as referring more explicitly to pain and pleasure.

8. We have one philosopher, who says, there is no harm in anything in the world but in telling a lie: and that if, for example, you were to murder your own father, this would only be a particular way of saying, he was not your father. Of course, when the philosopher sees anything that he does not like, he says, it is a particular way of telling a lie. It is saying, that the act ought to be done, or may be done, when, *in truth,* it ought not to be done.

9. The fairest and openest of them all is that sort of man who speaks out, and says, I am of the number of the Elect: now God himself takes care to inform the

Elect what is right: and that with so good effect, and let them strive ever so, they cannot help not only knowing it but practising it. If therefore a man wants to know what is right and what is wrong, he has nothing to do but to come to me.

It is upon the principle of antipathy that such and such acts are often reprobated on the score of their being *unnatural:* the practice of exposing children, established among the Greeks and Romans, was an unnatural practice. Unnatural, when it means anything, means unfrequent: and there it means something: although nothing to the present purpose. But here it means no such thing: for the frequency of such acts is perhaps the great complaint. It therefore means nothing: nothing, I mean, which there is in the act itself. All it can serve to express is, the disposition of the person who is talking of it: the disposition he is in to be angry at the thoughts of it. Does it merit his anger? Very likely it may: but whether it does or no is a question, which, to be answered rightly, can only be answered upon the principle of utility.

Unnatural, is as good a word as moral sense, or common sense; and would be as good a foundation for a system. Such an act is unnatural; that is, repugnant to nature: for I do not like to practise it: and, consequently, do not practise it. It is therefore repugnant to what ought to be the nature of every body else.

The mischief common to all these ways of thinking and arguing (which, in truth, as we have seen, are but one and the same method, couched in different forms of words) is their serving as a cloke, and pretence, and aliment, to despotism: if not a despotism in practice, a despotism however in disposition: which is but too apt, when pretence and power offer, to show itself in practice. The consequence is, that with intentions very commonly of the purest kind, a man becomes a torment either to himself or his fellow-creatures. If he be of the melancholy cast, he sits in silent grief, bewailing their blindness and depravity: if of the irascible, he declaims with fury and virulence against all who differ from him;

blowing up claims with fury and virulence against all who differ from him; blowing up the coals of fanaticism, and branding with the charge of corruption and insincerity, every man who does not think, or profess to think, as he does.

If such a man happens to possess the advantage of style his book may do a considerable deal of mischief before the nothingness of it is understood.

These principles, if such they can be called, it is more frequent to see applied to morals than to politics; but their influence extends itself to both. In politics, as well as morals, a man will be at least equally glad of a pretence for deciding any question in the manner that best pleases him, without the trouble of inquiry. If a man is an infallible judge of what is right and wrong in the actions of private individuals, why not in the measures to be observed by public men in the direction of those actions? accordingly (not to mention other chimeras) I have more than once known the pretended law of nature set up in legislative debates, in opposition to arguments derived from the principle of utility.

But is it never, then, from any other considerations than those of utility, that we derive our notions of right and wrong? I do not know: I do not care. Whether a moral sentiment can be originally conceived from any other source than a view of utility, is one question: whether upon examination and reflection it can, in point of fact, be actually persisted in and justified on any other ground, by a person reflecting within himself, is another; whether in point of right it can properly be justified on any other ground, by a person addressing himself to the community, is a third. The two first are questions of speculation: it matters not, comparatively speaking, how they are decided. The last is a question of practice: the decision of it is of as much importance as that of any can be.

"I feel in myself," (say you) "a disposition to approve of such or such an action in a moral view: but this is not owing to any notions I have of its being useful or not: it may be, for aught I know, a mischievous one." "But is it then," (say I) "a mischievous one? examine; and if you can make yourself sensible that it is so, then, if duty means any thing, that is, moral duty, it is your *duty* at least to abstain from it: and more than that, if it is what lies in your power, and can be done without too great a sacrifice, to endeavour to prevent it. It is not your cherishing the notion of it in your bosom, and giving it the name of virtue, that will excuse you."

"I feel in myself," (say you again) "a disposition to detest such or such an action in a moral view; but this is not owing to any notions I have of its being a mischievous one to the community. I do not pretend to know whether it be a mischievous one or not; it may be not a mischievous one: it may be, for aught I know, an useful one."—"May it indeed," (say I) "an useful one? but let me tell you then, that unless duty, and right and wrong, be just what you please to make them, if it really be not a mischievous one, and any body has a mind to do it, it is no duty of yours, but, on the contrary, it would be very wrong in you, to take upon you to prevent him: detest it within yourself as much as you please; that may be a very good reason (unless it be also a useful one) for your not doing it yourself: but if you go about, by word or deed, to do anything to hinder him, or make him suffer for it, it is you, and not he, that have done wrong: it is not your setting yourself to blame his conduct, or branding it with the name of vice, that will make him culpable, or you blameless. Therefore, if you can make yourself content that he shall be of one mind, and you of another, about that matter, and so continue, it is well: but if nothing will serve you, but that you and he must needs be of the same mind, I'll tell you what you have to do: it is for you to get the better of your antipathy, not for him to truckle to it."

XV. It is manifest, that the dictates of this principle will frequently coincide with those of utility, though perhaps without intending any such thing. Probably more frequently than not: and hence it is that the business of penal justice is carried on upon that tolerable sort of footing upon which we see it carried on in common at this day. For what more natural or more general ground of hatred to a practice can there be, than the mischievousness of such practice? What all men are exposed to suffer by, all men will be disposed to hate. It is far yet, however, from being a constant ground: for when a man suffers, it is not always that he knows what it is he suffers by. A man may suffer grievously, for instance, by a new tax, without being able to trace up the cause of his sufferings to the injustice of some neighbour, who has eluded the payment of an old one.

XVI. The principle of sympathy and antipathy is most apt to err on the side of severity. It is for applying punishment in many cases which deserve none: in many cases which deserve some, it is for applying more than they deserve. There is no incident imaginable, be it ever so trivial, and so remote from mischief, from which this principle may not extract a ground of punishment. Any difference in taste: any difference in opinion: upon one subject as well as upon another. No disagreement so trifling which perseverance and altercation will not render serious. Each becomes in the other's eyes an enemy, and, if laws permit, a criminal. This is one of the circumstances by which the human race is distinguished (not much indeed to its advantage) from the brute creation.

King James the First of England had conceived a violent antipathy against Arians: two of whom he burnt. This gratification he procured himself without much difficulty: the notions of the times were favourable to it. He wrote a furious book against Vorstius, for being what was called an Arminian: for Vorstius was at a distance. He also wrote a furious book, called "A Counterblast to Tobacco," against the use of that drug, which Sir Walter Raleigh had then lately introduced. Had the notions of the times co-operated with him, he would have burnt the Anabaptist and the smoker of tobacco in the same fire. However he had the satisfaction of putting Raleigh to death afterwards, though for another crime.

Disputes concerning the comparative excellence of French and Italian music have occasioned very serious bickerings at Paris. One of the parties would not have been sorry (says Mr. D'Alembert) to have brought government into the quarrel. Pretences were sought after and urged. Long before that, a dispute of like nature, and of at least equal warmth, had been kindled at London upon the comparative merits of two composers at London; where riots between the approvers and disapprovers of a new play are, at this day, not infrequent. The ground of quarrel between the Bigendians and the Little-endians in the fable, was not more frivolous than many an one which has laid empires desolate. In Russia, it is said, there was a time when some thousands of persons lost their lives in a quarrel, in which the government had taken part, about a number of fingers to be used in making the sign of the cross. This was in the days of yore: the ministers of Catherine II are better *instructed* than to take any other part in such disputes, than that of preventing the parties concerned from doing one another a mischief.

XVII. It is not, however, by any means unexampled for this principle to err on the side of lenity. A near and perceptible mischief moves antipathy. A remote and imperceptible mischief, though not less real, has no effect. Instances in proof of this will occur in numbers in the course of the work. It would be breaking in upon the order of it to give them here.

XVIII. It may be wondered, perhaps, that in all this while no mention has been made of the *theological* principle; meaning that principle which professes to recur for the standard of right and wrong to the will of God. But the case is, this is not in fact a distinct principle. It is never any thing more or less than one or other of the three before-mentioned principles presenting itself under another shape. The *will* of God here meant cannot be his revealed will, as contained in the sacred writings: for that is a system which nobody ever thinks of recurring to at this time of day, for the details of political administration: and even before it can be applied to the details of private conduct, it is universally allowed, by the most eminent divines of all persuasions, to stand in need of pretty ample interpretations; else to what use are the works of those divines? And for the guidance of these interpretations, it is also allowed, that some other standard must be assumed. The will then which is meant on this occasion, is that which may be called the *presumptive* will: that is to say, that which is presumed to be his will on account of the conformity of its dictates to those of some other principle. What then may be this other principle? It must be one or other of the three mentioned above: for there cannot, as we have seen, be any more. It is plain, therefore, that, setting revelation out of the question, no light can ever be thrown upon the standard of right and wrong, by any thing that can be said upon the question, what is God's will. We may be perfectly sure, indeed, that whatever is right is conformable to the will of God: but so far is that from answering the purpose of showing us what is right, that it is necessary to know first whether a thing is right, in order to know from thence whether it be conformable to the will of God.

XIX. There are two things which are very apt to be confounded, but which it imports us carefully to distinguish:—the motive or cause, which, by operating on the mind of an individual, is productive of any act: and the ground or reason which warrants a legislator, or other by-stander, in regarding that act with an eye of approbation. When the act happens, in the particular instance in question, to be productive of effects which we approve of, much more if we happen to observe that the same motive may frequently be productive, in other instances, of the like effects, we are apt to transfer our approbation to the motive itself, and to assume, as the just ground for the approbation we bestow on the act, the circumstance of its originating from that motive. It is in this way that the sentiment of antipathy has often been considered as a just ground of action. Antipathy, for instance, in such or such a case, is the cause of an action which is attended with good effects: but this does not make it a right ground of action in that case, any more than in any other. Still farther. Not only the effects are good, but the agent sees beforehand that they will be so. This may make the action indeed a perfectly right action: but it does not make antipathy a right ground of action. For the same sentiment of antipathy, if implicitly deferred to, may be, and very frequently is, productive of the very worst effects. Antipathy, therefore, can never be a right ground of action. No more, therefore, can resentment, which, as will be seen more particularly hereafter, is but a modification of antipathy. The only right ground of action, that can possibly subsist, is, after all, the consideration of utility, which, if it is a right principle of action, and of approbation, in any one case, is so in every other. Other principles in abundance, that is, other motives, may be the reasons why such and such an act *has* been done: that is, the reasons or causes of its being done: but it is this alone that can be the reason why it might or ought to have been done. Antipathy or resentment requires always to be regulated, to prevent its doing mischief: to be regulated by what? always by the principle of utility. The principle of utility neither requires nor admits of any other regulator than itself.

III. OF THE FOUR SANCTIONS OR SOURCES OF PAIN AND PLEASURE

I. It has been shown that the happiness of the individuals, of whom a community is composed, that is their pleasures and their security, is the end and the sole end which the legislator ought to have in view: the sole standard, in conformity to which each individual ought, as far as depends upon the legislator, to be *made* to fashion his behaviour. But whether it be this or any thing else that is to be *done,* there is nothing by which a man can ultimately be *made* to do it, but either pain or pleasure. Having taken a general view of these two grand objects (*viz.* pleasure, and what comes to the same thing, immunity from pain) in the character of *final* causes; it will be necessary to take a view of pleasure and pain itself, in the character of *efficient* causes or means.

II. There are four distinguishable sources from which pleasure and pain are in use to flow: considered separately, they may be termed the *physical,* the *political,* the *moral,* and the *religious:* and inasmuch as the pleasures and pains belonging to each of them are capable of giving a binding force to any law or rule of conduct, they may all of them be termed *sanctions.*

Sanctio, in Latin, was used to signify the *act of binding,* and, by a common grammatical transition, *anything which serves to bind a man:* to wit, to the observance of such or such a mode of conduct. According to a Latin grammarian, the import of the word is derived by rather a far-fetched process (such as those commonly are, and in a great measure indeed must be, by which intellectual ideas are derived from sensible ones) from the word *sanguis,* blood: because, among the Romans, with a view to inculcate into the people a persuasion that such or such a mode of conduct would be rendered obligatory upon a man by the force of what I called the religious sanction (that is, that he would be made to suffer by the extraordinary interposition of some superior being, if he failed to observe the mode of conduct in question) certain ceremonies were contrived by the priests: in the course of which ceremonies the blood of victims was made use of.

A Sanction then is a source of obligatory powers or *motives:* that is, of *pains* and *pleasures;* which, according as they are connected with such or such modes of conduct, operate, and are indeed the only things which can operate, as *motives.* See Chap. X. [Motives].

III. If it be in the present life, and from the ordinary course of nature, not purposely modified by the interposition of the will of any human being, nor by any extraordinary interposition of any superior invisible being, that the pleasure or the pain takes place or is expected, it may be said to issue from or to belong to the *physical sanction.*

IV. If at the hands of a *particular* person or set of persons in the community, who under names correspondent to that of *judge,* are chosen for the particular purpose of dispensing it, according to the will of the sovereign or supreme ruling power in the state, it may be said to issue from the *political sanction.*

V. If at the hands of such *chance* persons in the community, as the party in question may happen in the course of his life to have concerns with, according to each man's spontaneous disposition, and not according to any settled or concerted rule, it may be said to issue from the *moral* or *popular sanction.*

VI. If from the immediate hand of a superior invisible being, either in the present life, or in a future, it may be said to issue from the *religious sanction.*

VII. Pleasures or pains which may be expected to issue from the *physical, political,* or *moral* sanctions, must all of them be expected to be experienced, if ever, in the *present* life: those which may be expected to issue from the *religious* sanction, may be expected to be experienced either in the *present* life or in a future.

VIII. Those which can be experienced in the present life, can of course be no others than such as human nature in the course of the present life is susceptible of: and from each of these sources may flow all the pleasures or pains of which, in the course of the present life, human nature is susceptible. With regard to these then (with which alone we have in this place any concern) those of them which belong to any one of those sanctions, differ not ultimately in kind from those which belong to any one of the other three: the only difference there is among them lies in the circumstances that accompany their production. A suffering which befalls a man in the natural and spontaneous course of things, shall be styled, for instance, a calamity; in which case, if it be supposed to befall him through any imprudence of his, it may be styled a punishment issuing from the physical sanction. Now this same suffering, if inflicted by the law, will be what is commonly called a *punishment;* if incurred for want of any friendly assistance, which the misconduct, or supposed misconduct, of the sufferer has occasioned to be withholden, a punishment issuing from the *moral* sanction; if through the immediate interposition of a particular providence, a punishment issuing from the religious sanction.

IX. A man's goods, or his person, are consumed by fire. If this happened to him by what is called an accident, it was a calamity: if by reason of his own imprudence (for instance, from his neglecting to put his candle out) it may be styled a punishment of the physical sanction: if it happened to him by the sentence of the political magistrate, a punishment belonging to the political sanction; that is, what is commonly called a punishment: if for want of any assistance which his *neighbour* withheld from him out of some dislike to his *moral* character, a punishment of the *moral* sanction: if by an immediate act of *God's* displeasure, manifested on account of some sin committed by him, or through any distraction of mind, occasioned by the dread of such displeasure, a punishment of the *religious* sanction.

X. As to such of the pleasures and pains belonging to the religious sanction, as regard a future life, of what kind these may be we cannot know. These lie not open to our observation. During the present life they are matter only of expectation: and, whether that expectation be derived from natural or revealed religion, the particular kind of pleasure or pain, if it be different from all those which lie open to our observation, is what we can have no idea of. The best ideas we can obtain of such pains and pleasures are altogether unliquidated in point of quality. In what other respects our ideas of them *may* be liquidated will be considered in another place.

XI. Of these four sanctions the physical is altogether, we may observe, the ground-work of the political and the moral: so is it also of the religious, in as far as the latter bears relation to the present life. It is included in each of those other three. This may operate in any case, (that is, any of the pains or pleasures belonging to it may operate) independently of *them:* none of *them* can operate but by means of this. In a word, the powers of nature may operate of themselves; but neither the magistrate, nor men at large, *can* operate, nor is God in the case in question *supposed* to operate, but through the powers of nature.

XII. For these four objects, which in their nature have so much in common, it seemed of use to find a common name. It seemed of use, in the first place, for the convenience of giving a name to certain pleasures and pains, for which a name equally characteristic could hardly otherwise have been found: in the second place, for the sake of holding up the efficacy of certain moral forces, the influence of which is apt not to be sufficiently attended to. Does the political sanction exert an influence over the conduct of mankind? The moral, the religious sanctions do so too. In every inch of his career are the operations of the political magistrate liable to be aided or impeded by these two foreign powers: who one or other of them, or both, are sure to be either his rivals or his allies. Does it happen to him to leave them out in his calculations? He will be sure almost to find himself mistaken in the result. Of all this we shall find abundant proofs in the sequel of this work. It behoves him, therefore, to have them continually before his eyes; and that under such a name as exhibits the relation they bear to his own purposes and designs.

IV. VALUE OF A LOT OF PLEASURE OR PAIN, HOW TO BE MEASURED

I. Pleasures then, and the avoidance of pains, are the *ends* which the legislator has in view: it behoves him therefore to understand their *value.* Pleasures and pains are the *instruments* he has to work with: it behoves him therefore to understand their force, which is again, in other words, their value.

II. To a person considered *by himself,* the value of

a pleasure or pain considered by *itself,* will be greater
or less, according to the four following circumstances:

1. Its *intensity.*
2. Its *duration.*
3. Its *certainty* or *uncertainty.*
4. Its *propinquity* or *remoteness.*

III. These are the circumstances which are to be
considered in estimating a pleasure or a pain considered
each of them by itself. But when the value of any pleasure or pain is considered for the purpose of estimating
the tendency of any act by which it is produced, there
are two other circumstances to be taken into the account; these are,

5. Its *fecundity,* or the chance it has of being followed by sensations of the *same* kind: that is, pleasures,
if it be a pleasure: pains, if it be a pain.

6. Its *purity,* or the chance it has of *not* being followed by sensations of the *opposite* kind: that is, pains,
if it be a pleasure: pleasures, if it be a pain.

These two last, however, are in strictness scarcely to
be deemed properties of the pleasure or the pain itself;
they are not, therefore, in strictness to be taken into the
account of the value of that pleasure or that pain. They
are in strictness to be deemed properties only of the act,
or other event, by which such pleasure or pain has been
produced; and accordingly are only to be taken into the
account of the tendency of such act or such event.

IV. To a *number* of persons, with reference to each
of whom the value of a pleasure or a pain is considered,
it will be greater or less, according to seven circumstances: to wit, the six preceding ones; *viz.*

1. Its *intensity.*
2. Its *duration.*
3. Its *certainty* or *uncertainty.*
4. Its *propinquity* or *remoteness.*
5. Its *fecundity.*
6. Its *purity.*

And one other; to wit:

7. Its *extent;* that is, the number of persons to whom

it *extends;* or (in other words) who are affected by it.

V. To take an exact account then of the general tendency of any act, by which the interests of a community are affected, proceed as follows. Begin with any one person of those whose interests seem most immediately to be affected by it: and take an account,

1. Of the value of each distinguishable *pleasure* which appears to be produced by it in the *first* instance.

2. Of the value of each *pain* which appears to be produced by it in the *first* instance.

3. Of the value of each pleasure which appears to be produced by it *after* the first. This constitutes the *fecundity* of the first *pleasure* and the *impurity* of the first *pain*.

4. Of the value of each *pain* which appears to be produced by it after the first. This constitutes the *fecundity* of the first *pain,* and the *impurity* of the first pleasure.

5. Sum up all the values of all the *pleasures* on the one side, and those of all the pains on the other. The balance, if it be on the side of pleasure, will give the *good* tendency of the act upon the whole, with respect to the interests of that *individual* person; if on the side of pain, the bad tendency of it upon the whole.

6. Take an account of the *number* of persons whose interests appear to be concerned; and repeat the above process with respect to each. *Sum up* the numbers expressive of the degrees of *good* tendency, which the act has, with respect to each individual, in regard to whom the tendency of it is *good* upon the whole: do this again with respect to each individual, in regard to whom the tendency of it is *good* upon the whole: do this again with respect to each individual, in regard to whom the tendency of it is *bad* upon the whole. Take the *balance;* which, if on the side of *pleasure,* will give the general *good tendency* of the act, with respect to the total number or community of individuals concerned; if on the side of pain, the general *evil tendency,* with respect to the same community.

VI. It is not to be expected that this process should

be strictly pursued previously to every moral judgement, or to every legislative or judicial operation. It may, however, be always kept in view: and as near as the process actually pursued on these occasions approach to the character of an exact one.

VII. The same process is alike applicable to pleasure and pain, in whatever shape they appear: and by whatever shape they appear: and by whatever denomination they are distinguished: to pleasure, whether it be called *good* (which is properly the cause or instrument of pleasure) or *profit* (which is distant pleasure, or the cause or instrument of distant pleasure,) or *convenience,* or *advantage, benefit, emolument, happiness,* and so forth: to pain, whether it be called *evil,* (which corresponds to *good*) or *mischief,* or *inconvenience,* or *disadvantage,* or *loss,* or *unhappiness,* and so forth.

VIII. Nor is this a novel and unwarranted, any more than it is a useless theory. In all this there is nothing but what the practice of mankind, wheresoever they have a clear view of their own interest, is perfectly conformable to. An article of property, an estate in land, for instance, is valuable, on what account? On account of the pleasures of all kinds which it enables a man to produce, and what comes to the same thing the pains of all kinds which it enables him to avert. But the value of such an article of property is universally understood to rise or fall according to the length or shortness of the time which a man has in it: the certainty or uncertainty of its coming into possession: and the nearness or remoteness of the time at which, if at all, it is to come into possession. As to the *intensity* of the pleasures which a man may derive from it, this is never thought of, because it depends upon the use which each particular person may come to make of it; which cannot be estimated till the particular pleasures he may come to derive from it or the particular pains he may come to exclude by means of it, are brought to view. For the same person, neither does he think of *fecundity,* of *purity* of those pleasures.

Thus much for pleasure and pain, happiness and

unhappiness, in *general*. We come now to consider the several particular kinds of *pain* and *pleasure*.

V. PLEASURES AND PAINS, THEIR KINDS

I. Having represented what belongs to all sorts of pleasures and pains alike, we come now to exhibit, each by itself, the several sorts of pains and pleasures. Pains and pleasures may be called by one general word, interesting perceptions. Interesting perceptions are either simple or complex. The simple ones are those which cannot any one of them be resolved into more: complex are those which are resolvable into divers simple ones. A complex interesting perception may accordingly be composed either, 1. Of pleasures alone: 2. Of pains alone: or, 3. Of a pleasure or pleasures, and a pain or pains together. What determines a lot of pleasure, for example to be regarded as one complex pleasure, rather than as divers simple ones, is the nature of the exciting cause. Whatever pleasures are excited all at once by the action of the same cause, are apt to be looked upon as constituting all together but one pleasure.

II. The several simple pleasures of which human nature is susceptible, seem to be as follows: 1. The pleasures of sense. 2. The pleasures of wealth. 3. The pleasures of skill. 4. The pleasures of amity. 5. The pleasures of a good name. 6. The pleasures of power. 7. The pleasures of piety. 8. The pleasures of benevolence. 9. The pleasures of malevolence. 10. The pleasures of memory. 11. The pleasures of imagination. 12. The pleasures of expectation. 13. The pleasures dependent on association. 14. The pleasures of relief.

III. The several simple pains seem to be as follows: 1. The pains of privation. 2. The pains of the senses. 3. The pains of awkwardness. 4. The pains of enmity. 5. The pains of an ill name. 6. The pains of piety. 7. The pains of benevolence. 8. The pains of malevolence. 9. The pains of the memory. 10. The pains of the imagination. 11. The pains of expectation. 12. The pains dependent on association.

IV. 1. The pleasures of sense seem to be as follows: 1. The pleasures of the taste or palate; including whatever pleasures are experienced in satisfying the appetites of hunger and thirst. 2. The pleasure of intoxication. 3. The pleasures of the organ of smelling. 4. The pleasures of the touch. 5. The simple pleasures of the ear; independent of association. 6. The simple pleasures of the eye; independent of association. 7. The pleasure of the sexual sense. 8. The pleasure of health: or, the internal pleasureable feeling or flow of spirits (as it is called), which accompanies a state of full health and vigour; especially at times of moderate bodily exertion. 9. The pleasures of novelty: or, the pleasures derived from the gratification of the appetite of curiosity, by the application of new objects to any of the senses.

V. 2. By the pleasures of wealth may be meant those pleasures which a man is apt to derive from the consciousness of possessing any article or articles which stand in the list of instruments of enjoyment or security, and more particularly at the time of his first acquiring them; at which time the pleasure may be styled a pleasure of gain or a pleasure of acquisition: at other times a pleasure of possession.

3. The pleasures of skill, as exercised upon particular objects, are those which accompany the application of such particular instruments of enjoyment to their uses, as cannot be so applied without a greater or less share of difficulty or exertion.

VI. 4. The pleasures of amity, or self-recommendation, are the pleasures that may accompany the persuasion of a man's being in the acquisition or the possession of the good-will of such or such assignable person or persons in particular: or, as the phrase is, of being upon good terms with him or them: and as a fruit of it, of his being in a way to have the benefit of their spontaneous and gratuitous services.

VII. 5. The pleasures of a good name are the pleasures that accompany the persuasion of a man's being in the acquisition or the possession of the good-will of the world about him; that is, of such members of society as he is likely to have concerns with; and as a means of it, either their love or their esteem, or both: and as a fruit of it, of his being in the way to have the benefit of their spontaneous and gratuitous services. These may likewise be called the pleasures of good repute, the pleasures of honour, or the pleasures of the moral sanction.

VIII. 6. The pleasures of power are the pleasures that accompany the persuasion of a man's being in a condition to dispose people, by means of their hopes and fears, to give him the benefit of their services: that is, by the hope of some service, or by the fear of some disservice, that he may be in the way to render them.

IX. 7. The pleasures of piety are the pleasures that accompany the belief of a man's being in the acquisition or in possession of the good-will or favour of the Supreme Being: and as a fruit of it, of his being in a way of enjoying pleasures to be received by God's special appointment, either in this life, or in a life to come. These may also be called the pleasures of religion, the pleasures of a religious disposition, or the pleasures of the religious sanction.

X. 8. The pleasures of benevolence are the pleasures resulting from the view of any pleasures supposed to be possessed by the beings who may be the objects of benevolence; to wit, the sensitive beings we are acquainted with; under which are commonly included, 1. The Supreme Being. 2. Human beings. 3. Other animals. These may also be called the pleasures of good-will, the pleasures of sympathy, or the pleasures of the benevolent or social affections.

XI. 9. The pleasures of malevolence are the pleasures resulting from the view of any pain supposed to be suffered by the beings who may become the objects of malevolence: to wit, 1. Human beings. 2. Other animals. These may also be styled the pleasures of ill-will, the pleasures of the irascible appetite, the pleasures of antipathy, or the pleasures of the malevolent or dissocial affections.

XII. 10. The pleasures of the memory are the pleasures which, after having enjoyed such and such pleasures, or even in some case after having suffered such and such pains, a man will now and then experience, at recollecting them exactly in the order and in the circumstances in which they were actually enjoyed or suffered. These derivative pleasures may of course be distinguished into as many species as there are of original perceptions, from whence they may be copied. They may also be styled pleasures of simple recollection.

XII. 11. The pleasures of the imagination are the pleasures which may be derived from the contemplation of any such pleasures as may happen to be suggested by the memory, but in a different order, and accompanied by different groups of circumstances. These may accordingly be referred to any one of the three cardinal points of time, present, past, or future. It is evident they may admit of as many distinctions as those of the former class.

XIV. 12. The pleasures of expectation are the pleasures that result from the contemplation of any sort of pleasure, referred to time *future,* and accompanied with the sentiment of *belief.* These also may admit of the same distinctions.

XV. 13. The pleasures of association are the pleasures which certain objects or incidents may happen to afford, not of themselves, but merely in virtue of some association they have contracted in the mind with certain objects or incidents which are in themselves pleasureable. Such is the case, for instance, with the pleasure of skill, when afforded by such a set of incidents as compose a game of chess. This derives its pleasurable quality from its association partly with the pleasures of skill, as exercised in the production of incidents pleasurable of themselves: partly from its association with the pleasures of power. Such is the case also with the pleasure of good luck, when afforded by such incidents as compose the game of hazard, or any other game of chance, when played at for nothing. This derives its pleasurable quality from its association with one of the pleasures of wealth; to wit, with the pleasure of acquiring it.

XVI. 14. Farther on we shall see pains grounded upon pleasures; in like manner may we now see pleasures grounded upon pains. To the catalogue of pleasures may accordingly be added the pleasures of *relief:* or, the pleasures which a man experiences when, after he has been enduring a pain of any kind for a certain time, it comes to cease, or to abate. These may of course be distinguished into as many species as there are of pains: and may give rise to so many pleasures of memory, of imagination, and of expectation.

XVII. 1. Pains of privation are the pains that may result from the thought of not possessing in the time present any of the several kinds of pleasures. Pains of privation may accordingly be resolved into as many kinds as there are of pleasures to which they may correspond, and from the absence whereof they may be derived.

XVIII. There are three sorts of pains which are only so many modifications of the several pains of privation. When the enjoyment of any particular pleasure happens to be particularly desired, but without any expectation approaching to assurance, the pain of privation which thereupon results takes a particular name, and is called the pain of *desire,* or of unsatisfied desire.

XIX. Where the enjoyment happens to have been looked for with a degree of expectation approaching to assurance, and that expectation is made suddenly to cease, it is called a pain of disappointment.

XX. A pain of privation takes the name of a pain of regret in two cases: 1. Where it is grounded on the memory of a pleasure, which having been once enjoyed, appears not likely to be enjoyed again: 2. Where it is grounded on the idea of a pleasure, which was never actually enjoyed, nor perhaps so much as expected, but which might have been enjoyed (it is supposed), had such or such a contingency happened, which, in fact, did not happen.

XXI. 2. The several pains of the senses seem to be as follows: 1. The pains of hunger and thirst: or the disagreeable sensations produced by the want of suitable substances which need at times to be applied to the alimentary canal. 2. The pains of the taste: or the disagreeable sensations produced by the application of various substances to the palate, and other superior parts of the same canal. 3. The pains of the organ of smell: or the disagreeable sensations produced by the effluvia of various substances when applied to that organ. 4. The pains of the touch: or the disagreeable sensations produced by the application of various substances to the skin. 5. The simple pains of the hearing: or the disagreeable sensations excited in the organ of that sense by various kinds of sounds: independently (as before), of association. 6. The simple pains of sight: or the disagreeable sensations if any such there be, that may be excited in the organ of that sense by visible images, independent of the principle of association. 7. The pains resulting from excessive heat or cold, unless these be referable to the touch. 8. The pains of disease: or the acute and uneasy sensations resulting from the several diseases and indispositions to which human nature is liable. 9. The pain of exertion, whether bodily or mental: or the uneasy sensation which is apt to accompany any intense effort, whether of mind or body.

XXII. 3. The pains of awkwardness are the pains which sometimes result from the unsuccessful endeavour to apply any particular instruments of enjoyment or security to their uses, or from the difficulty a man experiences in applying them.

XXIII. 4. The pains of enmity are the pains that may accompany the persuasion of a man's being obnoxious to the ill-will of such or such an assignable person or persons in particular: or, as the phrase is, of being upon ill terms with him or them: and, in consequence, of being obnoxious to certain pains of some sort or other, of which he may be the cause.

XXIV. 5. The pains of an ill-name, are the pains that accompany the persuasion of a man's being obnoxious, or in a way to be obnoxious to the ill-will of the world about him. These may likewise be called the pains of ill-repute, the pains of dishonour, or the pains of the moral sanction.

XXV. 6. The pains of piety are the pains that accompany the belief of a man's being obnoxious to the displeasure of the Supreme Being: and in consequence to certain pains to be inflicted by his especial appointment, either in this life or in a life to come. These may also be called the pains of religion; the pains of a religious disposition; or the pains of the religious sanction. When the belief is looked upon as well-grounded, these pains are commonly called religious terrors; when looked upon as ill-grounded, superstitious terrors.

XXVI. 7. The pains of benevolence are the pains resulting from the view of any pains supposed to be endured by other beings. These may also be called the pains of good-will, of sympathy, or the pains of the benevolent or social affections.

XXVII. 8. The pains of malevolence are the pains resulting from the view of any pleasures supposed to be enjoyed by any beings who happen to be the objects of a man's displeasure. These may also be styled the pains of ill-will, of antipathy, or the pains of the malevolent or dissocial affections.

XXVIII. 9. The pains of the memory may be grounded on every one of the above kinds, as well of pains of privation as of positive pains. These correspond exactly to the pleasure of the memory.

XXIX. 10. The pains of the imagination may also be grounded on any one of the above kinds, as well of pains of privation as of positive pains: in other respects they correspond exactly to the pleasures of the imagination.

XXX. 11. The pains of expectation may be grounded on each one of the above kinds, as well of pains of privation as of positive pains. These may be also termed pains of apprehension.

XXXI. 12. The pains of association correspond exactly to the pleasures of association.

XXXII. Of the above list there are certain pleasures and pains which suppose the existence of some pleasure or pain of some other person, to which the pleasure or pain of the person in question has regard: such pleasures and pains may be termed *extra-regarding*. Others do not suppose any such thing: these may be termed *self-regarding*. The only pleasures and pains of the extra-regarding class are those of benevolence and those of malevolence: all the rest are self-regarding.

XXXIII. Of all these several sorts of pleasures and pains, there is scarce any one which is not liable, on more accounts than one, to come under the consideration of the law. Is an offense committed? It is the tendency which it has to destroy, in such or such persons, some of these pleasures, or to produce some of these pains, that constitutes the mischief of it, and the ground for punishing it. It is the prospect of some of these pleasures, or of security from some of these pains, that constitutes the motive or temptation, it is the attainment of them that constitutes the profit of the offence. Is the offender to be punished? It can be only by the production of one or more of these pains, that the punishment can be inflicted.

VI. OF CIRCUMSTANCES INFLUENCING SENSIBILITY

Pain and pleasure not uniformly proportioned to their causes
Degree or *quantum* of sensibility, what
Bias or *quality* of sensibility, what
Exciting causes pleasurable and *dolorific*
Circumstances *inflencing sensibility,* what
Circumstances influencing sensibility enumerated
  Extent and intricacy of this subject
   1. *Health*
   2. *Strength*
      Measure of strength, the weight a man can lift
      Weakness, what
   3. *Hardiness*

Difference between strength and hardiness
   4. *Bodily imperfection*
   5. Quantity and quality of *knowledge*
   6. *Strength* of *intellectual powers*
   7. *Firmness of mind*
   8. *Steadiness*
   9. *Bent* of *inclinations*
   10. *Moral sensibility*
   11. *Moral biases*
   12. *Religious sensibility*
   13. *Religious biases*
   14. *Sympathetic sensibility*
   15. *Sympathetic biases*
   16, 17. *Antipathetic sensibility* and *biases*
   18. *Insanity*
   19. *Habitual occupations*
   20. *Pecuniary* circumstances
   21. *Connexions* in the way of *sympathy*
   22. Connexions in the way of *antipathy*
   23. Radical *frame* of *body*
   24. Radical frame of *mind*
       Idiosyncrasy, what
This distinct from the circumstance of frame of body
     Whether the soul be *material* or *immaterial* makes
        no difference
—and from all others
Yet the result of them is not separately discernible
Frame of body indicates, but not certainly, that of mind
Secondary influencing circumstances
   25. *Sex*
   26. *Age*
   27. *Rank*
   28. *Education*
   29. *Climate*
   30. *Lineage*
   31. *Government*
   32. *Religious profession*
Use of the preceding observations
How far the circumstances in question can be taken
   into account

IX. OF CONSCIOUSNESS

Connexion of this chapter with the foregoing
Acts *advised* and *unadvised; consciousness,* what
Unadvisedness may regard either *existence,* or *materiality*
The circumstance may have been *present, past,* or *future*
An unadvised act may be *heedless,* or *not heedless*
A *misadvised* act, what,—a *missupposal*
The supposed circumstance might have been material in the way either of *prevention* or of *compensation*
It may have been supposed *present, past,* or *future*
Example, continued from the last chapter
In what case consciousness extends the intentionality from the act to the consequences
Example continued
A misadvised act may be *rash* or *not rash*
The intention may be good or bad *in itself,* independently of the *motive* as well as the eventual consequences
It is better, when the *intention* is meant to be spoken of as being good or bad, not to say, the *motive*
Example
Intention, in what cases it may be *innocent*
Intentionality and consciousness, how spoken of in the *Roman* law
Use of this and the preceding chapter

X. OF MOTIVES

1. Different sense of the word Motive.

Motives, why considered
Purely *speculative* motives have nothing to do here
Motives to the *will*
Figurative and *unfigurative senses* of the word
Motives *interior* and *exterior*
Motive in *prospect*—motive in *esse*
Motives *immediate* and *remote*
Motives to the *understanding* how they may influence the *will*

2. No Motives either constantly good or constantly bad.

Nothing can act of itself as a motive, but the idea of *pleasure* or *pain*

No sort of motive is in itself a *bad* one

Inaccuracy of expressions in which *good* or *bad* are applied to motives

Any sort of *motive* may give birth to any sort of *act*

Difficulties which stand in the way of an analysis of this sort

3. Catalogue of Motives corresponding to that of Pleasures and Pains.

Physical desire corresponding to pleasures of *sense* in general

The *motive* corresponding to the *pleasures* of the *palate*

Sexual desire corresponding to the *pleasures* of the *sexual* sense

Curiosity, etc. corresponding to the *pleasures* of *curiosity*

None to pleasures of sense

Pecuniary interest to the *pleasures* of *wealth*

None to the pleasures of *skill*

To the pleasures of *amity,* the *desire* of *ingratiating* one's self

To the *pleasures* of a *good name,* the *love* of *reputation*

To the *pleasures* of *power,* the *love of power*

The *motive* belonging to the *religious sanction*

Good-will, etc. to the *pleasures* of *sympathy*

Ill-will, etc. to the *pleasures of antipathy*

Self-preservation, to the several kinds of *pains*

To the *pains* of *exertion,* the love of *ease*

Motives can only be *bad* with reference to the most frequent complexion of their *effects*

How it is that motives, such as *lust, avarice,* etc., are constantly *bad*

Under the above restrictions, motives may be distinguished into *good, bad,* and *indifferent* or *neutral*

Inconveniences of this distribution

It is only in *individual* instances that motives can be good or bad

The disposition is to be inferrred, 1. From the apparent *tendency* of the act: 2. From the nature of the *motive*

Case 1. Tendency, *good*—motive, *self-regarding*

Case 2. Tendency, *bad*—motive, *self-regarding*

Case 3. Tendency, *good*—motive, *good-will*

Case 4. Tendency, *bad*—motive, *good-will*

This case not an impossible one

Example I.

Example II.

Example III.

Case 5. Tendency, *good*—motive, *love of reputation*
    The bulk of mankind apt to depreciate this motive

Case 6. Tendency, *bad*—motive, *honour*

Example I.

Example II.

Case 7. Tendency, *good*—motive, *piety*

Case 8. Tendency, *bad*—motive, *religion*

The disposition may be bad in this case

Case 9. Tendency, *good*—motive, *malevolence*

Example

Case 10. Tendency, *bad*—motive, *malevolence*

Example

Problem—to measure the *depravity* in a man's disposition

A man's disposition is constituted by the *sum* of his *intentions*

—which owe their birth to *motives*

A *seducing* or *corrupting* motive, what—a *tutelary* or *preservatory* motive

Tutelary motives are either *standing* or *occasional*

Standing tutelary motives are,

  1. *Good-will*
  2. The *love* of *reputation*
  3. The *desire* of *amity*
  4. The *motive* of *religion*

Occasional tutelary motives *may* be any whatsoever

Motives that are *particularly apt* to act in this character are, 1. *Love of ease.* 2. *Self-preservation.*

XII. OF THE CONSEQUENCES OF A MISCHIEVOUS ACT

—applied to the preceding cases

—to examples of other cases where the mischief is less conspicuous

Example I. An act of self-intoxication

Example II. Non-payment of a tax

No alarm, when no assignable person is the object

2. How intentionality, &c. may influence the mischief of an Act.

Secondary mischief influenced by the state of the agent's mind

Case 1. *Involuntariness*

Case 2. *Unintentionality* with *heedlessness*

Case 3. *Missupposal* of a *complete justification,* without rashness

Case 4. Missupposal of a *partial* justification, without rashness

Case 5. Missupposal, with *rashness*

Case 6. Consequences *completely intentional,* and *free from missupposal*

The nature of a motive *takes not away* the mischief of the secondary consequences

Nor the beneficialness

But it may *aggravate* the mischievousness, where they are mischievous

But not the *most* in the case of the *worst* motives

It does the more, the more considerable the *tendency* of the motive to *produce* such acts

—which is as its *strength* and *constancy*

General *efficacy* of a species of motive, how measured

A mischievous act is more so, when issuing from a *self-regarding* than when from a *dissocial* motive

—so even when issuing from the motive of *religion*

How the secondary mischief is influenced by *disposition*

Connexion of this with the succeeding chapter

XIII. CASES UNMEET FOR PUNISHMENT

1. General View of Cases unmeet for Punishment

The end of law is, to augment happiness

But punishment is an evil

What concerns the *end,* and several other topics, relative to punishment, dismissed to another work

Concise view of the ends of punishment

Therefore ought not to be admitted

1. Where *groundless*
2. *Inefficacious*
3. *Unprofitable*
4. Or *needless*

2. Cases in which Punishment is groundless.

1. Where there has never been any mischief: as in the case of *consent*
2. Where the mischief was *outweighed:* as in *precaution* against *calamity,* and the exercise of *powers*
3. —or will, for a certainty, be *cured* by *compensation*
   Hence the favours shown to the offences of responsible offenders: such as *simple mercantile frauds*

3. Cases in which Punishment must be inefficacious.

1. Where the penal provision comes *too late:* as in 1. An *ex-post-facto* law. 2. An *ultra-legal sentence*
2. Or is *not* made *known:* as in a law *not* sufficiently *promulgated*
3. Where the *will* cannot be *deterred* from *any* act, as in,
   [a] *Infancy*
   [b] *Insanity*
   [c] *Intoxication*
       In infancy and intoxication the case can hardly be proved to come under the rule
       The reason for not punishing in these three cases is commonly put upon a wrong footing
4. Or not from the *individual* act in question, as in,
   [a] *Unintentionality*
   [b] *Unconsciousness*
   [c] *Missupposal*
5. Or is acted on by an opposite *superior force:* as by,
   [a] *Physical danger*

[b] *Threatened mischief*

Why the influence of the *moral* and *religious* sanctions is not mentioned in the same view

6. —or the *bodily organs* cannot *follow* its *determination:* as under *physical compulsion* or *restraint*

4. Cases where Punishment is unprofitable.

1. Where, in the *sort* of case in question, the punishment would produce more evil than the offence would

Evil producible by a *punishment*—its four branches— viz.

[a] *Restraint*
[b] *Apprehension*
[c] *Sufferance*
[d] *Derivative* evils

The *evil* of the *offence,* being different according to the nature of the offence, cannot be represented here

2. —Or in the *individual* case in question: by reason of

[a] *The multitude* of *delinquents*
[b] The *value* of a *delinquent's* service
[c] The *displeasure* of the *people*
[d] The *displeasure* of *foreign powers*

5. Cases where Punishment is needless.

1. Where the mischief is to be *prevented* at a *cheaper* rate: as by instruction

XIV. OF THE PROPORTION BETWEEN PUNISHMENTS AND OFFENCES

Recapitulation

Four *objects* of punishment

1st Object—to *prevent all offences*
2nd Object—to prevent the *worst*
3rd Object—to keep down the *mischief*
4th Object—to act at the least *expense*

Rules of *proportion* between *punishments* and offences

The same rules applicable to *motives* in general

Rule 1.—*Outweigh* the *profit* of the offence

Recapitulation
The nicety here observed vindicated from the charge
  of inutility

XV. OF THE PROPERTIES TO BE
GIVEN TO A LOT OF PUNISHMENT

Properties are to be governed by *proportion*
Property 1. *Variability*
Property 2. *Equability*
Punishments which are apt to be deficient in this respect
Property 3. *Commensurability* to other punishments
How two lots of punishment may be rendered perfectly
  commensurable
Property 4. *Characteristicalness*
The mode of punishment the most eminently character-
  istic, is that of *retaliation*
Property 5. *Exemplarity*
The most effectual way of rendering a punishment
  exemplary is by means of *analogy*
Property 6. *Frugality*
Frugality belongs in perfection to *pecuniary punishment*
Exemplarity and *frugality* in what they differ and agree
Other properties of inferior importance
Property 7. *Subserviency* to *reformation*
—applied to *offences* originating in *ill-will*
—to offences originating in *indolence* joined to *pe-
  cuniary interest*
Property 8. *Efficacy* with respect to *disablement*
—is most conspicuous in *capital* punishment
Other punishments in which it is to be found
Property 9. Subserviency to *compensation*
Property 10. *Popularity*
  Characteristicalness renders a punishment, 1.
    memorable: 2. *exemplary*: 3. *popular*
Mischiefs resulting from the *unpopularity* of a punishment—*discontent* among the people, and *weakness
  in the law*
This property supposes a *prejudice* which the legislature
  ought to cure

Property 11. *Remissibility*

To obtain all these properties, punishments must be *mixed*

The foregoing properties recapitulated

Connexion of this with the ensuing chapter

XVI. DIVISION OF OFFENCES

1. Classes of Offences.

Method pursued in the following division

Distinction between what *are* offences and what *ought to be*

No act *ought to be* an offence but what is *detrimental* to the *community*

To be so, it must be detrimental to some one or more of its *members*

These may be *assignable* or *not*

Persons *assignable,* how

If assignable, the *offender* himself, or *others*

Class 1. *Private* offences

Class 2. *Semi-public* offences

Limits between private, semi-public, and public offences, are, strictly speaking, undistinguishable

Class 3. *Self-regarding* offences

Class 4. *Public* offences

Class 5. *Multiform* offences, viz. 1. Offences *by falsehood*. 2. Offences *against trust*

The imperfections of language an obstacle to arrangement

Irregularity of this class

—which could not be avoided on any other plan

2. Divisions and sub-divisions.

Divisions of *Class*. 1. 1—Offences against *person*. 2—*Property*. 3—*Reputation*. 4—*Condition*. 5—*Person and property*. 6—*Person and reputation*

In what manner pleasure and pain depend upon the *relation* a man bears to exterior objects

Divisions of *Class* 2. 1. Offences through *calamity*

Sub-divisions of offences through calamity, dismissed

2. Offences of *mere delinquency,* how they correspond
with the divisions of private offences

Divisions of *Class* 3 coincide with those of Class 1

Divisions of *Class* 4
    Exhaustive method departed from

Connexion of the *nine first divisions* one with another

Connexion of offences against *religion* with the foregoing ones

Connexion of offences against the *national interest in
general* with the rest

Sub-Divisions of *Class* 5 enumerated

Divisions of offences by *falsehood*

Offences by falsehood, in what they agree with one
another

—in what they differ

Sub-divisions of offences by falsehood are determined
by the divisions of the preceding classes

Offences of this class, in some instances, change their
names; in others, not

A *trust,* what
    Power and *right,* why no complete definition is
    here given of them

Offences against *trust, condition,* and *property,* why
ranked under separate divisions

Offences against *trust*—their connexion with each other

Prodigality in trustees dismissed to Class 3

The *sub-divisions* of offences *against trust* are also determined by the divisions of the preceding classes

Connexion between offences *by falsehood* and offences
against trust

3. Genera of Class 1.

Analysis into *genera* pursued no further than Class 1

Offences against an *individual* may be *simple* in their
effects or *complex*

Offences *against* person—their *genera*

Offences against *reputation*

Offences against *property*
    Payment, what

Offences against *person and reputation*

Offences against *person and property*

Offences against *condition*—Conditions *domestic* or *civil*

Domestic conditions grounded on *natural* relationships

Relations—*two* result from every two objects

Domestic relations which are purely of *legal institution*

Offences touching the *condition* of a *master*

Various *modes* of *servitude*

Offences touching the *condition* of a *servant*

Guardianship, what—Necessity of the institution

Duration to be given to it

Powers that may, and *duties* that ought to be, annexed to it

Offences touching the *condition* of a *guardian*

Offences touching the condition of a *ward*

Offences touching the condition of a *parent*

Offences touching the *filial condition*

Condition of a *husband.*—*Powers, Duties,* and *rights,* that may be annexed to it

Offences touching the condition of a husband

Offences touching the condition of a *wife*

Civil conditions

4. Advantages of the present method.

General idea of the *method* here pursued

Its *advantages*

—1. It is convenient for the *apprehension* and the *memory*

—2. It gives room for *general* propositions

—3. It points out the *reason* of the *law*

—4. It is alike applicable to the laws of *all nations*

5. Characters of the five classes.

Characters of the classes, how deducible from the above method

Characters of *class* 1

Characters of *class* 2

Characters of *class* 3

Characters of *class* 4

Characters of *class* 5

XVII. OF THE LIMITS OF THE
PENAL BRANCH OF JURISPRUDENCE

2. Jurisprudence, its branches.

Jurisprudence, *expository—censorial*

Expository jurisprudence, *authoritative—unauthoritative*

Sources of the distinctions yet remaining

Jurisprudence, *local—universal*

—internal and *international*

Internal jurisprudence, *national* and *provincial, local* or *particular*

Jurisprudence, *ancient—living*

Jurisprudence, *statutory—customary*

Jurisprudence, *civil—penal—criminal*

Question, concerning the distinction between the civil branch and the penal, stated

    I. Occasion and purpose of this concluding note

    II. By a *law* here is not meant a *statute*

   III. Every law is either a *command,* or a *revocation* of one

   IV. A *declaratory law* is not, properly speaking, a law

    V. Every *coercive* law creates an offence

   VI. A law creating an *offence,* and one appointing *punishment,* are *distinct* laws

  VII. A *discoercive* law can have *no punitory* one appertaining to it but through the intervention of a *coercive* one

 VIII. But a punitory law involves the *simply imperative* one it belongs to

   IX. The simply imperative one might therefore be spared, but for its *expository* matter

    X. *Nature* of such expository matter

   XI. The vastness of its comparative bulk is not peculiar to legislative commands

  XII. The same mass of expository matter may serve in common for *many* laws

 XIII. The *imperative* character essential to law, is apt to be *concealed* in and by *expository* matter

 XIV. The concealment is favoured by the multitude

of *indirect* forms in which imperative matter is capable of being couched.

THE BOOK OF FALLACIES*

[*The Book of Fallacies* is an analysis by which Bentham hoped to show up the devices made use of by political reactionaries when they lack reasonable or valid arguments to present against a measure they hate.

In the version here presented the 100,000 words of Bingham's edition have been reduced to about 15,000. Each fallacy is included, however, and every word is Bentham's as he wrote it.

One form of the design was to make the classification of motives to be appealed to by the fallacies in Latin terms, and as these still appear at times in the present version, they are here listed and translated:

ad verecundiam	(to modesty)
ad superstitionem	(to superstition)
ad amicitiam	(to friendship)
ad metum	(to fear)
ad odium	(to hatred)
ad superbiam	(to pride)
ad judicium	(to judgment)
ad quietem	(to peace)
ad invidentiam	(to envy)
ad socordiam	(to weak-mindedness)
ad imaginationem	(to imagination)]

POLITICAL FALLACIES THE SUBJECT OF THIS WORK

The present work confines itself to the examination and exposure of only one class of fallacies, which class is

*Edited from Bentham's mss. by Peregrine Bingham, 1824; reprinted in *Works* (1843), Vol. II, pp. 379ff.

determined by the nature of the occasion in which they are employed.

The occasion here in question is that of the formation of a decision procuring the adoption or rejection of some measure of *government:* including under the notion of a measure of legislation as well as of administration—two operations so intimately connected, that the drawing of a boundary line between them will in some instances be a matter of no small difficulty, but for the distinguishing of which on the present occasion, and for the purpose of the present work, there will not be any need.

Sophistry is a hydra, of which, if all the necks could be exposed, the force would be destroyed. In this work they have been diligently looked out for, and in the course of it the principal and most active of them have been brought to view.

First, fallacies of *authority* (including laudatory personalities); the subject-matter of which is authority in various shapes—and the immediate object, *to repress,* on the ground of the weight of such authority, *all exercise of the reasoning faculty*.

Secondly, fallacies of *danger* (including vituperative personalities); the subject-matter of which is the suggestion of danger in various shapes—and the object, *to repress altogether,* on the ground of such danger, the *discussion* proposed to be entered on.

Thirdly, fallacies of *delay;* the subject-matter of which is an assigning of reasons for delay in various shapes—and the object, to *postpone* such *discussion,* with a view of eluding it altogether.

Fourthly, fallacies of *confusion;* the subject-matter of which consists chiefly of vague and indefinite generalities—while the object is *to produce,* when discussion can no longer be avoided, such *confusion* in the minds of the hearers as to incapacitate them for forming a correct judgment on the question proposed for deliberation.

PART I. FALLACIES OF AUTHORITY
The Subject of Which Is Authority
In Various Shapes, and The Object to Repress
All Exercise of the Reasoning Faculty

At the top of the scale of trustworthiness stands that mass of authority which is constituted by what may be termed *scientific* or professional *opinion:* that is, opinion entertained in relation to the subject in question by a person who, by special means and motives attached to a particular situation in life, may with reason be considered as possessed of such *means* of insuring the correctness of his opinion, as cannot reasonably be expected to have place on the part of a person not so circumstanced.

1. The legitimately persuasive force of professional authority being taken as the highest term in the scale, the following may be noticed as expressive of so many other species of authority, occupying so many inferior degrees in the same scale:—

2. Authority derived from *power*. The greater the quantity of power a man has, no matter in what shape, the nearer the authority of his opinion comes to professional authority, in respect of the facility of obtaining the means conducive to correctness of decision.

3. Authority derived from *opulence*. Opulence— being an instrument of power, and to a considerable extent applicable in a direct way to many or most of the purposes to which power is applicable—seems to stand next after power in the scale of instruments of facility as above.

4. Authority derived from *reputation,* considered as among the efficient causes of respect. By reputation, understand, on this occasion, general reputation, not special and relative reputation, which would rank the species of authority under the head of professional authority as above.

By authority, support, the strength of which is proportioned to the number of the persons joining in it, is given to systems of opinions at once absurd and pernicious—to the religion of Buddh, of Brama, of Foh, of Mahomet.

And hence it may be inferred that the probative force of authority is not increased by the number of those who may have professed a given opinion—unless, indeed, it could be proved that each individual of the multitudes who professed the opinion, possessed in the highest degree the means and motives for ensuring its correctness.

Take any part of the field of moral science, private morality, constitutional law, private law—go back a few centuries, and you will find argument consisting of reference to authority, not exclusively, but in as large a proportion as possible. As experience has increased, authority has been gradually set aside, and reasoning, drawn from facts, and guided by reference to the end in view, true or false, has taken its place.

Of the enormous mass of Roman law heaped up in the school of Justinian—a mass, the perusal of which would employ several lives occupied by nothing else— materials of this description constitute by far the greater part. A throws out at random some loose thought: B, catching it up, tells you what A thinks—at least, what A said: C tells you what has been said by A and B; and thus, like an avalanche, the mass rolls on.

The Wisdom of Our Ancestors; or Chinese Argument—(ad verecundiam)

"Our wise ancestors"—"The wisdom of our ancestors" —"The wisdom of ages"—"Venerable antiquity"— "Wisdom of old times:"—

This fallacy affords one of the most striking of the numerous instances in which, under the conciliatory influence of *custom*—that is, of *prejudice*—opinions the most repugnant to one another are capable of maintaining their ground in the same intellect.

This fallacy, prevalent as it is in matters of law, is directly repugnant to a principle or maxim universally admitted in almost every other department of human intelligence, and which is the foundation of all useful knowledge and of all rational conduct.

"Experience is the mother of wisdom," is among the maxims handed down to the present and all future ages, by the wisdom, such as it has been, of past ages.

No! says this fallacy, the true mother of wisdom is not *experience,* but *inexperience.*

So long as they keep to vague generalities—so long as the two objects of comparison are each of them taken in the lump—wise ancestors in one lump, ignorant and foolish mob of modern times in the other—the weakness of the fallacy may escape detection.

Take, for example, any year in the reign of Henry the Eighth, from 1509 to 1546.

On no one branch of legislation was any book extant, from which, with regard to the circumstances of the then present times, any useful instruction could be derived: distributive law, penal law, international law, political economy, so far from existing as sciences, had scarcely obtained a name: in all those departments, under the head of *quid faciendum,* a mere blank: the whole literature of the age consisted of a meagre chronicle or two, containing short memorandums of the usual occurrences of war and peace, battles, sieges, executions, revels, deaths, births, processions, ceremonies, and other external events; but with scarce a speech or an incident that could enter into the composition of any such work as a history of the human mind—with scarce an attempt at investigation into causes, characters, or the state of the people at large. Even when at last, little by little, a scrap or two of political instruction came to be obtainable, the proportion of error and mischievous doctrine mixed up with it was so great, that whether a blank unfilled might not have been less prejudicial than a blank thus filled, may reasonably be matter of doubt.

If we come down to the reign of James the First, we shall find that Solomon of his time, eminently eloquent as well as learned, not only among the crowned but among uncrowned heads, marking out for prohibition and punishment the practices of devils and witches, and without any the slightest objection on the part of the great characters of that day in their high situations, consigning men to death and torment for the misfortune of not being so well acquainted as he was with the composition of the Godhead.

1. Fallacy of Irrevocable Laws
2. Fallacy of Vows—(ad superstitionem)

The two fallacies brought to view in this chapter are intimately connected, and require to be considered together: the object in view is the same in both—the difference lies only in the instrument employed; and both of them are in effect the fallacy of *the wisdom of our ancestors,* pushed to the highest degree of extravagance and absurdity.

The object is to tie up the hands of future legislators by obligations supposed to be indissoluble.

Let us examine the various kinds of contract to which statesmen have endeavoured to impart this character of perpetuity:—1. Treaties between state and foreign state, by which each respectively engages its government and people; 2. Grant of privileges from the sovereign to the whole community in the character of subjects; 3. Grant of privileges from the sovereign to a particular class of subjects; 4. New arrangement of power between different portions or branches of the sovereignty, or new declaration of the rights of the community; 5. Incorporative union between two sovereignties having or not having a common head.

Take, then, for the subject and substance of the contract, any one of these arrangements: so long as the happiness of the whole community, taken in the aggregate, is in a greater degree promoted by the exact observance of the contract, than it would be by any alteration, exact ought to be the observance:—on the contrary, if, by any given change, the aggregate of happiness would be in a greater degree promoted than by the exact observance, such change ought to be made.

True it is, that, considering the alarm and danger which is the natural result of every breach of a contract to which the sovereignty is party, in case of any change with respect to such contact, the aggregate of public happiness will be in general rather diminished than promoted, unless, in case of disadvantage produced to any party by the change, such disadvantage be made up by adequate compensation.

No-Precedent Argument—(ad verecundiam)

"The proposition is of a novel and unprecedented complexion: the present is surely the first time that any such thing was ever heard of in this house."

To such an observation there could be no objection, if the object with which it were made was only to fix attention to a new or difficult subject: "Deliberate well before you act, as you have no precedent to direct your course."

But in the character of an argument, as a ground for the rejection of the proposed measure, it is obviously a fallacy.

Whether or no the alleged novelty actually exists, is an inquiry which it can never be worth while to make.

That it is impossible that it should in any case afford the smallest ground for the rejection of the measure,— that the observation is completely irrelevant in relation to the question, whether or no it is expedient that such a measure should be adopted,—is a proposition to which it seems difficult to conceive how an immediate assent can be refused.

It may be urged, that if the measure had been a fit one, it would have been brought upon the carpet before. But there are several obstacles, besides the inexpediency of a measure, which, for any length of time, may prevent its being brought forward:—

1. If, though beyond dispute promotive of the interest of the many, there be anything in it that is adverse to the interests the prejudices, or the humors of the ruling few, the wonder is, not that it should not have been

brought forward before, but that it should be brought forward even now.

2. If in the complexion of it there be anything which it required a particular degree of ingenuity to contrive and adapt to the purpose, this would of itself be sufficient to account for the tardiness of its appearance.

1. Self-assumed Authority
—(ad ignorantiam; ad verecundiam.)
2. The Self-trumpeter's fallacy

This fallacy presents itself in two shapes:

The first is commonly played off as follows:—An evil or defect in our institutions is pointed out clearly, and a remedy proposed, to which no objection can be made; up starts a man high in office, and, instead of stating any specific objection, says, "I am not prepared" to do so and so, "I am not prepared to say," &c. The meaning evidently intended to be conveyed is, "If I, who am so dignified, and supposed to be so capable of forming a judgment, avow myself incompetent to do so, what presumption, what folly, must there be in the conclusion formed by any one else!" In truth, this is nothing else but an indirect way of browbeating—arrogance under a thin veil of modesty.

If you are not prepared to pass a judgment, you are not prepared to condemn, and ought not, therefore, to oppose: the utmost you are warranted in doing, if sincere, is to ask for a little time for consideration.

Supposing the unpreparedness real, the reasonable and practical inference is—say nothing, take no part in the business.

A proposition for the reforming of this or that abuse in the administration of justice, is the common occasion for the employment of this fallacy.

The second of these two devices may be called the self-trumpeter's fallacy.

There are certain men in office, who in discharge of their functions arrogate to themselves a degree of probity which is to exclude all imputations and all inquiry; their assertions are to be deemed equivalent to proof; their virtues are guarantees for the faithful discharge of their duties; and the most implicit confidence is to be reposed in them on all occasions. If you expose any abuse, propose any reform, call for securities, inquiry, or measures to promote publicity, they set up a cry of surprise, amounting almost to indignation, as if their integrity were questioned, or their honour wounded. With all this, they dexterously mix up intimations that the most exalted patriotism, honour, and perhaps religion, are the only sources of all their actions.

These assertions of authority, therefore, by men in office, who would have us estimate their conduct by their character, and not their character by their conduct, must be classed among political fallacies. If there be any one maxim in politics more certain than another, it is, that no possible degree of virtue in the governor can render it expedient for the governed to dispense with good laws and good institutions.

Laudatory Personalities—(ad amicitiam)

The object of laudatory personalities is to effect the rejection of a measure on account of the alleged good character of those who oppose it; and the argument advanced is—"The measure is rendered unnecessary by the virtues of those who are in power; their opposition is a sufficient authority for the rejection of the measure."

"The measure proposed implies a distrust of the members of his Majesty's government; but so great is their integrity, so complete their disinterestedness, so uniformly do they prefer the public advantage to their own, that such a measure is altogether unnecessary:— their disapproval is sufficient to warrant an opposition: precautions can only be requisite where danger is apprehended; here, the high character of the individuals in question is a sufficient guarantee against any ground of alarm."

In every public trust, the legislator should, for the

purpose of prevention, suppose the trustee disposed to break the trust in every imaginable way in which it would be possible for him to reap, from the breach of it, any personal advantage. This is the principle on which public institutions ought to be formed; and when it is applied to all men indiscriminately, it is injurious to none. The practical inference is, to oppose to such possible (and what will always be probable) breaches of trust every bar that can be opposed, consistently with the power requisite for the efficient and due discharge of the trust. Indeed, these arguments, drawn from the supposed virtues of men in power, are opposed to the first principles on which all laws proceed.

PART II. FALLACIES OF DANGER
The Subject-Matter of Which is Danger
in Various Shapes, and the Object
To Repress Discussion Altogether,
by Exciting Alarm

Vituperative Personalities—(ad odium)

The fallacies that belong to this cluster may be denominated—

1. Imputation of bad design.
2. Imputation of bad character.
3. Imputation of bad motive.
4. Imputation of inconsistency.
5. Imputation of suspicious connexions—*Noscitur ex sociis*.
6. Imputation founded on identity of denomination —*Noscitur ex cognominibus*.

The argument in its various shapes amounts to this:— In bringing forward or supporting the measure in question, the person in question entertains a bad design; therefore the measure is bad:—he is a person of a bad character; therefore the measure is bad:—he is actuated by a bad motive; therefore the measure is bad:—he has fallen into inconsistencies; on a former occasion, he either opposed it, or made some observation not reconcilable with some observation which he has advanced on the present occasion; therefore the measure is bad:——he is on a footing of intimacy with this or that person, who is a man of dangerous principles and designs, or has been seen more or less frequently in his company, or has professed, or is suspected of entertaining some opinion which the other has professed, or been suspected of entertaining; therefore the measure is bad: ——he bears a name that at a former period was borne by a set of men now no more, by whom bad principles were entertained, or bad things done; therefore the measure is bad.

"Give not your sanction to this measure; for though there may be no particular harm in it, yet if you do give your sanction to it, the same man by whom this is proposed, will propose to you others that will be bad; and such is your weakness, that, however bad they may be, you will want either the discernment necessary to enable you to see them in their true light, or the resolution to enable you to put a negative upon measures, of the mischief of which you are fully convinced."

The proposer of the measure, it is asserted, is actuated by bad motives, from whence it is inferred that he entertains some bad design. This, again, is no more than a modification of *the fallacy of distrust;* but one of the very weakest—1. Because motives are hidden in the human breast; 2. Because, if the measure is beneficial, it would be absurd to reject it on account of the motives of its author.

Imputation founded on identity of denomination—(noscitur ex cognominibus)

It is in matters touching religious persuasion, and to the prejudice of certain sects, that this fallacy has been played off with the greatest and most pernicious effect. In England, particularly against measures for the relief of the Catholics, "those of our ancestors, who, professing the same branch of the Christian religion as that which you now profess, were thence distinguished by the same name, entertained pernicious designs, that for some time showed themselves in pernicious measures; therefore you, entertaining the same pernicious designs, would now, had you but power enough, carry into effect the same pernicious measures:—they, having the power, destroyed by fire and faggot those who, in respect of religious opinions and ceremonies, differed from them; therefore, had you but power enough, so would you."

In vain is it observed (not that to this purpose this or any other part of the history of the 17th century is worth observing)—in vain is it observed, and truly observed, the Church of England continued her fires after the Church of Rome had discontinued hers.*

The Hobgoblin Argument, or,
No Innovation!—(ad metum)

The hobgoblin, the eventual appearance of which is denounced by this argument, is *anarchy;* which tremendous spectre has for its forerunner the monster *innovation.* The forms in which this monster may be denounced are as numerous and various as the sentences in which the word *innovation* can be placed. Whatever is now *establishment,* was once *innovation.*

He who on this ground condemns a proposed measure, condemns, in the same breath, whatsoever he would be most averse to be thought to disapprove:—he condemns the Revolution, the Reformation, the assumption made by the House of Commons of a part in the penning of the laws in the reign of Henry VI, the institution of the House of Commons itself in the reign of Henry III:—all these he bids us regard as sure forerunners of the monster anarchy, but particularly the birth and first efficient agency of the House of Commons—an innovation, in comparison of which all others, past or future, are for efficiency, and consequently mischievousness, but as grains of dust in the balance.

*Under James I, when, for being Anabaptists or Arians, two men were burnt in Smithfield. [Bentham's note.]

*Fallacy of Distrust,
or, What's at the Bottom?*—(ad metum)

This argument may be considered as a particular modification of the *No-Innovation* argument. An arrangement or set of arrangements has been proposed, so plainly beneficial, and at the same time so manifestly innoxious, that no prospect presents itself of bringing to bear upon them with any effect the cry of No innovation. Is the anti-innovationist mute? No; he has this resource:—In what you see as yet (says he) there may perhaps be no great mischief; but depend upon it, in the quarter from whence these proposed innoxious arrangements come, there are *more behind* that are of a very different complexion; if these innoxious ones are suffered to be carried, others of a noxious character will succeed without end, and will be carried likewise.

But think, not only what sort of man he must be who can bring himself to employ such an argument; but moreover, what sort of men they must be to whom he can venture to propose it—on whom he can expect it to make any impression, but such a one as will be disgraceful to himself. "Such drivellers," says he to them in effect, "such drivellers are you, so sure of being imposed upon by anyone that will attempt it, that you know not the distinction between good and bad; and when, at the suggestion of this or that man, you have adopted any one measure, good or bad, let but that same man propose any number of other measures, whatever be their character, ye are such idiots and fools that without looking at them yourselves, or vouch-safing to learn their character from others, you will adopt them in a lump." Such is the compliment wrapt up in this sort of argument.

Official Malefactor's Screen—(ad metum)
"Attack us, you attack Government."

The fallacy here in question is employed almost as of

ten as, in speaking of the persons by whom, or of the system on which, the business of the government is conducted, any expressions importing condemnation or censure are uttered. The fallacy consists in affecting to consider such condemnation or censure as being, if not in design, at least in tendency, pregnant with mischief to government itself:—"Oppose us, you oppose government;" "Disgrace us, you disgrace government;" "Bring us into contempt, you bring government into contempt; and anarchy and civil war are the immediate consequences." Such are the forms it assumes.

But so far is it from being true that a man's aversion or contempt for the hands by which the powers of government, or even for the system under which they are exercised, is a proof of his aversion or contempt towards government itself, that, even in proportion to the strength of that aversion or contempt, it is a proof of the opposite affection. What, in consequence of such contempt or aversion, he wishes for, is, not that there be no hands at all to exercise these powers, but that the hands may be better regulated;—not that those powers should not be exercised at all, but that they should be better exercised;—not that, in the exercise of them, no rules at all should be pursued, but that the rules by which they are exercised should be a better set of rules.

All government is a trust—every branch of government is a trust, and immemorially acknowledged so to be: it is only by the magnitude of the scale, that public differ from private trusts.

I complain of the conduct of a person in the character of guardian—as domestic guardian, having the care of a minor or insane person. In so doing, do I say that guardianship is a bad institution? Does it enter into the head of anyone to suspect me of so doing?

Accusation-Scarer's Device—(ad metum)
"Infamy must attach somewhere."

This fallacy consists in representing the imputation of

purposed calumny as necessarily and justly attaching upon him who, having made a charge of misconduct against any person or persons possessed of political power or influence, fails of producing evidence sufficient for conviction.

Its manifest object, accordingly, is, as far as possible, to secure impunity to crimes and transgressions in every shape, on the part of persons so situated; viz. by throwing impediments in the way of accusation, and in particular, by holding out to the eyes of those persons who have in view the undertaking the functions of accusers, in case of failure, in addition to disappointment, the prospect of disgrace.

PART III. FALLACIES OF DELAY
in Various Shapes—and the Object,
The Subject-Matter of Which Is Delay
with a View of Eluding It
To Postpone Discussion,

The Quietist, or "No Complaint"—(ad quietem)

A new law or measure being proposed in the character of a remedy for some incontestable abuse or evil, an objection is frequently started, to the following effect: —"The measure is unnecessary; nobody complains of disorder in that shape in which it is the aim of your measure to propose a remedy to it: even when *no* cause of complaint has been found to exist, especially under governments which admit of complaints, men have in general not been slow to complain; much less where any just cause of complaint has existed." The argument amounts to this:—Nobody complains, therefore nobody suffers. It amounts to a *veto* on all measures of precaution or prevention, and goes to establish a maxim in legislation, directly opposed to the most ordinary prudence of common life;—it enjoins us to build no parapets to a bridge till the number of accidents has raised an universal clamour.

Fallacy of False Consolation—(ad quietem)

"What is the matter with you?" "What would you have?" "Look at the people there, and there: think how much better off *you* are than *they* are. Your prosperity and liberty are objects of envy to them;—your institutions are the models which they endeavour to imitate."

Were the prosperity of the country ever so much greater than at present—take for the country any country whatsoever, and for present time any time whatsoever —neither the injustice of the argument, nor the absurdity of it, would in any the smallest degree be diminished.

Seriously and pointedly, in the character of a bar to any measure of relief—no, nor to the most trivial improvement, can it ever be employed. Suppose a bill brought in for converting an impassable road anywhere into a passable one, would any man stand up to oppose it who could find nothing better to urge against it than the multitude and goodness of the roads we have already? No: when in the character of a serious bar to the measure in hand, be that measure what it may, an argument so palpably inapplicable is employed, it can only be for the purpose of creating a diversion—of turning aside the minds of men from the subject really in hand, to a picture which by its beauty it is hoped, may engross the attention of the assembly, and make them forget for the moment for what purpose they came there.

Procrastinator's Argument—(ad socordiam)
"Wait a little, this is not the time."

A serious refutation would be ill bestowed upon so frivolous a pretence. The objection exists in the will, not in the judgment, of the objector. "Is it lawful to do good on the sabbath day?" was the question put by Jesus to the official hypocrites. Which is the properest day to do good?—which is the properest day to remove a nuisance? Answer: The very first day that a man can be found to propose the removal of it; and whosoever opposes the removal of it on that day, will, if he dare, oppose the removal on every other.

The doubts and fears of the parliamentary procrastinator are the conscientious scruples of his prototype the Pharisee; and neither the answer nor the example of Jesus has succeeded in removing these scruples. To him, whatsoever is too soon to-day, be assured that to-morrow, if not too soon, it will be too late.

True it is, that, the measure being a measure of reform or improvement, an observation to this effect may be brought forward by a friend to the measure: and in this case, it is not an instrument of deception, but an expedient of unhappily necessary prudence.

Snail's-Pace Argument—(ad socordiam)
"One thing at a time! Not too fast! Slow and sure!"

Importance of the business—extreme difficulty of the business—danger of innovation—need of caution and circumspection—impossibility of foreseeing all consequences—danger of precipitation—everything should be gradual—one thing at a time—this is not the time—great occupation at present—wait for more leisure—people well satisfied—no petitions presented—no complaints heard—no such mischief has yet taken place—stay till it has taken place:—such is the prattle which the magpie in office, who, understanding nothing, understands that he must have something to say on every subject shouts out among his auditors as a succedaneum to thought.

Fallacy of Artful Diversion—(ad verecundiam)

Hold up to view some other measure, such as, whether it bear any relation or none to the measure on the carpet, will, in the conception of your hearers, present itself as superior in the order of importance. Your language then is,—Why that? (meaning the measure already proposed)—why not this? or this? mentioning some other, which it is your hope to render more acceptable, and by means of it to create a diversion, and turn aside from the obnoxious measure the affections and attention of those whom you have to deal with.

The intention is of too great importance to be framed and carried into act in the compass of the same year or session: you accordingly announce your intention for next session. When the next session comes, the measure is of too great importance to be brought on the carpet at the commencement of the session; at that period it is not yet mature enough. If it be not advisable to delay it any longer, you bring it forward just as the session closes. Time is thus gained, and without any decided loss in the shape of reputation; for what you undertook, has to the letter been performed. When the measure has been once brought in, you have to take your choice, in the first place, between operations for delay and operations for rejection. Operations for delay exhibit a manifest title to preference: so long as their effect can be made to last, they accomplish their object, and no sacrifice either of design or of reputation has been made. The extreme importance and extreme difficulty are themes on which you blow the trumpet, and which you need not fear the not hearing sufficiently echoed.

PART IV. FALLACIES OF CONFUSION
Of Which the Object Is To Produce,
When Discussion Can No Longer Be Avoided,
Such Confusion in the Minds of the
Hearers as To Incapacitate Them
from Forming a Correct Judgment.

Question-begging Epithets (ad judicium)

There are names to which the idea of general approbation is habitually attached, such as: industry, honor, piety, generosity, gratitude, and so on. These are termed *eulogistic* or laudatory. There are still others to which the idea of general disapprobation is habitually attached, such as: lust, avarice, luxury, covetousness, prodigality, and so on. These may be termed *dyslogistic* or vituperative.

In speaking of the conduct, behavior, intention, motive, or disposition of this or that man, if he is one who is indifferent to you, and if you care not whether he is ill or well thought of, you will employ a *neutral* term. If he is a man whom you wish to recommend to favor, especially a member of your own party, you will employ the *eulogistic* term. But if he is a man whom it is your aim to consign to aversion or contempt, you will employ the *dyslogistic* term.

By appropriate eulogistic and dyslogistic terms many sorts of misrule find justifying arguments that are conclusive in too many eyes. Take, for example, the following eulogistic terms:

1. In war, *honor* and *glory*.
2. In international affairs, *honor, glory,* and *dignity*.
3. In finance, *liberality*. It is always at the expense of unwilling contributors that this virtue is exercised.
4. In the higher levels of all official departments, *dignity,* though not in itself depredation, operates as a pretense for, and hence as a cause of depredation. Wherever you see *dignity,* you may be sure that money is requisite for the support of it; and that public money raised by taxes imposed upon all other individuals, on the principle of *liberality,* must be found to supply it.

Take, for example, *improvement* and *innovation*. To pass censure on anything called an improvement would be too bold, and would even seem to be verging upon self-contradiction and nonsense. But *improvement* means something new, and so does *innovation*. Now, happily for your purpose, *innovation* has contracted a bad name. It now means something new which is new and bad at the same time.

Impostor Terms (ad judicium)

This fallacy is similar to the one which has just been exposed, but it is applied chiefly to the defense of things which under their proper names are manifestly indefensible. For instance, persecutors in matters of religion have no such word as persecution in their vocabularies; *zeal* is the word by which they characterize all their actions. There is a sort of man who, whether or not he is ready to commit any act or acts of adultery, would gladly be thought to have been habituated to the commission of such acts. But even this sort of man would neither be found to say of himself, "I am an adulterer"; nor would he be pleased to have it said of him, "He is an adulterer." But to have it said of him that he is a man of gallantry—that epithet the sort of man in question would regard as a compliment.

Vague Generalities (ad judicium)

Take for example the terms *government, laws, morals,* and *religion.* The genus comprehended in each of these terms may be divided into two species, the good and the bad. For no one can deny that there have been and still are in the world, bad governments, bad laws, bad systems of morals, and bad religions. The bare circumstance, therefore, of a man's attacking government or law, morals or religion, does not of itself afford the slightest presumption that he is engaged in anything blameable. If his attack is directed only against that which is bad in each, his efforts may indeed be productive of any amount of good. This essential distinction the defender of abuse takes care to keep out of sight, and boldly imputes to his antagonist the intention to subvert all government, laws, morals, or religion.

The word *order* is in a peculiar degree adapted to the purpose of a cloak for tyranny, for order is more extensive than law, or even than government. But, what is still more material, it has a eulogistic cast; whereas the words *government* and *law* still remain tolerably neutral in spite of the praise bestowed upon them in the lump. In this respect they are closer to the words *constitution* and *institutions.* Who is there who would have the boldness to assert that order ought not to be maintained?

Establishment. In the same way again, *establishment*

is a word used to protect the bad parts of establishments. It does so by charging all those who wish to remove or alter them with the wish to subvert all establishments, or all good establishments.

Matchless Constitution. The constitution has some good points. It has also some bad ones. It gives facility, and until radical reform shall have been accomplished, security and continual increase to waste, depredation, oppression, and corruption in every variety of shape and in every department.

Now in their own names respectively, waste, depredation, oppression, and corruption cannot be toasted. Gentlemen would not cry out: "Waste forever! Depredation forever! Corruption forever!" But "The constitution forever!" This a man may cry, and does cry, and makes a merit of it.

Matchless constitution. There's your sheet-anchor! There's your true standard! Rally round the constitution, that is—rally round waste, rally round depredation, rally round oppression, rally round corruption, rally round election terrorism, rally round imposture—imposture on the hustings, imposture in the honorable House, imposture in every court of law.

The constitution, why must it not be looked into? Why is it that under pain of being *ipso facto* convicted of anarchism, we must never presume to look at it except with our eyes shut?

Because it was the work of our ancestors, of legislators, few of whom could so much as read, and those few having nothing before them that was worth reading. First theoretical presupposition: *wisdom of barbarian ancestors.*

And when from their ordinary occupation, the cutting of one another's throats, or those of Welshmen, or Scotchmen, or Irishmen, they could now and then steal a holiday, how did they employ it? In cutting Frenchmen's throats in order to get their money. This was active virtue: leaving Frenchmen's throats uncut was indolence, slumber, inglorious ease. Second theoretical presupposition: *virtue of barbarian ancestors.*

Thus fraught with habitual wisdom and habitual virtue, they sat down and devised; and setting before them the best ends, and pursuing those best ends by the best means, they framed in outline—at any rate—they planned and executed our matchless constitution—the constitution as it stands, and may it forever stand!

Planned and executed? On what occasion? On none. At what place? At none. By whom? By nobody.

At no time? Oh, yes, says everything-as-it-should-be Blackstone. Oh, yes, says Whig after Whig. Anno Domini 1660; it was then in its perfection, about fourteen years before James the Second mounted the throne with a design to govern in politics as they do in Morocco, and in religion as they do in Rome: to govern without parliament, or in spite of parliament.

Balance of power. There is one instance in which a balance of forces may be employed with propriety, namely—in international law and international relations. Supposing it to be attainable, what is meant by a balance of forces or balance of power is in that field a legitimate object, beneficial to all the parties concerned. What is that object? It is, in one word, *rest* or *peace*, the absence of all hostile action, together with the absence of all coercion exercised by one of the parties over another: that rest which is the fruit of mutual and universal independence. Here then, as between nation and nation, the result is peace and prosperity.

But has the state of rest brought about by balance the same prosperous result internally? No; on the contrary; the consequence of universal rest in the body politic, as in the natural body, is death. No action on the part of the officers of government, no money collected, no service, and everything falls to pieces.

Glorious Revolution. The real uses of the revolution of 1688 were: the putting to an end of the tyranny, political and religious, of the Stuarts:—the political tyranny, governing without parliament, and forcing the people to pay taxes without even so much as a show of consenting to them through their chosen deputies; the religious tyranny, forcing men to join in a system of religion which they believed not to be true. But the deficiencies of the revolution were:—leaving the power of governing, and especially that of taxing, in the hands of men whose interest it was to make the amount of the taxes excessive, and to exercise misrule in a great variety of other ways.

Allegorical Idols (ad imaginationem)

The use of this fallacy is the securing of respect to persons in public office independently of their good behavior. It consists in substituting for men's proper official label the name of a fictitious entity to whom, by customary language, the attribute of excellence has been attached.

Examples: *Government,* for members of the governing body; *The law,* for lawyers; and *The church,* for churchmen. The advantage is that it obtains more respect for them than would otherwise be bestowed upon the class under its correct name.

Sweeping Classification (ad judicium)

By its nature, this fallacy is equally applicable to undeserved eulogy as well as undeserved censure; but it is more frequently used for the purpose of censure, since its efficiency is greater in that direction. Example 1. Kings—the crimes of kings. Example 2. Catholics—Cruelties of Catholics.

Sham Distinctions (ad judicium)

Example 1. Liberty and licentiousness of the press.

To shut the door against such imputations as are either unjust or useless, leaving it open at the same time to such as are just and useful, would require a precise, determinate, correct, and complete definition of the term by which the abuse, the (supposedly) preponderantly pernicious use of the press is to be characterized. This definition would have to be established by those in whom the supreme power of the State is vested. No such definition has ever been given, nor can such a definition be reasonably expected at the hands of any persons so situated, since the act of establishing it would curtail their power and prejudice their interests. Until that definition is given, every disclosure by the press of any abuse from the practice of which they derive any advantage is *licentiousness*. The *liberty* of the press is only such disclosure as will occasion them no apprehension of inconvenience.

Example. 2. Reform, temperate and intemperate.

Suppose a person inwardly determined to prevent the adoption of any reform, but convinced that it is necessary or advisable to present the appearance of a desire to contribute to reform. Using the device or fallacy here in question, he will represent that which goes by the name of reform as distinguishable into two species: one of them a fit subject for approbation, the other for disapprobation. The class which he professes to approve he will characterize by some epithet of the eulogistic cast, such as moderate or temperate or practicable. To the other of these two nominally distinct species he will, at the same time, attach an epithet of the dyslogistic cast, such as violent, intemperate, extravagant, outrageous, theoretical, speculative, and so forth.

Popular Corruption (ad superbiam)

The argument of this fallacy may be expressed in the following terms:—The source of corruption is in the minds of the people. So rank and extensively seated is that corruption that no political reform can ever have any effect in removing it.

"So bad are men in themselves, that no matter how badly they are treated, they cannot be treated worse than they deserve to be. Of a bad bargain, says the proverb, make the best; of so bad a crew, let us make the best for ourselves. No matter what they may suffer, they deserve it." If Nero had thought it worth his while to look around for a justification, he could not have found a more pat one than this.

Nearly akin to the cry of popular corruption is the following common exhortation: "Instead of reforming others, instead of reforming your betters, instead of re-

forming the state, the constitution, the church, everything that is most excellent—let each man reform himself, let him look at home, he will find there enough to
do, and what is within his power, without looking
abroad and aiming at what is out of his power, and so
on." [Here] is a tacit assumption of incompatibility
between the operation condemned and the operation
recommended. When closely examined, it will be seen
that no assumption could be more groundless. But it is
certain that if every man's time and labor is exclusively
employed in the correcting of his own personal imperfections, no part of it can be employed in the endeavor
to correct the imperfections and abuses of government;
—which is exactly what is wanted.

Anti-rational Fallacies (ad verecundiam)

When reason is found or supposed to operate in opposition to a man's interests, his endeavor will naturally
be to render the faculty itself, and whatever issue from
it, an object of hatred and contempt. As long as a government tolerates any sort of abuse from which its
members derive a profit and in the continuance of
which they consequently have an interest, if reason is
against them, they will to the same extent be against
reason. Sooner than fail of its object, sarcasm is directed not merely at reason, but against all thought, as
if there were something about thought itself which rendered its exercise incompatible with useful and successful living. Some examples of this fallacy are:

1. Sometimes a plan whose adoption would be contrary to the official person's interests is without more
ado pronounced a *speculative* one. By this observation
all need of rational and deliberate discussion, such as
objections that the end proposed is not a fit one, or that
the means are unfit means, is considered as being superseded. To the word *speculative* may be added or
substituted a number of synonymous terms, such as:
theoretical, visionary, chimerical, romantic, utopian.

2. Sometimes the following distinction is taken, and a
concession made: the plan is good in *theory*, but would

be bad in *practice*. That is to say, its being good in theory does not hinder its being bad in practice. What is here meant to be denied, however, is that a plan which is essentially incapable of proving good in practice can be said to be good in theory.

The fear of theory has, to a certain extent, its foundation in reason. There is a general propensity in those who adopt this or that theory to push it too far. They are prone to set up a general proposition which is not true until certain exceptions have been noted, without any of those exceptions, and to pursue it, without regard to them, into instances in which it is false, fallacious, and repugnant to reason and utility. The propensity to push theory too far is acknowledged to be almost universal. But what is the just inference? Only that in the particular case inquiry should be made. A plan proposes a wrong end; or, the end being all right, it proposes a wrong set of means. If this be what a man means, why can he not say so?

3. Sometimes, as if in consequence of further progress made in the art of irrationality, the plan is pronounced to be *too good to be practicable;* and furthermore its being as good as it is, is thus represented as the very cause of its being bad in practice.

Paradoxical Assertions (ad judicium)

Utility, method, simplification, reason, sincerity—A person inexperienced in the arts of political and verbal warfare would not imagine that such concepts could be pointed out as fit objects of hatred and contempt by anyone. Yet so it is.

1. Dangerousness of the principle of utility.
2. Uselessness of classification.
3. Mischievousness of simplification
4. Disinterestedness as a mark of profligacy.

[Examples given].

Non Causa Pro Causa, or Cause and Obstacle Confounded (ad judicium)

When in a system which has good points in it you have also a set of abuses to defend, after a general eulo-

gy bestowed upon the system, indicating more or less
explicitly the undisputed good effects, you take the
abuses which you wish to defend, either separately or
collectively (the latter is the safer course) and to them
you ascribe the credit for having given birth to the good
effects.

1. Effect, good government; obstacle represented as a
cause, station of the Bishops in the House of Lords.

2. Effect, useful national learning; obstacle stated as
a cause, system of education pursued in Church-of-
England universities.

In virtue and knowledge, as in every feature of felicity, the empire of Montezuma outshines, as everyone
knows, all the surrounding states, even the Common-
wealth of Tlascala not excepted. "Where is it," said
an inquirer once to the high priest of the temple of Vitzlipultzli, "that we are to look for the true cause of so
glorious a pre-eminence?" "Look for it!" answered the
holy pontiff, "Where shouldst thou look for it, blind
sceptic, but in the copiousness of the streams in which
the sweet and precious blood of innocents flows daily
down the altars of the great God?"

"Yes," answered in full convocation and full chorus
the archbishops, bishops, deans, canons, and prebends
of the religion of Vitzlipultzli. "Yes," answered in semi-
chorus the vice-chancellor, with all the doctors, both
the proctors and masters regent and non-regent of the
as yet uncatholicized university of Mexico. "Yes, in the
copiousness of the streams in which the sweet and precious blood flows daily down the altars of the great
God."

The End Justifies the Means (ad judicium)

Yes; but on three conditions, any one of which failing,
no such justification exists.

1. The first is, that the end be good.

2. That the means chosen be either purely good, or
if evil, having less evil in them on a balance than there
is of real good in the end.

3. That the means have more of good in them, or less

of evil, as the case may be, than any others which might have been used to attain the end.

Opposer-General's Justification: Not Measures but Men, or, Not Men but Measures (ad invidiam)

This oracular party adage was invented by the Whigs. On one occasion we have one form of the aphorism from the pen of Charles Fox himself. "How vain, how idle, how presumptuous (says the declaimer in his attempt to assume the mantle of historian) is the opinion that laws can do everything! And how weak and pernicious the maxim founded upon it, *that measures not men are to be attended to.*" Weak enough as thus expressed, it must be confessed, too weak to be worth noticing; as if anyone ever thought of denying that both men and measures should be "attended to."

Rejection instead of Amendment (ad judicium)

This fallacy consists in urging as a bar or conclusive objection against the proposed measure some consideration which, if presented in the character of a mere amendment, might have more or less claim to notice. It generally consists of some real or imaginary inconvenience that may be the eventual result of the measure's adoption. But such an inconvenience constitutes a conclusive objection only if it is irremediable and accompanied by losses which outweigh its promised gains.

Characters common to all these fallacies.

1. Whatever the measure in hand, they are irrelevant to it.

2. They are all of them such that their application affords a presumption either of weakness or of the total lack of relevant arguments on the side on which they are employed.

3. To any good purpose they are all of them unnecessary.

4. All of them are not only capable of being applied, but are actually in the habit of being applied to bad purposes, that is—to the obstruction and defeat of all

such measures as have for their object the removal of abuses or other imperfections still discernible in the frame and practice of the government.

5. By means of their irrelevancy they all consume and misapply time, thereby obstructing the course and retarding the progress of all necessary business.

The causes of the utterance of these fallacies may be named and enumerated as follows:

1. Sinister interest—self-conscious type.
2. Interest-begotten prejudice.
3. Authority-begotten prejudice.
4. Self-defense, meaning a sense of the need of self-defense against counter-fallacies.

ESSAY ON UNIVERSAL PEACE. ESSAY IV. A PLAN FOR AN UNIVERSAL AND PERPETUAL PEACE*

The object of the present Essay is to submit to the world a plan for an universal and perpetual peace. The globe is the field of dominion to which the author aspires,—the press of the engine, and the only one he employs,—the cabinet of mankind the theatre of his intrigue.

The happiest of mankind are sufferers by war; and the wisest, nay, even the least wise, are wise enough to ascribe the chief of their sufferings to that cause.

The following plan has for its basis two fundamental propositions:—1. The reduction and fixation of the force of the several nations that compose the European system; 2. the emancipation of the distant dependencies of each state.† Each of these propositions has its distinct advantages; but neither of them, it will appear, would completely answer the purpose without the other.

As to the utility of such an universal and lasting peace, supposing a plan for that purpose practicable, and likely to be adopted, there can be but one voice. The objection, and the only objection to it, is the apparent impracticability of it;—that it is not only hopeless, but that to such a degree that any proposal to that effect deserves the name of visionary and ridiculous. This objection I shall endeavour in the first place to remove;

---

*A work written in 1789, but first published in Bowring's *Works* (1843), Vol. II, pp. 561 ff.

†Two original writers have gone before me in this line, Dean Tucker and Dr. Anderson. The object of the first was to persuade the world of the inutility of war, but more particularly of the war then raging when he wrote; the object of the second to show the inutility of the colonies. [Bentham's note.]

for the removal of this prejudice may be necessary to procure for the plan a hearing.

What can be better suited to the preparing of men's minds for the reception of such a proposal than the proposal itself?

Let it not be objected that the age is not ripe for such a proposal: the more it wants of being ripe, the sooner we should begin to do what can be done to ripen it; the more we should do to ripen it. A proposal of this sort, is one of those things that can never come too early nor too late.

Who that bears the name of Christian can refuse the assistance of his prayers? What pulpit can forbear to second me with its eloquence,—Catholics and Protestants, Church-of-England-men and Dissenters, may all agree in this, if in nothing else. I call upon them all to aid me with their countenance and their support.

The ensuing sheets are dedicated to the common welfare of all civilized nations; but more particularly of Great Britain and France.

The end in view is to recommend three grand objects,—simplicity of government, national frugality, and peace.

Reflection has satisfied me of the truth of the following propositions—

I. That it is not the interest of Great Britain to have any foreign dependencies whatsoever.

II. That it is not the interest of Great Britain to have any treaty of alliance, offensive or defensive, with any other power whatever.

III. That it is not the interest of Great Britain to have any treaty with any power whatsoever, for the purpose of possessing any advantage whatsoever in point of trade, to the exclusion of any other nation whatsoever.

IV. That it is not the interest of Great Britain to keep up any naval force beyond what may be sufficient to defend its commerce against pirates.

V. That it is not the interest of Great Britain to keep on foot any regulations whatsoever of distant preparation for the augmentation or maintenance of its naval force; such as the Navigation Act, bounties on the Greenland trade, and other trades regarded as nurseries for seamen.

VI. VII. VIII. IX. & X. That all these several propositions are also true of France.

As far as Great Britain is concerned, I rest the proof of these several propositions principally upon two very simple principles.

I. That the increase of growing wealth in every nation in a given period, is necessarily limited by the quantity of capital it possesses at that period.

II. That Great Britain, with or without Ireland, and without any other dependency, can have no reasonable ground to apprehend injury from any one nation upon earth.

Turning to France, I substitute to the last of the two just-mentioned propositions the following:—

III. That France, standing singly, has at present nothing to fear from any other nation than Great Britain: nor, if standing clear of her foreign dependencies, would she have anything to fear from Great Britain.

XI. That supposing Great Britain and France thoroughly agreed, the principal difficulties would be removed to the establishment of a plan of general and permanent pacification for all Europe.

XII. That for the maintenance of such a pacification, general and perpetual treaties might be formed, limiting the number of troops to be maintained.

XIII. That the maintenance of such a pacification might be considerably facilitated, by the establishment of a common court of judicature for the decision of differences between the several nations, although such court were not to be armed with any coercive powers.

XIV. That secresy in the operations of the foreign department ought not to be endured in England; being altogether useless, and equally repugnant to the interests of liberty and to those of peace.

Proposition I.—That it is not the interest of Great Britain to have any foreign dependencies whatsoever.

The truth of this proposition will appear if we consider, 1st, That distant dependencies increase the chances of war,—

1. By increasing the number of possible subjects of dispute.

2. By the natural obscurity of title in case of new settlements or discoveries.

3. By the particular obscurity of the evidence resulting from the distance.

4. By men's caring less about wars when the scene is remote, than when it is nearer home.

2d, That colonies are seldom, if ever, sources of profit to the mother country.

Profitable industry has five branches:—

1. Production of new materials, including agricultures, mining, and fisheries; 2. Manufactures; 3. Home trade; 4. Foreign trade; 5. Carrying trade. The quantity of profitable industry that can be carried on in a country being limited by that of the capital which the country can command, it follows that no part of that quantity can be bestowed upon any one branch, but it must be withdrawn from, or withholden from, all the others. No encouragement, therefore, can be given to any one, but it must be a proportionable discouragement to all the others. Nothing can be done by government to induce a man to begin or continue to employ his capital in any one of those branches, but it must induce him in the same degree to withdraw or withhold that capital from all the rest. Of these five branches, no one is to such a degree more beneficial to the public than the rest, as that it should be worth its while to call forth the powers of law to give it an advantage. But if there were any, it would unquestionably be the improvement and cultivation of land. Every fictitious encouragement to any one of these rival branches being a proportionable discouragement to agriculture. Every encouragement to any of those branches of manufacture which produce articles that are at present sold to the colonies, is a proportionable discouragement to agriculture.

When colonies are to be made out to be beneficial to the mother country, and the quantum of the benefit is to be estimated, the mode in which the estimate is made is curious enough. An account is taken of what they export, which is almost the whole of their produce. All this, it is said, while you have the colonies, is yours; this is exactly what you lose if you lose your colonies. How much of all this is really yours? Not one single halfpenny. When they let you take it from them, do they give it you for nothing? Not they indeed; they make you pay for it just as anybody else would do. How much? Just so much as you would pay them if they belonged to themselves or to anybody else.

For maintaining colonies there are several avowed reasons, besides others which are not avowed: of the avowed reasons, by far the principal one is, the benefit of trade. If your colonies were not subject to you, they would not trade with you; they would not buy any of your goods, or let you buy any of theirs; at least, you could not be sure of their doing so: if they were subject to anybody else they would not do so; for the colonies of other nations are, you see, not suffered to trade with you. Give up your colonies, you give up so much of your trade as is carried on with your colonies. No; we do not give up any such thing,—we do not give up anything whatsoever. Trade with colonies cannot, any more than with anywhere else, be carried on without capital: just so much of our capital as is employed in our trade with the colonies—just so much of it is not employed elsewhere—just so much is either kept or taken from other trades.

Suppose, then, any branch of trade or manufacture to decline—even suppose it lost altogether—is this any permanent loss to the nation? Not the smallest. We know the worst that can happen from any such loss; the capital that would otherwise have been employed in the lost branch will be employed in agriculture. The loss of the colonies, if the loss of the colony trade were the consequence of the loss of the colonies, would at the worst be so much gain to agriculture.

Other reasons against distant dominion may be found in a consideration of the good of the government.

Distant mischiefs make little impression on those on whom the remedying of them depends. A single murder committed in London makes more impression than if thousands of murders and other cruelties were committed in the East Indies. The situation of Hastings, only because he was present, excited compassion in those who heard the detail of the cruelties committed by him with indifference.

The communication of grievances cannot be too quick from those who feel them to those who have the power to relieve them. The reason which in the old writs the king is made to assign for his interfering to afford relief, is the real cause which originally gave birth to that interference,—it is one of those few truths which have contrived to make their way through the thick cloud of lies and nonsense they contain. "See what it is that these people want," says the sovereign to the ministers of justice, "that I may not any more be troubled with their noise." The motive assigned to the unjust judge in the Gospel, is the motive which the sovereign, who is styled the fountain of justice, is thus made to avow.

The following, then, are the final measures which ought to be pursued:—

1. Give up all the colonies.
2. Found no new colonies.

The following is a summary of the reasons for giving up all the colonies:—

1. Saving the expense of the establishments, civil and military.

2. Saving the danger of war—1. For enforcing their obedience; 2. On account of the jealousy produced by the apparent power they confer.

3. Saving the expense of defending them, in case of war on other grounds.

4. Getting rid of the means of corruption afforded by the patronage—1. Of their civil establishments; 2. Of the military force employed in their defence.

5. Simplifying the whole frame of government, and thereby rendering a competent skill in the business of

government more attainable—1. To the members of administration; 2. To the people.

The stock of national intelligence is deteriorated by the false notions which must be kept up, in order to prevent the nation from opening its eyes and insisting upon the enfranchisement of the colonies.

At the same time, bad government results to the mother-country from the complication of interests, the indistinct views, and the consumption of time, occasioned by the load of distant dependencies.

Interest of the colonies.

Diminishing the chance of bad government resulting from—1. Opposite interest; 2. Ignorance.

The real interests of the colony must be sacrificed to the imaginary interests of the mother-country. It is for the purpose of governing it badly, and for no other, that you can wish to get or to keep a colony. Govern it well, it is of no use to you. Govern it as well as the inhabitants would govern it themselves,—you must choose those to govern it whom they themselves would choose. You must sacrifice none of its interests to your own,—you must bestow as much time and attention to their interests as they would themselves: in a word, you must take those very measures, and none others, which they themselves would take. But would this be governing? and what would it be worth to you if it were?

After all, it would be impossible for you to govern them so well as they would govern themselves, on account of the distance.

The following are approximating measures:—

1. Maintain no military force in any of the colonies.

2. Issue no moneys for the maintenance of any civil establishment in any of the colonies.

3. Nominate to the offices in the colonies as long as they permit you;—yield as soon as they contest such nomination.

4. Give general instructions to governors to consent to all acts presented to them.

5. Issue no moneys for fortifications.

Proposition II.—That it is not the interest of Great

Britain to have any treaty of alliance, offensive or defensive, with any other power whatever.

Reason: saving the danger of war arising out of them.

And more especially ought not Great Britain to guarantee foreign constitutions.

Reason: saving the danger of war resulting from the odium of so tyrannical a measure.

Proposition III.—That it is not the interest of Great Britain to have any treaty with any power whatsoever, for the purpose of possessing any advantages whatsoever, in point of trade, to the exclusion of any other nation whatsoever.

That the trade of every nation is limited by the quantity of capital is so plainly and obviously true, as to challenge a place among self-evident propositions. But self-evident propositions must not expect to be easily admitted, if admitted at all, if the consequences of them clash with prevalent passions and confirmed prejudices.

Nations are composed of individuals. The trade of a nation must be limited by the same causes that limit the trade of the individual. Each individual merchant, when he has as much trade as his whole capital, and all the credit he can get by means of his capital can suffice for carrying on, can have no more. This being true of each merchant, is not less true of the whole number of merchants put together.

Many books directly recognise the proposition, that the quantity of trade a nation can carry on is limited— limited by the quantity of its capital. None dispute the proposition; but almost all, somewhere or other, proceed on the opposite supposition; they suppose the quantity of trade to have no limitation whatsoever.

It is a folly to buy manufactured goods; wise to buy raw materials. Why? because you sell them to yourselves, or, what is still better, to foreigners, manufactured; and the manufacturer's profit is all clear gain to you. What is here forgotten is, that the manufacturer, to carry on his business, must have a capital; and that just so much capital as is employed in that way, is prevented from being employed in any other.

Hence the perfect inutility and mischievousness of all laws and public measures of government whatsoever, for the pretended encouragement of trade—all bounties in every shape whatsoever—all non-importation agreements and engagements to consume home manufactures in preference to foreign—in any other view than to afford temporary relief to temporary distress.

But of the two—prohibitions and bounties—penal encouragements and remuneratory—the latter are beyond comparison the most mischievous. Prohibitions, except while they are fresh, and drive men at a great expense out of the employments they are embarked in, are only nugatory. Bounties are wasteful and oppressive: they force money from one man in order to pay another man for carrying on a trade, which, if it were not a losing one, there would be no need of paying him for.

What then, are all modes of productive industry alike? May not one be more profitable than another? Certainly. But the favourite one is it, in fact, more profitable than any other? That is the question and the only question that ought to be put; and that is the very question which nobody ever thinks of putting.

Were it ever put and answered, and answered ever so clearly, it never could be of any use as a ground for any permanent plan of policy. Why? Because almost as soon as one branch is known to be more profitable than the rest, so soon it ceases so to be.—Men flock to it from all other branches, and the old equilibrium is presently restored. Your merchants have a monopoly as against foreigners? True, but they have no monopoly as against one another. Men cannot, in every instance, quit the less productive branch their capitals are already employed in, to throw them into this more productive one? True—but there are young beginners as well as old stagers; and the first concern of a young beginner, who has a capital to employ in a branch of industry, is to look out for the most profitable.

Objection:—Oh! but it is manufacture that creates the demand for the productions of agriculture. You cannot, therefore, increase the productions of agri-

culture but by increasing manufactures. No such thing.
I admit the antecedent—I deny the consequence. Increase of manufactures certainly does create an increase
in the demand for the productions of agriculture.
Equally certain is it that the increase of manufactures is
not necessary to produce an increase in that demand.
Farmers can subsist without ribbons, gauzes, or fine
cambrics. Weavers of ribbons, gauzes, or fine cambrics,
cannot subsist without the productions of agriculture;
necessary subsistence never can lose its value. Those
who produce it are themselves a market for their produce. Is it possible that provisions should be too cheap?
Is there any present danger of it? Suppose (in spite of
the extreme absurdity of the supposition) that provisions were growing gradually too cheap, from the increase of the quantity produced, and the want of manufacturers to consume them, what would be the consequence? The increasing cheapness would increase the
facility and disposition to marry: it would thence increase the population of the country; and the children
thus produced, eating as they grew up, would keep
down this terrible evil of a superabundance of
provisions.

Provisions, the produce of agriculture, constantly
and necessarily produce a market for themselves. The
more provisions a man raises, over and above what is
necessary for his own consumption, the more he has to
give to others, to induce them to provide him with whatever, besides provisions, he chooses to have. In a word,
the more he has to spare, the more he has to give
to manufacturers; who, by taking it from him, and paying him with the produce of their labours, afford the
encouragement requisite for the productions of the
fruits of agriculture.

It is impossible, therefore, that you can ever have too
much agriculture. It is impossible that while there is
ground untilled, or ground that might be better tilled
than it is, that any detriment should ensue to the community from the withholding or withdrawing capital
from any other branch of industry, and employing it in

agriculture. It is impossible, therefore, that the loss of any branch of trade can be productive of any detriment to the community, excepting always the temporary distress experienced by the individuals concerned in it for the time being, when the decline is a sudden one.

The following are the measures the propriety of which results from the above principles:—

1. That no treaties granting commercial preferences should be made.

2. That no wars should be entered into for compelling such treaties.

3. That no alliances should be contracted for the sake of purchasing them.

4. That no encouragements should be given to particular branches of trade, by—

    1. Prohibition of rival manufactures.

    2. Taxation of rival manufactures.

    3. Bounties on the trade meant to be favoured.

5. That no treaties should be entered into insuring commercial preferences.

They are useless as they add nothing to the mass of wealth; they only influence the direction of it.

Proposition IV.—That it is not the interest of Great Britain to keep up any naval force beyond what may be sufficient to defend its commerce against pirates.

It is unnecessary, except for the defence of the colonies, or for the purposes of war, undertaken either for the compelling of trade or the formation of commercial treaties.

Proposition V.—That it is not the interest of Great Britain to keep on foot any regulations whatsoever of distant preparation for the augmentation or maintenance of its naval force—such as the navigation act, bounties on the Greenland trade, and other trades regarded as nurseries for seamen.

This proposition is a necessary consequence of the foregoing one.

Propositions VI, VII, VIII, IX & X.

Propositions similar to the foregoing are equally true applied to France.

Proposition XI.—That supposing Great Britain and France thoroughly agreed, the principal difficulties would be removed to the establishment of a plan of general and permanent pacification for all Europe.

Proposition XII.—That for the maintenance of such a pacification, general and perpetual treaties might be formed, limiting the number of troops to be maintained.

If the simple relation of a single nation with a single other nation be considered, perhaps the matter would not be very difficult. The misfortune is, that almost everywhere compound relations are found. On the subject of troops,—France says to England, Yes I would voluntarily make with you a treaty of disarming, if there were only you; but it is necessary for me to have troops to defend me from the Austrians. Austria might say the same to France; but it is necessary to guard against Prussia, Russia, and the Porte. And the like allegation might be made by Prussia with regard to Russia.

Whilst as to naval forces, if it concerned Europe only, the difficulty might perhaps not be very considerable. To consider France, Spain and Holland, as making together a counterpoise to the power of Britain, —perhaps on account of the disadvantages which accompany the concert between three separate nations, to say nothing of the tardiness and publicity of procedures under the Dutch Constitution—perhaps England might allow to all together a united force equal to half or more than its own.

An agreement of this kind would not be dishonourable. If the covenant were on one side only, it might be so. If it regard both parties together, the reciprocity takes away the acerbity. By the treaty which put an end to the first Punic war, the number of vessels that the Carthaginians might maintain was limited. This condition was it not humiliating? It might be: but if it were, it must have been because there was nothing correspondent to it on the side of the Romans. A treaty which placed all the security on one side, what cause could it have had for its source? It could only have had one—that is the avowed superiority of the party thus incontestably secured,—such a condition could only have been a law dictated by the conqueror to the party conquered. The law of the strongest. None but a conqueror could have dictated it; none but the conquered would have accepted it.

On the contrary, whatsoever nation should get the start of the other in making the proposal to reduce and fix the amount of its armed force, would crown itself with everlasting honour. The risk would be nothing—the gain certain. This gain would be, the giving an incontrovertible demonstration of its own disposition to peace, and of the opposite disposition in the other nation in case of its rejecting the proposal.

The utmost fairness should be employed. The nation addressed should be invited to consider and point out whatever further securities it deemed necessary, and whatever further concessions it deemed just.

The proposal should be made in the most public manner:—it should be an address from nation to nation. This, at the same time that it conciliated the confidence of the nation addressed, would make it impracticable for the government of that nation to neglect it, or stave it off by shifts and evasions. It would sound the heart of the nation addressed. It would discover its intentions, and proclaim them to the world.

The cause of humanity has still another resource. Should Britain prove deaf and impracticable, let France, without conditions, emancipate her colonies, and break up her marine. The advantage even upon this plan would be immense, the danger none. The colonies I have already shown are a source of expense, not of revenue,—of burthen to the people, not of relief. This appears to be the case, even upon the footing of those expenses which appear upon the face of them to belong to the colonies, and are the only ones that have hitherto been set down to their account. But in fact the whole expense of the marine belongs also to that account, and no other. What other destination has it? What other can it have? None. Take away the colonies, what use would there be for a single vessel, more than the few necessary in the Mediterranean to curb the pirates.

In case of a war, where at present (1789) would England make its first and only attack upon France? In the colonies. What would she propose to herself from success in such an attack? What but the depriving France of her colonies. Were these colonies—these bones of contention—no longer hers, what then could England do? what could she wish to do?

There would remain the territory of France; with what view could Britain make any attack upon it in any way? Not with views of permanent conquest;—such madness does not belong to our age. Parliament itself, one may venture to affirm, without paying it any very extraordinary compliment, would not wish it. It would not wish it, even could it be accomplished without effort on our part, without resistance on the other. It would not, even though France herself were to solicit it. No parliament would grant a penny for such a purpose. If it did, it would not be a parliament a month. No king would lend his name to such a project. He would be dethroned as surely and as deservedly as James the Second. To say, I will be king of France, would be to say, in other words, I will be absolute in England.

Well, then, no one would dream of conquest. What other purpose could an invasion have? The plunder and destruction of the country. Such baseness is totally repugnant, not only to the spirit of the nation, but to the spirit of the times. Malevolence could be the only motive—rapacity could never counsel it; long before an army could arrive anywhere, everything capable of being plundered would be carried off. Whatever is portable, could be much sooner carried off by the owners, than by any plundering army. No expedition of plunder could ever pay itself.

Such is the extreme folly, the madness of war: on no supposition can it be otherwise than mischievous, especially between nations circumstanced as France and England. Though the choice of events were absolutely at your command, you could not make it of use to you. If unsuccessful, you may be disgraced and ruined: if successful, even to the height of your wishes, you are still but so much the worse. You would still be so much the worse, though it were to cost you nothing. For not even any colony of your own planting, still less a conquest of your own making, will so much as pay its own expenses.

The greatest acquisitions that could be conceived would not be to be wished for,—could they even be attained with the greatest certainty, and without the least expense. In war, we are as likely not to gain as to gain —as likely to lose as to do either: we can neither attempt the one, nor defend ourselves against the other, without a certain and most enormous expense.

Mark well the contrast. All trade is in its essence advantageous—even to that party to whom it is least so. All war is in its essence ruinous; and yet the great employments of government are to treasure up occasions of war, and to put fetters upon trade.

Ask an Englishman what is the great obstacle to a secure and solid peace, he has his answer ready:—It is the ambition, perhaps he will add, the treachery of France. I wish the chief obstacle to a plan for this purpose were the dispositions and sentiments of France!— were that all, the plan need not long wait for adoption.

Of this visionary project, the most visionary part is without question that for the emancipation of distant dependencies. What will an Englishman say, when he sees two French ministers of the highest reputation, both at the head of their respective departments, both joining in the opinion, that the accomplishment of this event, nay the speedy accomplishment of it, is inevitable, and one of them scrupling not to pronounce it as eminently desirable.

It would only be the bringing things back on these points to the footing they were on before the discovery of America. Europe had then no colonies—no distant garrisons—no standing armies. It would have had no wars but for the feudal system—religious antipathy— the rage of conquest—and the uncertainties of succession. Of these four causes, the first is happily extinct everywhere—the second and third almost everywhere, and at any rate in France and England—the last might, if not already extinguished, be so with great ease.

The moral feelings of men in matters of national morality are still so far short of perfection, that in the scale of estimation, justice has not yet gained the ascendency over force. Yet this prejudice may, in a certain point of view, by accident, be rather favourable to this proposal than otherwise. Truth, and the object of this essay, bid me to say to my countrymen, it is for you to begin the reformation—it is you that have been the greatest sinners. But the same considerations also lead me to say to them, you are the strongest among nations: though justice be not on your side, force is; and it is your force that has been the main cause of your injustice. If the measure of moral approbation had been brought to perfection, such positions would have been far from popular, prudence would have dictated the keeping them out of sight, and the softening them down as much as possible.

Humiliation would have been the effect produced by them on those to whom they appeared true—indignation on those to whom they appeared false. But, as I have observed, men have not yet learned to tune their feelings in unison with the voice of morality in these points. They feel more pride in being accounted strong, than resentment at being called unjust: or rather, the imputation of injustice appears flattering rather than otherwise, when coupled with the consideration of its cause. I feel it in my own experience; but if *I*, listed as I am as the professed and hitherto the only advocate in my own country in the cause of justice, set a less value on justice than is its due, what can I expect from the general run of men?

Proposition XIII.—That the maintenance of such a pacification might be considerably facilitated, by the establishment of a common court of judicature, for the decision of differences between the several nations, although such court were not to be armed with any coercive powers.

It is an observation of somebody's, that no nation ought to yield any evident point of justice to another. This must mean, evident in the eyes of the nation that is to judge,—evident in the eyes of the nation called upon to yield. What does this amount to? That no nation is to give up anything of what it looks upon as its rights—no nation is to make any concessions. Wherever there is any difference of opinion between the negotiators of two nations, war is to be the consequence.

While there is no common tribunal, something might be said for this. Concession to notorious injustice invites fresh injustice.

Establish a common tribunal, the necessity for war no longer follows from difference of opinion. Just or unjust, the decision of the arbiters will save the credit, the honour of the contending party.

Can the arrangement proposed be justly styled visionary, when it has been proved of it—that

1. It is the interest of the parties concerned.
2. They are already sensible of that interest.
3. The situation it would place them in is no new one, nor any other than the original situation they set out from.

Difficult and complicated conventions have been effectuated: for examples, we may mention,—

1. The armed neutrality.
2. The American confederation.
3. The German diet.
4. The Swiss league.

Why should not the European fraternity subsist, as well as the German diet or the Swiss league? These latter have no ambitious views. Be it so; but is not this already become the case with the former?

How then shall we concentrate the approbation of the people, and obviate their prejudices?

One main object of the plan is to effectuate a reduction, and that a mighty one, in the contributions of the people. The amount of the reduction for each nation should be stipulated in the treaty; and even previous to the signature of it, laws for the purpose might be prepared in each nation, and presented to every other, ready to be enacted, as soon as the treaty should be ratified in each state.

By these means the mass of the people, the part most exposed to be led away by prejudices, would not be sooner apprized of the measure, than they would feel the relief it brought them. They would see it was for their advantage it was calculated, and that it could not be calculated for any other purpose.

The concurrence of all the maritime powers, except England, upon a former occasion, proved two points: the reasonableness of that measure itself, and the weakness of France in comparison with England. It was a measure not of ambition, but of justice—a law made in favour of equality—a law made for the benefit of the weak. No sinister point was gained, or attempted to be gained by it. France was satisfied with it. Why? because she was weaker than Britain; she *could* have no other motive—on no other supposition could it have been of any advantage to her. Britain was vexed at it. Why? For the opposite reason: she could have no other.

Oh my countrymen! purge your eyes from the film of prejudice—extirpate from your hearts the *black specks* of excessive jealousy, false ambition, selfishness, and insolence. The operations may be painful; but the rewards are glorious indeed! As the main difficulty, so will the main honour be with you.

What though wars should hereafter arise? The intermediate savings will not the less be so much clear gain.

Though, in the generating of the disposition for war, unjust ambition has doubtless had by far too great a share, yet jealousy, sincere and honest jealousy, must be acknowledged to have had a not inconsiderable one. Vulgar prejudice, fostered by passion, assigns the heart as the seat of all the moral diseases it complains of; but the principal and more frequent seat is really the head: it is from ignorance and weakness that men deviate from the path of rectitude, more frequently than from selfishness and malevolence. This is fortunate;—for the power of information and reason, over error and ignorance is much greater and much surer than that of exhortation, and all the modes of rhetoric, over selfishness and malevolence.

It is because we do not know what strong motives other nations have to be just, what strong indications they have given of the disposition to be so, how often we ourselves have deviated from the rules of justice,—that we take for granted, as an indisputable truth, that the principles of injustice are in a manner interwoven into the very essence of the hearts of other men.

The diffidence, which forms part of the character of the English nation, may have been one cause of this jealousy. The dread of being duped by other nations—the notion that foreign heads are more able, though at the same time foreign hearts are less honest than our own, has always been one of our prevailing weaknesses. This diffidence has perhaps some connexion with the *mauvaise honte* which has been remarked as commonly showing itself in our behaviour, and which makes public speaking and public exhibition in every line a task so much more formidable to us than to other people.

This diffidence may, perhaps, in part be accounted for, from our living less in society, and accustoming ourselves less to mixed companies, than the people of other nations.

But the particular cast of diffidence in question, the apprehension of being duped by foreign powers, is to be referred in part, and perhaps principally, to another cause—the jealousy and slight opinion we entertain of our ministers and public men; we are jealous of them as our superiors, contending against us in the perpetual struggle for power; we are diffident of them as being our fellow-countrymen, and of the same mould as ourselves.

Jealousy is the vice of narrow minds;—confidence the virtue of enlarged ones. To be satisfied that confidence between nations is not out of nature where they have worthy ministers, one need but read the account of the negotiation between De Wit and Temple, as given by Hume. I say, by Hume:—for as it requires negotiators like De Wit and Temple to carry on such a negotiation in such a manner, so it required a historian like Hume to do it justice. For the vulgar among historians know no other receipt for writing that part of history than the finding out whatever are the vilest and basest motives capable of accounting for men's conduct in the situation in question, and then ascribing it to those motives without ceremony and without proof.

Temple and De Wit, whose confidence in each other was so exemplary and so just—Temple and De Wit were two of the wisest as well as most honourable men in Europe. The age which produced such virtue, was, however, the age of the pretended popish plot, and of a thousand other enormities which cannot now be thought of without horror. Since then, the world has had upwards of a century to improve itself in experience, in reflection, in virtue. In every other line its improvements have been immense and unquestioned. Is it too much to hope that France and England might produce not a Temple and a De Wit,—virtue so transcendent as theirs would not be necessary,—but men who, in happier times, might achieve a work like theirs with less extent of virtue.

Such a Congress or Diet might be constituted by each power sending two deputies to the place of meeting; one of these to be the principal, the other to act as an occasional substitute.

The proceedings of such Congress or Diet should all be public.

Its power would consist,—1. In reporting its opinion;

2. In causing that opinion to be circulated in the dominions of each state.

Manifestoes are in common usage. A manifesto is designed to be read either by the subjects of the state complained of, or by other states, or by both. It is an appeal to them. It calls for their opinion. The difference is, that in that case nothing of proof is given; no opinion regularly made known.

The example of Sweden is alone sufficient to show

the influence which treaties, the acts of nations, may be expected to have over the subjects of the several nations, and how far the expedient in question deserves the character of a weak one, or the proposal for employing and trusting to it, that of a visionary proposal.

The war commenced by the king of Sweden against Russia, was deemed by his subjects, or at least a considerable part of them, offensive, and as such, contrary to the constitution established by him with the concurrence of the states. Hence a considerable part of the army either threw up their commissions or refused to act; and the consequence was, the king was obliged to retreat from the Russian frontier and call a diet.

This was under a government, commonly, though not truly, supposed to be changed from a limited monarchy, or rather aristocracy, to a despotic monarchy. There was no act of any recognised and respected tribunal to guide and fix the opinion of the people. The only document they had to judge from was a manifesto of the enemy, couched in terms such as resentment would naturally dictate, and therefore none of the most conciliating,—a document which had no claim to be circulated, and of which the circulation, we may be pretty well assured, was prevented as much as it was in the power of the utmost vigilance of the government to prevent it.

3. After a certain time, in putting the refractory state under the ban of Europe.

There might, perhaps, be no harm in regulating, as a last resource, the contingent to be furnished by the several states for enforcing the decrees of the court. But the necessity for the employment of this resource would, in all human probability, be superseded for ever by having recourse to the much more simple and less burthensome expedient, of introducing into the instrument by which such court was instituted, a clause guaranteeing the liberty of the press in each state, in such sort, that the diet might find no obstacle to its giving, in every state, to its decrees, and to every paper whatever which it might think proper to sanction with its signature, the most extensive and unlimited circulation.

Proposition XIV.—That secresy in the operations of the foreign department in England ought not to be endured, being altogether useless, and equally repugnant to the interests of liberty and peace.

The existence of the rule which throws a veil of secrecy over the transactions of the Cabinet with foreign powers, I shall not take upon me to dispute—my objection is to the propriety of it.

Being asked in the House of Lords by Lord Stormont about secret articles, the minister for foreign affairs refuses to answer. I blame him not. Subsisting rules, it seems to be agreed, forbid reply. They throw a general veil of secrecy over the transactions of the Cabinet with foreign powers. I blame no man for the fault of the laws. It is these laws that I blame as repugnant to the spirit of the constitution, and incompatible with good government.

I take at once the boldest and the broadest ground— I lay down two propositions:—

1. That in no negotiation, and at no period of any negotiation, ought the negotiations of the cabinet in this country to be kept secret from the public at large; much less from parliament and after inquiry made in parliament.

2. That whatever may be the case with preliminary negotiations, such secrecy ought never to be maintained with regard to treaties actually concluded.

In both cases, to a country like this, such secrecy is equally mischievous and unnecessary.

It is mischievous. Over measures of which you have no knowledge, you can apply no control. Measures carried on without your knowledge you cannot stop,— how ruinous soever to you, and how strongly soever you would disapprove of them if you knew them. Of negotiations with foreign powers carried on in time of peace, the principal terminations are treaties of alliance, offensive or defensive, or treaties of commerce. But by one accident or other, everything may lead to war.

That in new treaties of commerce as such, there can be no cause for secrecy, is a proposition that will hardly be disputed. Only such negotiations, like all others, may eventually lead to war, and everything connected with war, it will be said, may come to require secrecy.

But rules which admit of a minister's plunging the nation into a war against its will, are essentially mischievous and unconstitutional.

It is admitted that ministers ought not to have it in their power to impose taxes on the nation against its will. It is admitted that they ought not to have it in their power to maintain troops against its will. But by plunging it into war without its knowledge they do both.

Parliament may refuse to carry on a war after it is begun:—Parliament may remove and punish the minister who has brought the nation into a war.

Sorry remedies these; add them both together, their efficacy is not worth a straw. Arrestment of the evil, and punishment of the authors, are sad consolations for the mischief of a war, and of no value as remedies in comparison with prevention. Aggressive war is a matter of choice: defensive, of necessity. Refusal of the means of continuing a war is a most precarious remedy, a remedy only in name. What, when the enemy is at your doors, refuse the materials for barricading them?

Before aggression, war or no war depends upon the aggressor;—once begun, the party aggrieved acquires a vote: He has his negative upon every plan for terminating the war.—What is to be one? Give yourself up without resistance to the mercy of a justly exasperated enemy? But this or the continuance of the war, is all the choice that is now left. In what state of things can this remedy be made to serve? Are you unsuccessful?—the remedy is inapplicable. Are you successful?—nobody will call for it.

Punishment of the authors of the war, punishment whatever it may be to the personal adversaries of the ministers, is no satisfaction to the nation. This is self-evident; but what is closer to the purpose and not less true, is, that in a case like this, the fear of punishment on such an account is not check to them: of a majority in parliament they are in possession, or they would not be ministers. That they should be abandoned by this majority is not in the catalogue of events that ought to be looked upon as possible: but between abandoning them and punishing them, there is a wide difference. Lord North was abandoned in the American war: he was not punished for it. His was an honest error in judgment, unstained by any *malafide* practice, and countenanced by a fair majority in parliament. And so may any other impolitic and unjust war be. This is not a punishing age. If bribe-taking, oppression, peculation, duplicity, treachery, every crime that can be committed by statesmen sinning against conscience, produce no desire to punish, what dependence can be placed on punishment in a case where the mischief may so easily happen without any ground for punishment? Mankind are not yet arrived at that stage in the track of civilization. Foreign nations are not yet considered as objects susceptible of an injury. For the citizens of other civilized nations, we have not so much feeling as for our negroes. There are instances in which ministers have been punished for making peace—there are none where they have been so much as questioned for bringing the nation into war; and if punishment had been ever applied on such an occasion, it would be not for the mischief done to the foreign nation, but purely for the mischief brought upon their own; not for the injustice, but purely for the imprudence.

It has never been laid down as a rule that you should pay any regard to foreign nations: it has never been laid down that you should stick at anything which would give you an advantage in your dealings with foreign nations. On what ground could a minister be punished for a war, even the most unsuccessful, brought on by any such means? I did my best to serve you, he would say—the worse the measure was for the foreign nation, the more I took upon me: the greater therefore the zeal I showed for your cause: the event has proved unfavourable. Are zeal and misfortune to be represented as crimes?

A war unjust on the part of our own nation, by

whose ministers it is brought on, can never be brought on but in pursuit of some advantage which, were it not for the injustice towards the foreign nation it would be for our interests to pursue. The injustice and the danger of retaliation being on all hands looked upon as nothing, the plea of the minister would always be,—"It was *your* interest I was pursuing." And the uninformed and unreflecting part of the nation, that is, the great body of the nation would echo to him,—"Yes, it was our interest you were preserving." The voice of the nation on these subjects can only be looked for in newspapers. But on these subjects the language of all newspapers is uniform:—"It is we that are always in the right, without a possibility of being otherwise. Against us other nations have no rights. If according to the rules of judging between individual and individual, we are right —we are right by the rules of justice: if not, we are right by the laws of patriotism, which is a virtue more respectable than justice."—Injustice, oppression, fraud, lying, whatever acts would be crimes, whatever habits would be vices, if manifested in the pursuit of individual interests, when manifested in pursuit of national interests, become sublimated into virtues. Let any man declare who has ever read or heard an English newspaper, whether this be not the constant tenor of the notions they convey. Party on this one point makes no difference. However hostile to one another on all other points, on this they have never but one voice—they write with the utmost harmony. Such are the opinions, and to these opinions the facts are accommodated as of course. Who would blush to misrepresent, when misrepresentation is a virtue?

But newspapers, if their voice make but a small part of the voice of the people, the instruction they give makes on these subjects the whole of the instruction which the people receive.

Such being the national propensity to error on these points, and to error on the worst side, the danger of parliamentary punishment for misconduct of this kind must appear equivalent to next to nothing, even in the eyes of an unconcerned and cool spectator. What must it appear then in the eyes of ministers themselves, acting under the seduction of self-partiality, and hurried on by the tide of business? No; the language which a minister on such occasions will hold to himself will be uniformly this,—"In the first place what I do is not wrong: in the next place, if it were, nothing should I have to fear from it."

Under the present system of secrecy, ministers have, therefore, every seduction to lead them into misconduct while they have no check to keep them out of it. And what species of misconduct? That in comparison of which all others are peccadillos. Let a minister throw away £30,000 or £40,000 in pensions to his creatures. Let him embezzle a few hundred thousand for himself. What is that to fifty or a hundred millions, the ordinary burthen of a war? Observe the consequence. This is the department of all others in which the strongest checks are needful; at the same time, thanks to the rules of secrecy of all the departments, this is the only one in which there are no checks at all. I say, then, the conclusion is demonstrated. The principle which throws a veil of secrecy over the proceedings of the foreign department of the cabinet is pernicious in the highest degree, pregnant with mischiefs superior to everything to which the most perfect absence of all concealment could possibly give rise.

There still remains a sort of inexplicit notion which may present itself as secretly furnishing an argument on the other side. Such is the condition of the British nation: peace and war may be always looked upon as being to all human probability in good measure in her power. When the worst comes to the worst, peace may always be had by some unessential sacrifice. I admit the force of the argument: what I maintain is that it operates in my favour. Why? It depends upon two propositions,—the matchless strength of this country, and the uselessness of her foreign dependencies. I admit both. But both operate as arguments in my favour. Her strength places her above the danger of surprise, and above the necessity of having recourse to it to defend herself. The uselessness of her foreign dependencies prove *a fortiori*, the uselessness of engaging in wars for their protection and defence. If they are not fit to keep without war, much less are they worth keeping at the price of war. The inutility of a secret cabinet is demonstrated by this short dilemma. For offensive measures, cabinet secrecy can never be necessary to this nation; for defence it can never be necessary to any.

My persuasion is that there is no state whatever in which any inconveniences capable of arisng from publicity in this department would not be greatly overbalanced by the advantages; be the state ever so great or ever so small; ever so strong or ever so weak; be its form of government pure or mixed, single or confederated, monarchical, aristocratical, or democratical. The observations already given seem in all these cases sufficient to warrant the conclusion.

But in a nation like Britain, the safety of publicity, the inutility of secrecy in all such business, stands upon peculiar grounds. Stronger than any two other nations, much stronger of course than any *one,* its superiority deprives it of all pretence of necessity of carrying points by surprise. Clandestine surprise is the resource of knavery and fear, of unjust ambition combined with weakness. Her matchless power exempts her from the one; her interest, if her servants could be brought to be governed by her evident interests, would forbid the other.

Taking the interest of the first servant of the state as distinct from and opposite to the nation, clandestinity may undoubtedly be, in certain cases, favourable to the projects of sceptred thieves and robbers. Without taking the precautions of a thief, the Great Frederic might probably enough not have succeeded in the enterprise of stealing Silesia from her lawful sovereign. Without an advantage of this sort, the triple gang might, perhaps, not have found it quite so easy to secure what they stole from Poland. Whether there can or cannot exist occasions on which it might, in this point of view, be the interest of a king of Great Britain to turn highwayman, is a question I shall waive: but a proposition I shall not flinch from is, that it never can be the interest of the nation to abet him in it. When those sceptred sinners sold themselves to the service of Mammon, they did not serve him for nought: the booty was all their own. Were we (I speak as one of the body of the nation) to assist our king in committing a robbery upon France, the booty would be his. He would have the naming to the new places, which is all the value that in the hands of a British robber such booty can be of to anybody. The privilege of paying for the horse and pistols is all that would be ours. The booty would be employed in corrupting our confidential servants: and this is the full and exact amount of what we should get by it.

Conquests made by New Zealanders have some sense in them; while the conquered fry, the conquerors fatten. Conquests made by the polished nations of antiquity,— conquests made by Greeks and Romans,—had some sense in them. Land, moveables, inhabitants, everything went into the pocket. The invasions of France in the days of the Edwards and the Henrys, had a rational object. Prisoners were taken, and the country was stripped to pay their ransom. The ransom of a single prisoner, a Duke of Orleans, exceeded one-third of the national revenue of England.

Conquests made by a modern despot of the continent have still some sense in them. The new property; the inhabitants, as many as he thinks fit to set his mark upon, go to increase his armies; their substance, as much as he thinks fit to squeeze from them, goes into his purse.

Conquests made by the British nation would be violations of common sense, were there no such thing as justice. They are bungling imitations of miserable originals, bating the essential circumstances. Nothing but confirmed blindness and stupidity can prompt us to go on imitating Alexander and Caesar, and the New Zealanders, and Catherine and Frederic, without the profit.

If it be the king alone who gets the appointment to the places, it is a part of the nation, it may be said, that gets the benefit of filling them. A precious lottery! Fifty or one hundred millions the cost of the tickets. So many years purchase of ten or twenty thousand a-year, the value of the prizes. This if the scheme succeed:—what if it fail?

I do not say there are no sharers in the plunder:—it is impossible for the head of a gang to put the whole of it into his own pocket. All I contend for is, that robbery by wholesale is not so profitable as by retail:—if the whole gang together pick the pockets of strangers to a certain amount, the ringleaders pick the pockets of the rest to a much greater. Shall I or shall I not succeed in persuading my countrymen that it is not their interest to be thieves?

"Oh, but you mistake!" cries somebody, "we do not now make war for conquests, but for trade." More foolish still. This is a still worse bargain than before. Conquer the whole world, it is impossible you should increase your trade one halfpenny:—it is impossible you should do otherwise than diminish it. Conquer little or much, you pay for it by taxes:—but just so much as a merchant pays in taxes, just so much he is disabled from adding to the capital he employs in trade. Had you two worlds to trade with, you could only trade with them to the amount of your capital, and what credit, you might meet with on the strength of it. This being true of each trader, is so of all traders. Find a fallacy in this short argument if you can. If you obtained your new right of trading given you for nothing, you would not be a halfpenny the richer: if you paid for them by war or preparations for war; by just so much as you paid for these you would be the poorer.

The good people of England, along with the right of self-government, conquered the prodigious right of trade. The revolution was to produce for them not only the blessings of security and power, but immense and sudden wealth. Year has followed after year, and to their endless astonishment, the progress to wealth has gone on no faster than before. One piece of good fortune still wanting, they have never thought of:—that on the day their shackles were knocked off, some kind sylph should have slipped a few thousand pounds into every man's pocket. There is no law against my flying to the moon. Yet I cannot get there. Why? Because I have no wings. What wings are to flying, capital is to trade.

There are two ways of making war for trade,—forcing independent nations to let you trade with them, and conquering nations, or pieces of nations, to make them trade with you. The former contrivance is to appearance the more easy, and the policy of it the more refined. The latter is more in the good old way, and the king does his own business and the nation's at the same time. He gets the naming to the places: and the nation cannot choose but join with him, being assured that it is all for the sake of getting them the trade. The places he lays hold of, good man, only out of necessity, and that they may not go a-begging:—on his account, he has no more mind for them than a new-made bishop for the mitre, or a new-made speaker for the chair. To the increase of trade, both these plans of war equally contribute. What you get in both cases is the pleasure of the war.

The legal right of trading to part of America was conquered by France from Britain in the last war. What have they got by it? They have got Tobago, bankruptcy, and a revolution, for their fifty millions. Ministers, who to account for the bankruptcy are forced to say something about the war, call it a national one:—the king has not got by it,—therefore the nation has. What has it got? A fine trade, were there but capital to carry it on. With such room for trade, how comes there to be no more to it? This is what merchants and manufacturers are putting themselves to the torture to account for. The sylph so necessary elsewhere, was still more necessary to France; since, over and above her other work, there was the fifty millions spent in powder and shot to replace.

The King of France, however, by getting Tobago,

probably obtained two or three thousand pounds worth of places to give away. This is what he got, and this is all that anybody got for the nation's fifty millions. Let us go on as we have begun, strike a bold stroke, take all their vessels we can lay hold of without a declaration of war, and who knows but what we may get it back again. With the advantages we now have over them, five times the success they are so pleased with, would be but a moderate expectation. For every fifty millions thus laid out, our king would get in places to the amount, not of two or three thousand pounds only, but say of ten, fifteen, or twenty thousand pounds. All this would be prodigious glory—and fine paragraphs and speeches, thanksgivings, and birth-day odes, might be sung and said for it: but for economy, I would much rather give the king new places to the same amount at home, if at this price his ministers would sell us peace.

The conclusion is, that as we have nothing to fear from any other nation or nations, nor want anything from other nations, we can have nothing to say to other nations, nor to hear from them,—that might not be as public as any laws. What then is the veil of secrecy that enwraps the proceedings of the cabinet? A mere cloak for wickedness and folly—a dispensation to ministers to save them from the trouble of thinking—a warrant for playing all manner of mad and silly pranks, unseen and uncontrolled—a license to play at hazard with their fellows abroad, staking our lives and fortunes upon the throw.

What, then, is the true use and effect of secrecy? That the prerogatives of place may furnish an aliment to petty vanity,—that the members of *the circulation* may have as it were a newspaper to themselves,—that under favour of the monopoly, ignorance and incapacity may put on airs of wisdom,—that a man, unable to write or speak what is fit to be put into a newspaper, may toss up his head and say, I don't read newspapers —as if a parent were to say I don't trouble my head about schoolmasters,—and that a minister, secure from scrutiny in that quarter, may have the convenient opportunity, upon occasion, of filling the posts with obsequious cyphers, instead of effective men:—anything will do to make a minister whose writing may be written for him, and whose duty in speaking consists in silence.

This much must be confessed:—if secrecy as against the nation be useless and pernicious to the nation, it is not useless and pernicious with regard to its servants. It forms part of the *douceurs* of office—a perquisite which will be valued in proportion to the insignificance of their characters and the narrowness of their views. It serves to pamper them up with notions of their own importance, and to teach the servants of the people to look down upon their masters.

"Oh!—but if everything that were written were liable to be made public, were published, who would treat with you abroad? Just the same persons as treat with you at present. Negotiations, for fear of misrepresentation, would perhaps be committed somewhat more to writing than at present;—and where would be the harm? The king and his ministers might not have quite such copious accounts, true or false, of the tittle-tattle of each court: or they must put into different hands the tittle-tattle, and the real business. And suppose your head servants were not so minutely acquainted with the mistresses and buffoons of kings and their ministers,— what matters it to you as a nation, who have no intrigues to carry on, no petty points to compass?

It were an endless task to fill more pages with the shadows that might be conjured up in order to be knocked down. I leave that task to any that will undertake it. I challenge party men—I invite the impartial lovers of their country and mankind to discuss the question—to ransack the stores of history, and imagination as well as history, for cases actual or possible, in which the want of secrecy in this line of business can be shown to be attended with any substantial prejudice.

As to the constitution, the question of cabinet-secrecy having never been tried by the principles of the constitution, has never received a decision. The good old

Tudor and Stuart principles have been suffered to remain unquestioned here. Foreign politics are questions of state. Under Elizabeth and James nothing was to be inquired into—nothing was to be known—everything was matter of state. On other points the veil has been torn away: but with regard to these, there has been a sort of tacit understanding between ministers and people.

Hitherto war has been the national rage: peace has always come too soon,—war too late. To tie up the ministers' hands and make them continually accountable, would be depriving them of numberless occasions of seizing those happy advantages that lead to war: it would be lessening the people's chance of their favourite amusement. For these hundred years past, ministers, to do them justice, have generally been more backward than the people—the great object has rather been to force them into war, than to keep them out of it. Walpole and Newcastle were both forced into war.

It admits of no doubt, if we are really for war, and fond of it for its own sake, we can do no better than let things continue as they are. If we think peace better than war, it is equally certain that the law of secrecy cannot be too soon abolished.

Such is the general confusion of ideas—such the power of the imagination—such the force of prejudice —that I verily believe the persuasion is not an uncommon one;—so clear in their notions are many worthy gentlemen, that they look upon war, if successful, as a cause of opulence and prosperity. With equal justice might they look upon the loss of a leg as a cause of swiftness.

Well, but if it be not directly the cause of opulence, it is indirectly; from the successes of war, come, say they, our prosperity, our greatness; thence the respect paid to us by Foreign Powers—thence our security: and who does not know how necessary security is to opulence?

No; war is, in this way, just as unfavourable to opulence as in the other. In the present mode of carrying on war—a mode which it is in no man's power to depart from, security is in proportion to opulence. Just so far then as war is, by its direct effects, unfavourable to opulence,—just so far is it unfavourable to security.

Respect is a term I shall beg leave to change; respect is a mixture of fear and esteem, but for constituting esteem, force is not the instrument, but justice. The sentiment really relied upon for security is fear. By respect then is meant, in plain English, fear. But in a case like this, fear is much more adverse than favourable to security. So many as fear you, join against you till they think they are too strong for you, and then they are afraid of you no longer;—meantime they all hate you, and jointly and severally they do you as much mischief as they can. You, on your part, are not behindhand with them. Conscious or not conscious of your own bad intentions, you suspect theirs to be still worse. Their notion of your intentions is the same. Measures of mere self-defence are naturally taken for projects of aggression. The same causes produce, on both sides, the same effects; each makes haste to begin for fear of being forestalled. In this state of things, if on either side there happen to be a minister or a would-be minister, who has a fancy for war, the stroke is struck, and the tinder catches fire.

At school, the strongest boy may perhaps be the safest. Two or more boys are not always in readiness to join against one. But though this notion may hold good in an English school, it will not bear transplanting upon the theatre of Europe.

Oh! but if your neighbours are really afraid of you, their fear is of use to you in another way—you get the turn of the scale in all disputes. Points that are at all doubtful, they give up to you of course. Watch the moment, and you may every now and then gain points that do not admit of doubt. This is only the former old set of fallacies exhibited in a more obscure form, and which, from their obscurity only, can show as new. The fact is, as has been already shown, there is no nation that has any points to gain to the prejudice of any other. Between the interests of nations, there is nowhere any real conflict: if they appear repugnant anywhere, it is only in proportion as they are misunderstood. What are these points? What points are these which, if you had your choice, you would wish to gain of them? Preferences in trade have been proved to be worth nothing,—distant territorial acquisitions have been proved to be worth less than nothing. When these are out of the question, what other points are there worth gaining by such means?

Opulence is the word I have first mentioned; but opulence is not the word that would be first pitched upon. The repugnancy of the connexion between war and opulence is too glaring:—the term opulence brings to view an idea too simple, too intelligible, too precise. Splendour, greatness, glory, these are terms better suited to the purpose. Prove first that war contributes to splendour and greatness, you may persuade yourself it contributes to opulence, because when you think of splendour you think of opulence. But splendour, greatness, glory, all these fine things, may be produced by useless success, and unprofitable and enervating extent of dominion obtained at the expense of opulence; and this is the way in which you may manage so as to prove to yourself, that the way to make a man run the quicker is to cut off one of his legs. And true enough it is, that a man who has had a leg cut off, and the stump healed, may hop faster than a man who lies in bed with both legs broken, can walk. And thus you may prove that Britain is in a better case after the expenditure of a glorious war, than if there had been no war; because France or some other country, was put by it into a still worse condition.

In respect, therefore, of any benefit to be derived in the shape of conquest, or of trade—of opulence or of respect—no advantage can be reaped by the employment of the unnecessary, the mischievous, and unconstitutional system of clandestinity and secrecy in negotiation.

THE CONSTITUTIONAL CODE*

In the Introduction to the *Constitutional Code* there is to be found a brief summing up of the whole body of the law as conceived by Bentham. Each of these subdivisions of two or three pages (it should be noted) is actually represented in his collected works by from one hundred thousand to over a million words. Even so, a few passages have been omitted in this reprint as indicated by the customary ellipses.

I. GENERAL DIVISION OF
THE AGGREGATE BODY OF THE LAW

On viewing the aggregate of that which in any country has the force of law, it will be found divisible, in first place, the whole of it, into two portions or branches, viz. in the first place, that in which the rule of action is laid down simply and absolutely, without reference to the functions of any such members of the community as those whose business it is, under some such name as that of judges, or ministers of justice, to secure the observance of it; in the next place, that in which a description is given of the course to be taken by those same official persons for securing the observance of, and giving execution and effect to, several arrangements contained in that same main or substantive branch. This branch may be distinguished by the name of the adjective branch, or law of judiciary procedure.

The main or substantive portion, or branch of the law, may again be distinguished into two portions or branches. In the first place, that in which individuals are considered separately only, and in their private capacity. This may be distinguished by the name of private law. In the next place, that in which individuals are regarded collectively, and in some public capacity, with a view to the powers necessary to be exercised by some of them over others, for the good of the whole. This branch may be distinguished by the name of public or constitutional law.

The law cannot in any part of it operate without doing more or less towards the making distribution of benefits and burthens.

Burthens it may distribute or impose without distributing or conferring benefit, in any shape. Benefit in any shape it cannot confer, without, at the same time, imposing burthen in a correspondent shape, either on the individual benefited, or intended to be benefited, or on some other or others, most commonly even on all others, with little or no exception. . . .

Of the whole body of actual law one pre-eminently remarkable division, derived from a correspondently remarkable source, and pervading the whole mass, still remains. It is that by which it is distinguished into two branches—the arrangements of one of which are arrangements that have really been made—made by hands universally acknowledged as duly authorized, and competent to the making of such arrangements, viz. the hands of a legislator-general, or set of legislators-general, or their respective subordinates. This branch of law may stand distinguished from that which is correspondent and opposite to it, by the name of *real* law, really existing law, legislator-made law;—under the English Government it stands already distinguished by the name of *statute* law, as also by the uncharacteristic, undiscriminative, and, in so far improper appellation, of *written* law. The arrangements supposed to be made by the other branch, in so far as they are arrangements of a general nature, applying not only to individuals assignable, but to the community at large, or to individuals not individuals assignable, may stand distinguished by the appellations of unreal, not really existing, imaginary, fictitious, spurious, judge-made law. Under the English Government the division actually distinguished by the unexpressive, uncharacteristic, and unappropriate names of *common* law and *unwritten* law. . . .

II. CONSTITUTIONAL LAW

The constitutional branch of law, is that branch, by which designation is made of that person, or those persons, to whose power it is intended, that on each occasion, the conduct of all the other members of the community in question shall be subjected.

The power which is here conferred is the supreme power.

Of the supreme power thus designated, that is to say, of the aggregate of the operations by which the exercise of it is performed, there are, of necessity, two perfectly distinct branches, the operative and the constitutive; the operative, is exercised by the declaration made of the all-directing will above alluded to; the constitutive, is exercised by the determination made of the individual or individuals, by whom the operative power is exercised.

Constitutional law has for its object, security against misrule: security against those adversaries of the community, in whose instance, while their situation bestows on them the denomination of rulers, the use they make of it, adds the adjunct evil, and thus denominates them evil rulers. . . .

So far as it wears the complexion of penal law, constitutional law has these two for its distinguishable and contrasted objects: first, the ordering matters so, that those who, to some purposes and on some occasions, occupy the situation of rulers, shall, in respect of their conduct in that and other situations, be liable to be dealt with, in the character of offenders, delinquents, criminals; could the ordering matters so, that to acts done in resistance to, or for prevention of, misrule, and thence productive of more good than evil,—to such acts, of whatever penal denomination they may appear susceptible, no such punishment, if any, shall be allotted, as might, with propriety, be allotted to them, if the applica-

But when a particular and practical application comes to be made of the word security, certain names of fictitious entities* in common use must be employed to designate so many objects, to and for which the security is afforded. Person, reputation, property, condition in life, by these four names of fictitious entities, all the objects to which, in the case of an individual, the security afforded by government can apply itself, may be designated.

Security has for its adversaries, against whose enterprises it is to be afforded, three classes of persons differently situated and denominated, viz. foreign adversaries considered as such, foreigners considered in so far as they are, or are liable to become, adversaries; rulers, viz. of the country in question considered in that same light; and fellow-citizens, or fellow-subjects, considered in that same light.

As to the acts against which security is to be afforded, and by which, in so far as they are performed, security is broken in upon and lessened, they are in themselves and their immediate effects, the same by which soever of the three species of adversaries they are exercised. Taken, however, in the aggregate, they are wont to be designated by a different denomination, according to the situation of the class to which the person or persons by whom they are exercised, is considered as belonging. If to that of foreign adversaries, they are denominated acts of hostility: if to that of domestic adversaries, considered in the character of rulers, acts of oppression—or, if the oppression be considered as to a certain degree flagrant, acts of tyranny; if to that of domestic adversaries, considered in the character of subjects, acts of delinquency. . . .

Section III. Subsistence

Original and all-comprehensive, derivative and incidental, means of subsistence. By these words may be designated the two branches of a division which it is nec-

---

*For an explanation of this division of entities see *Works,* Vol. III, p. 195, *et seq.* [Editor's note.]

essary in the first place to bring to view.

The original fund of each man's subsistence is each man's labour. The production of it is the work of nature without law, and antecedently to law. What it looks for at the hand of law is security: security against calamity, security against hostility from foreigners, from fellow-subjects, and from rulers.

Incidental and derivative means of subsistence. The need of these arises out of the deficiencies that are liable to have place in the produce of each man's labour, considered as a fund for each man's subsistence.

Certain and casual. By the two distinctions thus designated may be comprehended, in the first place, all the varieties of which the cause of this deficiency are susceptible.

Certain is the nature of those produced by time of life: by the time antecedent to the capacity for labour, and by the time subsequent to it: by immaturity and by caducity.

The time of immaturity endures for years: the time of caducity may endure for years, or may terminate in the same moment in which it commenced.

Want of capacity for labour, want of employment for labour. Under one or other of these heads may be comprehended all the *casual* causes of deficiency in regard to subsistence.

Casual want of capacity for labour is indisposition—relative indisposition. Indisposition may be of body or mind: the degree of indisposition in question is designated by the effect.

If against any of the causes of deficiency in regard to subsistence the government has failed to provide an efficient remedy, the consequence is death; security against calamity has so far failed to have been afforded.

But against deficiency in regard to subsistence, no remedy can ever be provided but at the expense of security for abundance. The fund of abundance is composed of the stock remaining of the produce of labour, deduction made of the several amounts, substracted by consumption, useful and useless, immediate and gradual, natural and human, in all their several shapes.

In his endeavour to provide a remedy against deficiency in regard to subsistence, the legislator finds himself all along under the pressure of this dilemma— forbear to provide supply, death ensues, and it has you for its author; provide supply, you establish a bounty upon idleness, and you thus give increase to the deficiency which it is your endeavour to exclude.

Under the pressure of this dilemma, how to act is a problem, the solution of which will, in a great degree, be dependent upon local circumstances: nor can anything like a complete solution be so much as attempted without continual reference to them. One leading observation applies to all places and all times. So long as any particle of the matter of abundance remains in any one hand, it will rest with those, to whom it appears that they are able to assign a sufficient reason, to show why the requisite supply to any deficiency in the means of subsistence should be refused.

Section IV. Abundance

Of the instruments of abundance, the fund is composed of the surplus of the means of subsistence, deduction made of the quantity destroyed by consumption in all its shapes.

Increase of production—decrease of consumption. Under one or other of these two heads may be comprehended all the possible causes of increase to the abundance fund.

Natural and factitious. Under one or other of these two heads may be comprehended all the possible modes of increase to production.

By natural, understand all those that have place without intervention on the part of the government in this particular view. Under this same head natural, is therefore comprehended whatsoever assistance is afforded to production, by the security afforded to produce.

By factitious modes of increase to production, understand all such as are employed by government in that special view.

Here comes in with propriety one general and all-comprehensive rule. In so far as the natural means of increase to the abundance fund suffice for the production of the effect, forbear to employ any factitious means for giving increase or acceleration to it.

Neither for this purpose nor for any other can the power of government be employed, but coercion must be applied immediately, in so far as the inducements employed are of the penal kind; unimmediately, in so far as the inducements employed are of the remunerative kind: but it is only by coercion that any means of remuneration can be collected.

In favour, and for the benefit of, A, you cannot seek to give increase to production in the hands of A, except in so far as coercion is applied either to A himself, or to B, C, and D, and so forth.

But why seek to benefit A by coercion applied to A? His regard for himself is greater than yours can be:— his knowledge of what is most beneficial to himself is greater than yours can be;—his experience of what has been most beneficial and most hurtful to himself is greater than yours can be.

Why seek to benefit A by coercion applied to B, C, and D, and so forth? Coercion is evil—positive evil—suffering: absence of increase is but negative evil. No suffering is the result of it. A is but one; B,C,D, and the rest of them are many: by the number of them all, after allowance made for the lessening of loss by the distribution of it is the quantity of the suffering, produced by the coercion, multiplied.

Increase cannot thus be sought to be given to production otherwise than at the expense of equality; by violations made of the rules of equality; by violations made of the rules of equality, for the importance of which to the greatest happiness of the greatest number, see further on.

For *security*, yes, without decrease, and with increase to the greatest happiness of the greatest number, the rules of equality may be infringed: for increase to abundance, without decrease to the great happiness of the greatest number, they cannot be infringed.

The negative means of increase to the abundance fund is by decrease of consumption. In so far as it is by voluntary decrease of consumption that decrease is made in the amount of the abundance fund, by the respective proprietors, pleasure and security, in all their various shapes are the effects of it, and are in proportion to it. In the case of by far the greatest portion, in quantity and value, of the produce of labour, subsistence, pleasure and security, in all their several shapes, have place only in so far as consumption has place. In each individual instance, from which of two causes, pleasure, or security, or both, are derived by him in greatest quantity, viz. from consumption or from avoidance of consumption—in a word, from preservation, is better known to the proprietor himself, than it can be to any body, and not at all known to you.

The great cause by which decrease is produced in the abundance fund, always without pleasure, and, in too great degree, without proportionable security to the possessors, is, that which consists of the draughts made upon it by government. . . .

Section V. Equality

Fourth on the list of the benefits which the civil branch of the law is occupied in distributing, is equality.

By equality is here meant, not the utmost conceivable equality, but only practicable equality. The utmost conceivable equality has place only in the field of physics; it applies only to weight, measure, time and thence to motion.

The utmost conceivable equality, say absolute equality, admits not of degrees,—practicable equality does admit of degrees.

Equality is not itself, as security, subsistence, and abundance are, an immediate instrument of felicity. It operates only through the medium of those three, especially through abundance and security. Of all three taken together, the use, fruit, and object is felicity—the maximum of felicity; of this maximum the magnitude depends upon the degree of equality that has place in the proportions in which those three are distributed.

Apply it first to subsistence,—means or instruments of subsistence,—subsistence taken in the strict sense. There is not in this case a place for degrees in the scale of equality; for, by the supposition, no inequality has place in this case. As contradistinguished from the instruments of abundance, by the means of subsistence, is meant that least quantity of those instruments, which is such, that with any lesser quantity existence could not have place: no subsistence, no existence.

It is when applied to abundance—to the elements or instruments of abundance, that the nature, and, with the nature, the importance, of political economy is most plainly discernible.

In the aggregate of the elements of abundance is included, as above, the aggregate of the means of subsistence. If the aggregate of felicity were as the aggregate of the elements of subsistence, no addition could be made, by any degree of equality, to the aggregate of felicity. But so far is this from being the case, that it is a question scarcely susceptible of solution, whether, where the aggregate of the elements of abundance is represented by the greatest number possible, the aggregate of felicity is so great as, or greater than, two. Take, on the one hand, the day-labourer, who throughout life has had complete means of subsistence, but at no time any portion of the elements of abundance: take, on the other part, the monarch, who throughout life has had the elements of abundance, together with all the other instruments of felicity, in the greatest quantity possible. Ages equal, scarcely can any one assure himself by full persuasion, that the quantity of felicity enjoyed by the monarch has been twice the amount of that enjoyed by the labourer; for the quantity of felicity is not as the quantity of the elements of felicity simply, but as the quantity of the elements of felicity, and the capacity of containing the felicity, taken together. In a basin of

water, introduce anywhere a secret waste-pipe: inject
through another pipe any quantity of water how great
soever, the vessel, it shall happen, will be never the fuller; for as fast as it flows in at one part, it flows out at
another. Just so it is with the elements or instruments of
felicity, when a stream of them, of boundless magnitude is injected into the human breast. Of pain, in all its
shapes, a monarch is no less susceptible than the labourer: and in its most common shapes the quantity of
pain may be, and frequently is, so great as to outweigh
the greatest quantity of pleasure in all its shapes, of
which human nature is susceptible. Even suppose pain,
in all its severe shapes, absent during the whole time:
the quantity experienced the whole time, suppose it a
minimum: this being the case in both situations, still the
question will remain insoluble as before. For in both
cases the quantity of felicity actually enjoyed depends
on the degree of sensibility to enjoyment, in each instance: and while in the labourer the sensibility is a
maximum, the degree of sensibility in the monarch may
be a minimum. Even supposing this sensibility to be at
the same degree, in both instances at a given time of
life, it is, in the case of the monarch, exposed to a cause
of diminution, which has no place in the case of the labourer; for by high doses of the exciting matter applied
to the organ, its sensibility is in a manner worn out.
And in fact, number for number, the certain probative
symptoms or circumstantial evidences of infelicity, as
exhibited on the countenance, are at least as frequent in
the case of the monarch as in the case of the labourer.

Apply the investigation to any of the situations intermediate between that of the labourer and that of the
monarch, the result will be the same.

The more closely the subject is looked into, the more
complete will the persuasion be.

Of the enjoyments or instruments of positive felicity,
the principal and most unquestionable will be found to
be, as constantly and in as high a degree, attached to
the situation of the labourer, as above delineated—the
labourer, to whom none of the means of subsistence

have been wanting, though none of the other elements of abundance have been present—as to that of the monarch.

The principal enjoyments of which human nature is susceptible, constancy of repetition being considered as well as magnitude, are—those produced by the operations by which the individual is preserved; those produced by the operations by which the species is preserved; that cessation from labour which is termed repose; and that pleasure of sympathy which is produced by the observation of others partaking in the same enjoyments. These four, with the exception of repose, are so many positive enjoyments upon the face of them.

Cessation from labour presents, it is true, upon the face of it no more than a negative idea; but when the condition of him by whom repose after corporeal labour is experienced, is considered, the enjoyment will be seen to be a positive quantity; for, in this case, not merely a cessation from discomfort, but a pleasurable feeling of a peculiar kind, is experienced, such as, without the antecedent labour, never can be experienced. In the case of the labourer, it may indeed be said, that before the time of repose, with its enjoyment, arrives, the labour is pushed to a degree of intensity of which pain (in those degrees, at least, in which it is denoted by the word discomfort) has been produced. But the greater the degree of the pain of suffrance, the greater the degree of the pleasure of expectation—the expectation of the pleasure of repose—with which it has been accompanied. And this pleasure of expectation has had for its accompaniment, the pleasures of expectation respectively appertaining to the other pleasures of enjoyment above-mentioned; sensibility with regard to each being increased by that very labour, to the intensity of which that of the pleasure of repose is proportioned.

Pursue the investigation throughout the several other enjoyments of which human nature is susceptible, the ultimate result will not be materially different. . . .

The usefulness of the benefit of equality stands, then, upon these positions:—

1. The quantity of *happiness* possessed by a man, is not as the quantity of *property* possessed by the same man.

2. The greater the quantity of the matter of property a man is already in possession of, the less is the quantity of happiness he receives by the addition of another quantity of the matter of property, to a given amount.

3. The addition made by property to happiness goes on increasing in such a ratio, that, in the case of two individuals—he who has *least*, having, at all times, a quantity of the matter of property sufficient for a subsistence, while he who has *most*, possesses it in a quantity as great as any individual ever had, or ever can have; it is a question scarce capable of solution, whether the one who has the greatest quantity of the matter property, has twice the quantity of happiness which he has whose quantity of the means of happiness, in that shape, is the least.

If this ratio, of two to one, be regarded as too small a ratio, substitute to it the ratio of 3 to 1, the ratio of 4 to 1, and so on, till you are satisfied you have fixed upon the proper ratio: still, the truth of the practical conclusion will not be affected.

This conclusion is, that, so far as consistent with security, the nearer to equality the distribution is, which the law makes of the matter of property among the members of the community, the greater is the happiness of the greatest number: and, accordingly, this is the proposition which, so far as can be done without preponderant prejudice to security, ought, at all times, and in all places, to be established and maintained.

As to absolute equality, in relation to property, such equality is neither possible nor desirable. . . .

Section VI. Rights and Obligations

Correspondent to rights, are obligations. Without the idea expressed by the word obligation, no clear or correct idea can be annexed to the word right.

Rights are either simple or complex: simple rights, are the elements out of which complex rights are composed. Those which first come to be considered, are simple rights.

An original or primary right, is that which is constituted by the absence of the correspondent obligation. This is the sort of right which has place antecedently to the formation of government. It belongs equally to every agent, and has place with relation to every subject. No man, as yet, being under any obligation to abstain from making any use of anything; every man has, as yet, a right to make every use of everything.

Next come those rights, the existence of which is constituted by the existence of correspondent obligations.

First comes that right which is constituted by an obligation imposed upon other men, inhibiting them from exercising, with relation to the subject in question, the sort of right above designated by the appellation of an original or primary right. Calls this a right by obligation, to wit, restrictive obligation,—imposed by the addition of this secondary right, the primary right acquires the character and name of an exclusive right.

If the birth of the exclusive right awaits a manifestation of the will of the person is whose favour it is created, it receives the appellation of a right of excluding, or say of exclusion.

In this case, the word *power,* is in use to be employed: and we say, accordingly, right of exclusion, or power of exclusion.

In the case of the right by exclusion, or the right of excluding, the subject to which the right and the exclusion apply, may be an individual or a species: an individual, for instance, the paper, and the collection of marks called letters which have been superinduced upon it: a species, for instance, any paper of the texture or appearance of this individual paper, or any marks presenting to view in the same order the same words, *i.e.* words of the same import as those which upon this paper are superinduced.

Of this species of exclusive right, to wit, the exclusive

right which applies to sorts of subjects, the origin is of date long posterior to that of the right which applies to individuals. When, as in the case of copyright, the duration proper to be given to it came in question, its nature and the mode of its formation were so imperfectly understood,—so far from being clear and correct, were the ideas suggested by the words employed in giving expression to it, that the mass of argument produced by the contest, exhibits a web of confusion no where unravelled. Of the original sort of right, it was said that it presented something tangible: of the more recently created sort of right, it was said that it presented nothing tangible: and in this supposed absence of tangible matter was found a sufficient reason for disallowing the right. But it has just been seen, that whereas in the case of the original right, the quantity of tangible matter belonging to the case is but individual, and therefore, finite; in the case of the more recently created right, that quantity is a species and therefore infinite.

On the occasion of these rights, will come to be considered the subjects to which they are applicable, and also their efficient causes: to wit, the several states of things or occurrences by which they are wont to be respectively brought into existence. . . .

IV. PENAL LAW

The penal branch of law has for its object and occupation, the giving execution and effect to the civil or distributive branch; as also a portion of the constitutional branch: such is the benefit conferred, or sought to be conferred by it. But no benefit, as we have seen, can have existence, but with, and by means of, a correspondent burthen. Nor profit without loss: without expenditure and expense, which is voluntary loss. What remains is, that in quantity and value, the benefit—the profit—be as great, the burthen—the loss—as small as possible.

For rendering it such, keep in mind this radical allusion. The community is the body politic. Misdeeds are its disorders. Occupied on the penal branch of law, the legislator is its medical practitioner—its surgeon. In a surgical operation the cure is the benefit: the pain of the patient the burthen. The operations of the surgeon have for their object, the rendering the cure as prompt and as complete as possible, at the expense of as little pain as possible.

The surgeon, when he cuts into the bladder of a patient for the extraction of a stone—does he say, the patient *deserves* to be so cut? Not he indeed: by no surgeon was any such absurdity ever uttered.

The possessor of political power—the magistrate—the legislator—has, at all times, in all places, uttered it without a blush. Why? Because, at all times, in all places, till yesterday, and in the new world, the magistrate—the legislator—such is man's nature—have been tyrants: tyrants having each of them, for the object of his acts as such—not the greatest happiness of the greatest number, but his own single greatest happiness.

In the origin from which he deduced the word, indicative of the demand for, as propriety of, the punishment, he was occupied in the application of,—he found a pretence for tyranny: for tyranny exercising itself in the taking of vengeance. The term *desert,* (which is not without hazarding the production of useless punishment to an indefinite extent), is, and ever was, in use to be employed (without hazard of any such evil), where, on the occasion of a contract for service between individual and individual, good, in the shape of reward, was to be applied: on the one part, the work contracted for, has been done—the service has been performed: at the hands, and at the expense of, the other, title has been made, to the correspondent service: the pay—the *reward* —has been *deserved.*

Hence arise two radical positions:—

1. Objects which punishment ought never to propose to itself, are vengeance, establishment of imaginary congruity and equality between transgression and punishment.

2. Objects which punishment ought ever to propose to itself are, compensation, in so far as the nature of the case admits of the application of it, for the evil produced by the misdeed: prevention of the commission of similar misdeeds in future, as well by the misdoer himself as by all other individuals taken at large.

Exacted at the expense of the evil doer, compensation necessitates suffering: exacted in consideration of, and in proportion to, the evil done by him, that suffering, by the whole amount of it, operates as punishment.

In the first place, compensation for the party injured: in the next place, over and above compensation, punishment for the benefit of the public, and punishment for appeasement of the wrath of the offended and wrathful monarch—such is the arithmetic of tyranny. Punishment, including to the profit of the monarch, the exaction of the whole of that matter by which compensation to the individual injured, might have been afforded; after that, compensation to the individual injured—such is the order, the method of tyranny. Compensation by one course of procedure: punishment by another, and a different course of procedure; reformation, by health given to the soul, by a third and different course of procedure: such is the arithmetic of lawyer-craft—confederate partner and instrument of tyranny; of lawyer-craft in its most rapacious character, and elaborate garb—the character and garb of the English lawyer.

Compensation and satisfaction are synonymous. Of the word compensation, the psychological import has its root in the physical idea of weight: compensation is weight for weight: satisfaction is giving enough for what has been suffered, in such sort that the weight of the good in the scale of enjoyment, shall be equal to the weight of the evil in the scale of suffering.

Satisfaction has been distinguished into lucrative and vindictive. Lucrative is satisfaction in any shape, considered otherwise than with a view to vengeance. Vindictive satisfaction, is satisfaction in any shape, considered with a view to vengeance.

In no shape or quantity should suffering be created, for the single purpose of affording satisfaction of the vindictive kind.

Only when, for the sake of the community at large, punishment is inflicted, if there be any shape by which (without increase of suffering to the wrong-doer) satisfaction to the individual wronged, may be administered, that shape may be employed.

By that shape, the apprehension of the eventual punishment may, moreover, be rendered the more impressive upon the mind of him, on whom the temptation to do the wrong is operating. . . .

In relation to punishment, considered as so much evil, employed as a means for excluding,—as far as possible, without greater evil, evil considered as producible by misdeeds, thus converted into offenses, three main questions on every occasion present themselves.

In what cases shall punishment be applied?

In what proportion?

In what shape?

In what cases shall it be applied? To a question of the opposite aspect,—the question, in what cases shall it not be applied?—a more commodious, howsoever indirect, answer, may be given.

Where it would be groundless.

Where it would be needless.

Where it would be inefficacious.

Where it would be unprofitable.

In each one of these cases, supposing them realized, punishment, it is evidently manifest, would be unapt: of all these cases, it may be said, they are unmeet for punishment.

Case the first.—Where punishment would be groundless: where the application of punishment would be unapt. Necessarily included in the notion of punishment is the notion of misdeed one, of offence given. Of the sort of operation by which, for the exclusion of greater evil, evil is purposely produced, the operation called punition, or more commonly punishment, is but one mode. For, taken by itself, government is in itself one vast evil: only except, in so far as evil, already produced by it, is done away or lessened, can any exercise of government be performed—can the power of government be in any way exercised, but evil is produced by it. But whereever, by evil thus produced, greater evil is excluded, the balance takes the nature, shape, and name of good; and government is justified in the production of it. In this case in the account of good and evil, the evil produced and applied in the shape of punishment would, unless it excluded some greater evil, or produced some preponderant good, be all loss.

Thus it is, that where evil applied as punishment would be groundless, what will often happen, is—that evil produced, though designedly, is not causeless—is not unjustifiable.

Where it would be needless. Here the circumstance from which the evil receives the denomination of punishment, viz. misdoing, offence has place: as such, evil is among the consequences of it. But, by the operation of some other cause, all the relative good that could be done by the evil of punishment, is done without it. In this case, therefore, whatsoever portion of punishment were applied, would be all loss.

Where it would be inefficacious. In this case, too, be the evil of the offence ever so great, the evil of punishment, though it could not be said to be needless, would, however, be all loss; to the undiminished evil of the offence, would be added the evil of the punishment.

Where the punishment would be unprofitable. Of the evil which, in its totality, would otherwise be produced by the offence, a portion, more or less considerable, would be excluded by the punishment; but the evil thus introduced is greater than the evil excluded by it.

In the three former cases, the evil of the punishment is all loss: in this last case, the evil produced is not all loss, but, after deducting, from the sum of what is produced by it the sum of what is excluded by it, there still remains on the balance a net remainder, or difference, which is so much loss.

Comprehensive, and on that account, theoretical as the description of these cases may appear, there is not one of them that has not, to a vast and deplorable extent, had its exemplification in practice. To afford an indication of every one of them, would be to give an all-comprehensive picture of whatever has been hitherto done on the field of penal law. . . .

V. PROCEDURE LAW

The penal branch of law, as already observed, has for its object and occupation the giving execution and effect to the civil or distributive branch, as also a portion of the constitutional branch. Both together, compose the *substantive* branch of law. The law of judicial procedure constitutes the *adjective* branch of law. This adjective branch has, for its object and occupation, the giving execution and effect to the aforesaid substantive branch.

For the production of this effect, the requisite means are right decision and conformable execution.

To the positive expression right decision, substitute an expression with a negative aspect, it will stand thus: —avoidance of misdecision.

In so far as the law is of a beneficial nature, giving execution and effect to it, will, bating accidental preponderant evil, be in a like manner a benefit. But as above, in the field of law no benefit can have place, without its attendant burthen.

The burthens inseparably attendant on judicial procedure stand comprised, the whole assemblage of them, within the import of three words—vexation, delay, and expense. . . .

On the occasion of each individual course of judicial procedure, there are two necessarily distinguishable questions,—the question of law, and the question of fact: whether the state of the law is as alleged, and whether the state of facts is as alleged.

If so it be that the state of the law is really as alleged, the bringing to the view of the judge that part of the law on which the claimant grounds his claim cannot be attended with much difficulty.

Not so the bringing to view the state of facts.

The means or instruments by which a state of facts is thus brought to view, and the persuasion of its existence endeavoured to be established, in the minds of those to whom it appertains to form a decision in relation to it, are called the evidences, or, by one collective appellation, the evidence. . . .

So far as depends upon the single exertions of the claimant himself in the bringing to view, on each occasion, the mass of evidence thus described, there will not, in general, be much difficulty.

But, most commonly for the production of the necessary mass of evidence, in addition to, or instead of, all operations performable by the claimant himself, appropriate operations, performed by other persons, (neither to the number of whom, nor to the distance of whose residence from the seat of judicature, can any determinate limits be assigned), may be necessary: and, in the instance of each such person, either willingness or reluctance may, to any degree, have place.

Here, then, for one main purpose, viz. the yielding evidence, there will, on each occasion, be a need, that either things, or persons, or both, should be forthcoming at the seat of judicature. Here, accordingly, one main problem presents itself for solution at the hands of the legislator—how to secure forthcomingness on the part of persons and things for the purpose of evidence. . . .

When the suit has commenced, let evidence be received from any and every source—exclude none. For, if any evidence is excluded, there will be danger of misdecision.*

As a security against improper conduct on the part of the judges and all other functionaries, the utmost publicity must be given to all judicial proceedings.

---

*See this subject considered in detail in the "Rationale of Evidence," in *Works*, Vols. VI and VII. [Editor's note.]

VI. FINANCIAL LAW

The financial department, is that by which is performed the extraction, custody, and expenditure of such money and money's worth, as is employed, or professed to be employed, in the public service: viz. in this and the several other branches of the public service.

Whatsoever be the public function, by the exercise of which service is rendered, or pretended to be rendered to the public, or to any part of it; money, or money's worth, or both, are, in a quantity more or less considerable, necessary to be employed and disbursed on the occasion of its being rendered: the financial branch is thus a branch which intertwines itself, and runs through the several other branches of the public service.

This branch of government has for its proper end, that branch of good economy which consists of appropriate frugality.

Of economy there are two branches: the one positive, or say, distributive; the other negative, or say, restrictive.

The distributive branch has for its object, the due appropriation of the aggregate of the sums levied, to the several services for which they are levied.

The restrictive branch has for its object, avoidance of all exaction, the burthensomeness of which is not outweighed by the usefulness of the application made of it.

For judging of the consistency of any mass of expenditure with the proper ends of economy, take for a test this directive rule: with the alleged benefit, alleged to be expected from the expenditure, compare the unquestionable burthen produced by a tax to the same amount: forego the benefit, the burthen is excluded.

. . .

Pay of useless offices, pay of needless, overpay of useful offices, pay of sinecures, *i.e.* of places to which no duty is attached—these are the shapes in which, at the expense of the greatest happiness of the greatest number, money in excess is extracted from the people, for the benefit of public functionaries.

Remains, that source or mode of wasteful expenditure in the wholesale way which, howsoever congenial, is not essential to the form of government. These are—unnecessary wars, and distant, and thence preponderately expensive, dependencies. . . .

Hand in hand with waste, is to be found taxation.

Considerable must have been the difference between the quantities of evil produced by the different sorts of taxes resorted to, and the different degrees of mischievousness of those several taxes, even in the best governed state: still more in every other state, in proportion as it is ill governed. Of this inferiority in the scale of aptitude as applied to a tax, the cause may be seen partly in a deficiency in the article of appropriate intellectual aptitude, partly in a deficiency in the article of appropriate moral aptitude, on the part of the authors of the tax: in other words, in a want of wisdom and in a want of feeling: in the one case, if he produces so much needless suffering it is for want of knowing how to find another sort of tax that shall not produce so much of that undesirable result: in the other case, it is because so as the money is but produced to the treasury, he cares not how much suffering is produced elsewhere by it. . . .

Be this as it may, what in every state ought to be expected, is, in the first place, that among the existing sorts of taxes there should be different degrees of mischievousness: in the next place, that the degrees of mischievousness should not exactly follow the chronological order of the taxes. To the perfection of appropriate intellectual aptitude on the part of the financier, suppose the perfection of appropriate probity added,—the degree of mischievousness will, on this supposition, be in the inverse ratio of the chronological order of the different sorts of taxes, as first in time, will come the least mischievous,—last in time, the most mischievous.

Compare now the mischief of the waste with the mischief of the tax.

To obtain an adequate conception of the quantity of evil produced by a quantity of waste to a given amount, find and compare with it, the quantity of evil produced by the levying of a correspondent and equal portion of the most mischievous of all the existing taxes. For, on condition of abstaining from the commission of the waste, you may relieve the people from the burthen of that portion of the produce of the tax—you may abolish so much of the tax.

Note that, to render this rule strictly conformable to the truth, the quantity of waste abstained from, must be equal to the whole amount of the tax; for, in the case of a tax, there will always be a portion of evil, the quantity of which, will be the same, be the produce ever so great or ever so small. For example, a certain portion of the expense attached to the official establishment employed in the collection of it.

By the above general observations, the reader will now have been in some sort prepared for the forming a just estimate of the evil produced in the shape of waste, by various branches of customary expenditure, hitherto very commonly regarded as justifiable, either on the ground of absolute necessity, or, at any rate, on the ground of utility. Take, for example, the splendour of the crown, the support of the dignity of the peerage,—jobs for the amusement of the ruling and influential few.